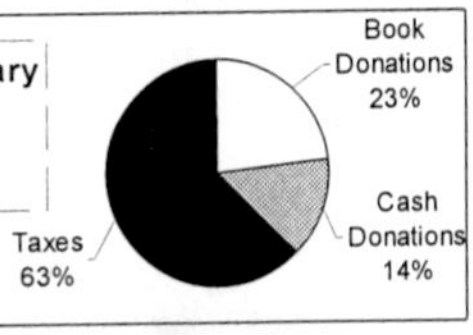

\<WEBONOMICS\>

< WEBONOMICS >

NINE ESSENTIAL PRINCIPLES FOR GROWING YOUR BUSINESS ON THE WORLD WIDE WEB

EVAN I. SCHWARTZ

BROADWAY BOOKS

BROADWAY

Broadway Books titles may be purchased for business or promotional use or for special sales. For information, please write to: Special Markets Department, Bantam Doubleday Dell Publishing Group, Inc., 1540 Broadway, New York, NY 10036.

BROADWAY BOOKS and its logo, a letter B bisected on the diagonal, are trademarks of Broadway Books, a division of Bantam Doubleday Dell Publishing Group, Inc.

Webonomics is a registered trademark of Evan I. Schwartz.
Library of Congress Cataloging-in-Publication Data
Schwartz, Evan I.
Webonomics : nine essential principles for growing your business on the World Wide Web / Evan I. Schwartz. — 1st ed.
p.   cm.
Includes bibliographical references (p. 221) and index.
ISBN 0-553-06172-0 (hardcover)
1. Internet marketing.   2. Electronic commerce.   3. World Wide Web (Information retrieval system)   I. Title.
HF5415.1265.S384   1997
658.8'00285'4678—dc21   96-47780
                                                        CIP

Designed by Julie Duquet

97 98 99 00 01 10 9 8 7 6 5 4 3 2

To Amy,

and to little Michaela,

born around the same time

as the idea for this book.

————————

Webonomics\,web-ə-'näm-iks\ *n*

the study of the production, distribution,

and consumption of goods, services,

and ideas over the World Wide Web

———————

<CONTENTS>

<INTRODUCTION><1>
The Foundation of Webonomics

<ONE><21>
The *Quantity* of People Visiting Your Site Is Less Important
Than the *Quality* of Their Experience

<TWO><47>
Marketers Shouldn't Be on the Web for *Exposure*,
but for *Results*

<THREE><72>
Consumers Must Be Compensated for Disclosing
Data About Themselves

<FOUR><92>
Consumers Will Shop Online Only for
Information-Rich Products

<FIVE><117>
Self-Service Provides for the Highest Level
of Customer Comfort

<SIX><138>
"Value-Based Currencies" Enable You to
Create Your Own Monetary System

<SEVEN><155>
Trusted Brand Names Matter Even More on the Web

<EIGHT><174>
Even the Smallest Business Can Compete
in the Web's Global "Marketspace"

<NINE><190>
Agility Rules—Web Sites Must Continually
Adapt to the Market

<EPILOGUE><201>
The Web Effect—How It's Changing Life As We Know It

<ACKNOWLEDGMENTS><218>

<NOTES><221>

<APPENDIX><227>
A Directory of Important and Intriguing Web Sites

<INDEX><235>

<INTRODUCTION>

The Foundation of Webonomics

New sites on the World Wide Web have been cropping up at the rate of one per minute. As it expands at this astounding pace, it's clear that the Web's colorful entanglement of words, pictures, sound, and motion is briskly becoming more than just the most important new communication medium since television. The Web is more like a parallel universe that mirrors the physical world in some ways but exhibits entirely unique properties in others. And if you hang out there long enough, you will slowly discover that there's nothing less than an entirely new economy taking shape on this digital terrain—and a new way of looking at how this marketplace of information and ideas works. Call it Webonomics.

Many of the businesses now piling onto the Web may totally misunderstand what this new medium is all about. They may end up losing millions of dollars and eventually decide that the Web isn't living up to its hype. Other businesses may totally ignore the Web and get left behind. Their competitors, meanwhile, will use the Web as a tool to literally steal their best customers away. Averting such scenarios will only come with a keen understanding of Webonomics.

Traditional economics is based on the notion of scarcity—that human desires will always exceed available resources such as food, clothing, and shelter. It was Thomas Malthus, the English economist, who first postulated that populations will always increase faster than the food supply. This pessimistic focus on the allocation of scarce resources is what earned economics the reputation as "the dismal science."

Webonomics is anything but dismal. On the Web, precisely the reverse is true. Since the Web is a fast-growing world of intellectual property that can be copied and downloaded ad infinitum, its supply of resources will continue to *soar past* human demand for these resources. Instead of a scarcity of supply, the Web economy exhibits a scarcity of demand. Indeed, one of the main complaints about the Web is that it's "mind-boggling" and "too overloaded" with information. On the Web, the main commodity in limited supply is the *attention* of the busy people using it. The underlying battle in the Web economy is the ability to command and sustain that attention.

As such, growth of the Web economy has everything to do with the *quality* of the information there—how interesting and engaging it is, how it is presented, and how it takes advantage of the unique attributes of the medium. As more and more people continue to enjoy the Web, as they find it worthy of their attention, the Web will continue to grow at its frenetic pace. Unlike a national economy with limited resources, there are no physical limits on this growth. Unlike real estate, steel, or even paper, computing power and computer storage is cheap and getting cheaper. There's an infinite number of bits in the universe and a virtually bottomless hunger for valuable information and knowledge.

The Web is also a world without borders in which the physical location of a company doing business there is of little importance. Despite efforts to do so, the Web economy will resist efforts by national governments to control or regulate it. It will be up to each citizen of the world to choose what they see and do. In this sense, a totally free-market economy had been considered to be only theoretically possible in the past; the Web makes it practically possible for the first time.

The nature of this beast is both good and bad. Because of the abundant choices available, the combat among companies is, in the words of Sun Microsystems CEO Scott McNealy, one of "fierce Darwinism." To succeed, businesses on the Web must invent new ways to market themselves, new ways to learn what customers want, new ways to forge lasting relationships with them.

The opportunities for creating entirely new businesses are vast. But the fear of losing your existing business should also be a prime motivator. It's kind of like the story of the two guys camping out in the jungle who suddenly see a tiger approaching them. One of the guys quickly puts on his running shoes. The other guy asks, "Do you really think those shoes will make you run faster than that tiger?"

"I don't have to outrun the tiger," comes the reply. "I just have to outrun *you.*"

In industry after industry, the Web is the pair of running shoes that can keep you ahead of the ferocious forces of change.

To put the principles of Webonomics into use, you have to first understand the motivations behind the four main groups settling the world's first large-scale, bit-based landscape:

- The consumers. Tens of millions of people worldwide are surfing the Web in search of surprises, cheap thrills, knowledge and entertainment, time-saving services, plus information on products that they hope will enhance their lives. They expect to make the Web a place of their own, a place of customized information and relationships. The consumers are in the driver's seat. Able to search for the best deals in an instant, they will obtain a product or service over the Web only if it is the best, cheapest, and most convenient alternative from a source they trust.

- The content creators. Hundreds of major publishing companies, television networks, movie studios, and new, hybrid media outlets are now colonizing the Web by creating perpetually updated Web pages meant to inform and amuse those who visit. They not only want to enhance their brand image among the demographically desirable Web surfers, but they are also desperately seeking a way to somehow make their Web sites profitable ventures.

- The marketers. Thousands of companies are promoting and selling products ranging from food and beverages to cars and

trucks to information and financial services. Some will advertise, market, and sell their products on the Web using out-
moded thinking from traditional, one-way media, and thereby
fail. Others will embrace the principles of Webonomics and
succeed.

- The infrastructure companies. Computer companies are selling Web server machines. Software companies are selling Web
browser programs and tools for building elaborate Web sites.
Developers of Web search engines are locked in fierce battle,
as are scores of Internet access providers offering gateways to
the Web. Meanwhile, advertising agencies and thousands of
consultants have set up practices to create custom Web sites
for clients. In this digital gold rush, these companies are selling the picks and shovels. But long term, they won't succeed
unless the other three groups do.

Things happen differently on the Web. First, the very behavior of consumers changes dramatically once they enter Web space. Just as your
expectations differ when you are in a fine French restaurant as opposed to a Taco Bell, consumers have different expectations when interacting with a company on the Web. Customers entering a Web site
will come to expect customized products and services. They will expect full access to their own account information. They will expect
their experience to be fun and entertaining. They will expect not just
to read an advertisement but to interact with it and place orders for the
advertised product.

Understanding how to forge lasting relationships with these demanding consumers is the key. One way to do that is to create what
amounts to a new monetary system. In the traditional economy, national governments can control supply and demand of resources by
tightening or loosening the value of money. On the Web, that power is
distributed among thousands of companies. A simple example comes
from the airline companies, which already issue frequent flier points

that have real value. To command the attention of consumers, an auto company's Web site could offer to pay 100 Web bucks to any person willing to spend an hour learning about the company's new cars and answering a few questions. Those 100 points could be credited to the consumer's "digital cash" account, redeemable for a CD player if they choose to buy a car. Such a system of currency will help determine customer loyalty—something that will become more and more important in the Web economy.

In short, Webonomics amounts to new economic rules, new forms of currency, and new consumer behavior. The process of putting these changes into perspective all begins with a look at where the Web came from.

THE VISION OF A UNIVERSAL LIBRARY

A hundred years from now, historians and anthropologists sifting through the artifacts of premillennial culture will come upon the strange symbols—http, www, URL—that suddenly began appearing in nearly every periodical and broadcast of the time. They will wonder why cyber-speak seeped so rapidly into, some would say warped, the speech and writing of that era. "W—as in WWW—seems suddenly to have become the most commonly encountered consonant in the English language," notes Neil Rudenstine, president of Harvard University. "And E—as in e-mail, e-prints, e-journals, e-groups, and e-lectronic everything else—seems to have emerged as our all-purpose, ever-present vowel."

As the future historians comb through our primitive newspapers, they'll see articles about the Web appearing with equal stature alongside accounts of the day's political conflicts, wars, natural disasters, and acts of violence. They won't be perplexed as to what this Web is, as they will be using a successor to this information retrieval technology to perform their research in the first place. But these historians and anthropologists may be scratching their heads as to why all this discussion of the Web happened so abruptly, so instantaneously, in the mid-1990s.

In fact, something like the World Wide Web had long been the stuff of dreams among a few visionaries. In the summer of 1945, as American bombers were preparing to end a world wide war, an electrical engineer named Vannevar Bush was busy laying out a vision for a world wide web of all human knowledge. A vice president of the Massachusetts Institute of Technology, Bush had been selected by Franklin D. Roosevelt to head the Wartime Office of Scientific Research and Development, a coalition of 6,000 scientists dedicated to applying scientific breakthroughs to modern warfare.

With the surrender of Germany in hand, and with the war appearing to be screeching to a halt in Japan, Bush turned his attention away from global combat and toward global sharing of information. In an article entitled "As We May Think," published that summer in the *Atlantic Monthly*, Bush wrote: "Instruments are at hand which, if properly developed, will give man access to and command over the inherited knowledge of the ages."

He went on to gripe about the problem of information overload and to articulate an overwhelming need for something that gives people control over all that information. "The summation of human experience is being expanded at a prodigious rate," he complained. "But the means we use for threading through the consequent maze to the momentarily important item is the same as was used in the days of square-rigged ships."

At the time Vannevar Bush wrote those words, computers as large as warehouses but less powerful than one of today's pocket calculators were just being invented. Bush's idea, however, transcended the current notion of the computer itself. He envisioned the ability to create information "trails" that linked related texts and illustrations. These trails could then be stored and used for future reference, he wrote. Bush believed this way of organizing and gathering information to be similar to the way the human mind worked, constantly associating one idea with another. He called this easy-to-use, searchable, personal storehouse of knowledge "the Memex."

Bush himself was not able to build the Memex. But he inspired others to work toward his vision.

One of those followers was Ted Nelson, a rebellious kid from Greenwich Village who became determined to create a "nonsequential writing system" during his freshman year at Harvard. A few years later, in a paper presented at an Association for Computer Machinery conference in 1965, Nelson called this concept "hypertext," drawing on a definition of the prefix meaning "in a space of more than three dimensions." Nelson wrote about documents that could contain built-in sets of tiny programs for taking you to another document located on some other far-off computer. If one document made a reference to Charles Dickens, you should be able to link instantly to the complete texts of Dickens for further research and then return back to where you were.

Nelson spent the better part of the next three decades trying to build this system out of software, the lines of computer code that perform the magic on the screen. He called this massive program Xanadu, a name taken from the poem "Kubla Khan," by Samuel T. Coleridge. In the 1797 poem, Xanadu is "the magic place of literary memory where nothing is forgotten." And so it would be with Nelson's universal hypertext system. Nelson believed that providing all people with the ability to get all information would wipe out ignorance, political misunderstandings, miscommunication, and ancient hatreds. In short, hypertext would save the world.

"The future of humanity is at the interactive computer screen," Nelson wrote in that 1965 paper, "The new writing and movies will be interactive and interlinked. It will be united by bridges of transclusion, and we need a worldwide network to deliver it with royalty."

But like Bush's Memex, Xanadu was not to be—at least not yet. Unfortunately, Nelson was beset with an acute case of attention deficit disorder. Ideas swirled around in his head at such a furious pace that he had trouble focusing on anything for more than a short instant. As such, he couldn't seem to get anything done in a reasonable amount of time. Instead of finishing what he began, his project expanded until the sheer weight of his ambition led to its inevitable collapse.

John Walker, the founder of the successful Silicon Valley software company Autodesk, saw what was happening. He believed in Nelson's dream, acquired Nelson's technology in 1988, and sank about $5 million into its development. But the work at Autodesk was abandoned four years later when it became known that programmers at the Switzerland-based European Particle Physics Laboratory (best known by its French acronym CERN), had already released something remarkably similar.

In 1989, while working at CERN, Tim Berners-Lee, an Oxford-trained physicist in his mid-thirties, proposed a global hypertext system that he named "WorldWideWeb." His goal was not only to create a universally accessible "information space" for all the world's citizens but also to enable groups of far-flung people to work together on large problems. By December 1990, he made his software for creating, searching, and retrieving hypertext documents available to the small community of CERN scientists.

Specifically, Berners-Lee invented three things: First, he defined the HyperText Transfer Protocol. Now represented by the ubiquitous "HTTP" symbol, the protocol is a standard format enabling all computers to look up documents. Second, he created the Uniform Resource Locator (URL). This is simply a standard for finding a document by typing in an address—such as www.website.com/document—much the way people address letters in a standard postal format. Third, he devised the HyperText Markup Language (HTML). A standard design for word processor-like functions, HTML enables people to add special codes to text. One piece of code would mark a sentence as a large-type headline, for instance, while another piece of code would mark a series of words as a link to another document.

The World Wide Web that Berners-Lee envisioned needed all three elements: HTML for creating and formatting documents, URL addressing for finding documents, and HTTP for transferring documents among different types of computers and networks.

In the summer of 1991, Berners-Lee put his trio of programs on the Internet. An energetic man who speaks quickly but coherently, Berners-Lee became all-consumed with driving the Web to new technological heights. He has compared the early work of conceiving, designing, and promoting the World Wide Web to jump-starting a bobsled by pushing it from the top of a mountain. When interest in the Web surged in the mid-1990s, he says that felt as if he were jumping into that bobsled, frantically trying to steer it as it careered downhill at accelerating speeds. His steering mechanism had been the World Wide Web Consortium, a group he established at MIT to promote technical and ethical standards for the Web.

Like Vannevar Bush and Ted Nelson before him, Berners-Lee was driven by a sense of idealism. In inventing the Web, he aimed to create a global hypertext library that would do nothing less than bring the people of the world closer together. In 1995, at an MIT symposium commemorating the fiftieth anniversary of Bush's seminal paper, Berners-Lee paid tribute not only to that work's technical foresight but also to its strong sense of morality. "Anyone who reads the *Atlantic Monthly* article today will be struck with the distance and accuracy of Bush's vision," Berners-Lee said. "To a large part, we have Memexes on our desks today."

But the centerpiece of Berners-Lee's talk was a challenge to those who are putting his technology to use:

We have access to information, but have we been solving problems? Well, there are many things it is much easier for individuals to do today than five years ago. But personally, I don't feel that the Web has made great strides in helping us work as a global team. I still have a dream that the Web could be less of a television and more of an interactive sea of shared knowledge. I imagine it immersing us in a warm, friendly environment made of the things we and our friends have seen, heard, believe, or have figured out. I would like it to bring our friends and colleagues closer, in that by working on this knowledge together, we can come to better understandings. If misunderstandings are the cause of many of the world's woes, then can we not work them out in cyberspace?

THE BATTLE FOR ATTENTION

The phenomenal growth of the Web clearly has been driven more by the roar of opportunism than by the whisper of idealism. The hopes and aspirations of Bush, Nelson, and Berners-Lee may indeed be guiding the Web in a subtle way. But for better or worse, ours is a world dominated by capitalism, commercialism, and consumerism. And the Web represents the next phase for all three of those forces.

The Web has already passed by the scientists who dreamed about it and made it happen. In the same way that Bell couldn't imagine all the uses of the telephone and Edison didn't foresee the rise of the music industry when he created sound recording, Berners-Lee cannot possibly dictate or even predict the many different ways the Web will change the world. It's now largely in the hands of the democratic masses of business people and consumers who hopelessly outnumber the population of idealistic scientists.

One business opportunity in particular set the Web afire. The opportunity arose due to the fact that Tim Berners-Lee purposely omitted a key element when he invented the Web. He left open the choice for individual computer owners to use any kind of "browser" program they liked. Browsers are necessary to view all the documents on the Web and jump from one page to another with ease. But Berners-Lee believed that people would want a choice of many different browsers, so long as they were compatible with his standards. So, he left the creation of browsers up to any programmer who so desired to design one.

Anyone who knows something about the technology will tell you that writing a basic Web browser is not all that momentous, as far as programming goes. The Dilbert comic strip had an amusing take on this phenomenon. One day, Dilbert instructs his colleague Ratbert to dance on his computer keyboard—in order to deliberately introduce bugs into a program he was writing. When Ratbert is done dancing, Dilbert glances at the screen and says: "I think you just authored a Web browser."

A programmer named Marc Andreessen was among the first to see the opportunity here. Andreessen didn't create just any old browser. A twenty-three-year old recent graduate of the University of Illinois who was working at the school's renowned supercomputer center in Champagne-Urbana, Andreessen completed a graphically elegant and fun-to-use version of a browser program that enabled users to call up Web documents by pointing and clicking the mouse—the way Microsoft Windows and the Apple Macintosh worked. While this first version of the software only ran on scientific computers that were powered by the Unix operating system, the program immediately developed a cult following upon its release in January 1993. Andreessen called the software Mosaic and made it available free to anyone who wanted to download it over the Internet.

From that point on, Web users and Web sites began proliferating like pachysandra. At the time Mosaic appeared, there were only fifty computers in the world that hosted and served up Web documents. In August, Andreessen released free versions of Mosaic for the Macintosh and Windows. By October, there were more than 500 Web servers. By June 1994, there were 1,500. Within a year after that, tens of thousands of such computers were hosting an even larger number of individual Web sites created by companies, newspapers, magazines, universities, and government agencies. Then, in the blink of an eye, there were hundreds of thousands of Web sites.

Compared to today's software, the Mosaic browser didn't do all that much. In this respect, it was like Microsoft's MS-DOS in the early 1980s. The main point was establishing it as the presumptive industry standard as quickly as possible. Then, programmers could "add functionality" later on.

The story of how former Silicon Graphics Chairman Jim Clark recruited Andreessen and a team of his colleagues at the supercomputer center, then parlayed their free browser program into the fastest rising start-up company ever is now part of computer industry legend. In March 1994, Clark flew to Illinois, rented a suite at a hotel near the university, and invited the members of the Mosaic programming team over for interviews. He hired them all and relocated the team to Silicon Valley within a matter of weeks. Now, instead of paying a $100,000 license fee plus royalties to the university and reselling Mosaic—like other software companies were doing already—Clark and his whiz kids could write an entirely new program from scratch without infringing on any copyrights.

The team went into overdrive to build a better browser, calling their creation and their new company Netscape. In the summer of 1995, the World Wide Web suddenly pierced mass consciousness when Netscape Communications Corp. went public in one of Wall Street history's most stratospheric stock offerings—despite the fact that the company was months away from reporting any profits. By the end of the year, Netscape's market value had soared to around $4 billion, about the same level as established corporations such as Delta Air Lines and Dow Jones.

Most people assumed that Netscape's stock took on such elephantine proportions because the company had a clear shot at monopolizing a crucial software market. The theory was that Netscape would do for the Internet what Microsoft's MS-DOS and Windows did for IBM-compatible PCs. The company would be at the center of a booming new industry for easy-to-use Internet programs.

But that was only a part of the reason for the surge. The other, more subtle reason had to do with the fact that anytime people logged onto the Web using the Netscape Navigator program, their eyes were first taken to Netscape's site on the Web. At the site, people can download the latest version of Netscape's growing list of software products, read about how the company was doing financially, view paid advertisements for other Web sites and services, even embark on searches of all the other content on the Web. By obtaining this captive audience, Netscape promised to do much more than monopolize a new market for software. Netscape was promising to monopolize the computer-using public's attention.

Sensing this, the world's richest man and the world's biggest software company made it priority number one to cut into Netscape's party. Beginning in 1995, Bill Gates and Microsoft began releasing new versions of its Internet Explorer browser in rapid succession. Microsoft's browser, of course, pointed consumers directly to its own Web site and its own Web content.

By the summer of 1996, product reviewers were impressed enough with version 3.0 of Microsoft's program to declare it at least the technological equal of the Netscape Navigator. By then, Netscape had succeeded in seeding the market with tens of millions of copies of its free program, capturing more than 80 percent of the market. And so, Clark decided it was time to charge customers $49 each for new versions. Microsoft, meanwhile, was gaining market share by giving away millions of copies and convincing many computer makers to bundle it on hard drives at no cost.

Suddenly, the two companies were locked in a colossal battle for the attention of consumers. At Netscape's urging, the U.S. Department of Justice began investigating whether Microsoft was using its monopoly in PC operating systems to gain the upper hand in what has come to be known as "the browser wars."

True, the browser wars grew so fierce so fast because an important new software market was at stake. But the reason why this market became so important has everything to do with the fact that whoever supplies the browser has the inside edge on the consumer's attention span. This battle for attention cuts right to the heart of Webonomics.

WHO SURFS THE WEB AND WHY

In retrospect, it shouldn't have come as a shock that the Web would quickly become the most widely embraced part of the Internet. After it was established by the Defense Department in the late 1960s, the Internet became the domain of techies, students, and academic researchers. It was composed of many separate and hard-to-use databases with such names as Gopher, WAIS, FTP, and others, each requiring a different set of commands. Whereas the Internet required a mastery of arcane instructions and esoteric computer concepts, the Web required little more than pointing and clicking the mouse.

Instead of all those incompatible databases, the Web pieced together all kinds of information for you—placing words, photos, sounds, and video snippets together on one electronic page. The page metaphor enabled people to publish not just plain text and numbers but beautifully illustrated layouts. That's why Web page design has become the newest pop art. And the Web itself has been called the biggest public art project in the history of the world. This relative ease of use and aesthetic appeal goes a long way toward explaining why the Web came to be known as the Internet's chief multimedia business district and entertainment zone.

But what got people paying attention to the Web in the first place? In the very beginning, the Web was like ham radio, the domain of hobbyists. In this case, it was hard-core software jocks, scientists, university students, librarians, and underground communities of artists who were designing and viewing Web pages. People weren't creating Web pages to make money, but rather to impress and amuse one another. Some of the earliest sites were dedicated to interactive frog dissection, comic book sagas, unpublished fiction, scientific drawings, and independent music samples.

In those days, 94 percent of Web users were male and 56 percent were between the ages of twenty-one and thirty, according to the first semiannual survey of Web users by the Georgia Institute of Technology. The Web was clearly dominated by techies back then: That January 1994 survey also showed 88 percent of the Web's users had computers that ran the hard-to-use Unix operating system.

Then, the Web went corporate. For many corporate employees, habitual surfing can be traced to a phenomenon known as "the water-cooler effect." Starting in 1994, techno-savvy office workers began populating the Web. Managers at companies with high-speed networks were reading about it or hearing about it through colleagues. High-profile sites like Hotwired and the White House home page started springing up and garnering press attention. Business people were simply curious to see what all the early hype was about. They were itching to type in some of the strange Web addresses that were beginning to appear in newspapers and magazines.

So they began browsing the Web during times they would normally be taking a break. They were doing it for the same reason that they would occasionally emerge from their office, hang around the water cooler, and find someone with whom to exchange gossip or shoot the breeze. As a popular communications medium, the Web started out as a diversion, as a way to see for yourself what was going on out there in the world. Instead of spending time chatting around the old water cooler, office workers began wandering down paths and byways in a new global information village. In many offices, a personal computer operated by someone who knew his way around the Web became the *new* water cooler—and without the messy pile of used cups.

The water-cooler effect was dutifully tracked by the so-called Webmasters who created and ran these early Web sites. The Webmasters had evidence that corporate employees were logging on in larger and larger numbers because their Web server computers kept "log files" that showed that visitors with Internet addresses at AT&T, Digital Equipment, Kodak, Hewlett-Packard, Microsoft, IBM, and other high-tech companies were the heaviest users. Even *Playboy* magazine reported that the heaviest usage of its new site was not late at night or during the weekend, as one might expect, but smack dab in the middle of the day. Demand for the Web began surging at 12:00 P.M. and again at 3:00 P.M. during business hours—precisely lunchtime on the East and West coasts of the United States. By the end of 1994, the overloaded network would slow to a crawl during those hours.

The April 1995 survey conducted by Georgia Tech reflected this shift away from techies and toward business users. The average age of users rose to thirty-five, while the proportion of males online dropped to 82 percent. Meanwhile, new data showed that Web surfers were unmistakably upscale, with an average income of $69,000.

After the influx of business people came the hoards of at-home users. In 1995, the three largest commercial online services, CompuServe, America Online, and Prodigy, all began offering their millions of members access to the World Wide Web. In the second half of 1995 alone, at-home use of the Web doubled, to nearly eight million U.S. households, according to Odyssey, a San Francisco research firm. In 1996, the number of households with Web connections doubled once again, to sixteen million.

As a result, the population of Web users began to resemble the population at large. The April 1996 survey by Georgia Tech showed the average income dropping to $59,000, and the percentage of males falling to 68.5 percent. The vast majority were nontechnical people who owned PCs running Windows. In addition, more than 25 percent of Web surfers came from outside the United States, with that percentage expected to grow rapidly in coming years.

Overall, the rate of growth of Web usage was beginning to look like the proliferation of television sets in the late 1940s. The phenomenon even got the attention of the A. C. Nielsen Company, which released a study projecting that more than 35 percent of the U.S. population will be using the Web by 1998.

Actually, the Web has begun to act as a source of competition to television. A Coopers & Lybrand survey of Internet users found that 58 percent of people surveyed were cutting back on television viewership to go online. This cutback was most pronounced among people surfing the Web. Subscribers to commercial services such as America Online reported spending five to seven hours per month online, while those with direct access to the Web though a corporate network, university, or an Internet service provider reported spending forty to forty-five hours per month. (Incidentally, this survey only showed Web time coming out of the time spent watching TV, with no drop-off in usage of newspapers or other media.)

If this trend holds, the Web may reverse some of TV's well-documented effects on society. The Web, in a sense, is the opposite of television. TV programs and Web content are indeed both delivered to electronic devices that shoot electrons at the back of a display screen. But television is a passive experience. You watch it at a distance, mostly in a semiconscious state, sprawled out on a couch. Often, you're not fully aware of all the advertising and entertainment seeping into your brain. But you are drawn to your favorite shows time after time.

When surfing the Web, you sit up close to the screen. You're alert. You are in an active, information-seeking mode. The clicker is yours and yours alone. In a report titled "The Interactive Consumer," Saatchi & Saatchi researchers call this entering a "flow state" in which users become totally absorbed, relaxed, and exhilarated in the experience. Often, the journey is the reward; browsing itself is often more important than actually reaching any specific destination. That's why, in these early days of the Web, it has been difficult to draw people to the same sites over and over. The authors of the study also compare entering this flow state to doing a hobby or other pleasant tasks that require concentration. This difference in mode helps explain why people respond differently and want fundamentally different things from their PCs as opposed to their TVs.

That people often get lost in the alleys and byways of the Web is not all that surprising. We all know that there's mountains of material on the Web. If you spent ten hours per day browsing Web pages and only spent a minute per page, it would take you more than four years—an entire college career!—to explore a million Web pages. And during that time, parents would have wasted good money on tuition.

Just how big can the Web get? Roy Williams, a researcher at the California Institute of Technology's Center for Advanced Computing Research, estimates that all the information from all of human history stored on paper in the world today amounts to about 200 *petabytes.* A byte roughly equals a printed character. So, a petabyte is about one quadrillion (or a thousand trillion) characters. That figure includes all the paper in all corporate filing cabinets, all government archives, all homes, all schools, universities, and libraries.

By the year 2000, Williams estimates, the amount of *online* information that will have accumulated in just the *few decades* leading up to the new millennium will be *about two and a half times* that amount now on paper. Much of that information will be on the Web. It's enough to make your head explode.

Most of the Web's massive array of content appeals to narrow niche audiences. Unlike radio, television, newspapers, and magazines, the Web is not a mass medium. Rather, it's the first interactive one. The interactive features of the Web enable people to personalize their experience by choosing for themselves among its huge array of content. In this sense, the Web is the ultimate Rorschach test—it reveals whatever you decide to see in it.

How personal does the experience get? One of the first things many people do when they first log on the Web is go to a search engine and type in their name, or their hometown, or their college, or their employer. Those who find themselves mentioned somewhere on the Web feel a sense of validation, not unlike Steve Martin in *The Jerk* when he exclaimed, "The new phone books are here!" This is why millions of people are creating their own personal Web pages. In the future, everyone will be the subject of a Web reference or his or her own Web site. Andy Warhol got it almost right: It's fifteen *megabytes* of fame.

Still, most newcomers to the Web feel overwhelmed. As a newbie, you might not immediately know how you should be using this deceptively simple but very powerful tool. After following a trail of links into some obscure Web site, you will start scratching your head. Like a digital David Byrne, you may ask yourself: "Well, how did I get here?" And you may ask yourself: "How do I work this?"

Such puzzlement is exacerbated by the traditional media. Every day, people hear about how the Web is the central component in the "digital revolution" that's sweeping the planet. The press dutifully reports all the new and improved Web sites, while marketers are all putting their cryptic Web addresses at the bottom of every print ad, at the end of every TV commercial, even on billboards. The fact that no individual, corporation, or government owns or controls this medium makes it all the more mysterious. It's kind of like NATO: Most people realize it's important, but they don't know why. They don't know whether they should be visiting all the sites they hear about. They don't know how to harness the Web's true power.

This is especially true for companies that have created Web sites to promote their products and their brand image. Promotion is only the tip of the iceberg. At its most powerful, the Web is about customer service, selling products directly, establishing a dialogue with consumers, and expanding the geographic base of a business. A Gartner Group study found that 90 percent of first-generation Web sites were created without asking existing customers what they wanted. The next generation of Web sites now under development don't have that luxury. Customers are voting every day on which are the most useful Web sites. And their tolerance for glorified electronic brochures is fading fast.

Most of the early marketing sites on the Net have temporarily drawn an audience for the same reason that people like to watch a baby learning to eat solid foods. These sites have garnered attention not because they are done well, but because they are being done *at all*. After a while, you'd like to see the kid actually get the food into her mouth. Once you've seen a few of these sites, you're ready to watch the medium grow up.

As the Web matures, its inhabitants are becoming more and more selective as to how they pay out their precious attention. This is where the principles of Webonomics come in. Consumers are returning again and again to quality Web sites that offer a real value proposition, ignoring ones they have no use for. They are looking to buy products and interact with companies, not just absorb the same brand positioning they see on TV. They are coming to expect rewards for disclosing data about themselves. They are shopping online in the global marketspace, but only for "information-rich," or high-involvement, products. They cherish self-service. They are accumulating and spending new digital currencies. They are aligning themselves with brand names that they can trust. They expect Web sites to quickly adapt to market changes. These are the principles for growing your business on the Web.

The story of how companies are implementing the principles of Webonomics is a story not just about the Web itself but about life in the Information Age. It's a story about new types of relationships, about the rise of new communities, about living in a technology-mediated society, about what it means to be personal and what it means to be private, about the next phase of capitalism and the new role of government, about accelerating change, about the relentless future.

<CHAPTER ONE>

The *Quantity* of People Visiting Your Site Is Less Important Than the *Quality* of Their Experience

PET ROCK OF THE '90S?

Let's start with the most basic of questions: What do people do when they are on the Web? What do people look for when such a wide array of stuff is at their disposal? To find out, one only has to get in touch with the people who run Alta Vista, Yahoo!, InfoSeek, Hotbot, Excite, Magellan, Lycos, or any of the Web's other "search engines" and computerized directories. These services enable users to find the Web sites that interest them, simply by browsing directory categories or by typing in key words.

The top ten search terms that people enter into Alta Vista happen to be these:

1. sex
2. nude
3. pictures
4. jpg (J-PEG is a format for online photos)
5. software
6. windows
7. adult
8. women
9. naked
10. erotic

"As you can see," says Louis Monier, Alta Vista's technology director, "the list is 20 percent Bill Gates and 80 percent James Exon," the senator who sponsored antipornography legislation for the Internet. Given that sex is a proven lure, especially among new users, it makes sense to begin our demonstration of the first principle of Webonomics at some of the most sexually charged sites.

Since the very first day it went live in the summer of 1994, the site created by Playboy Enterprises became one of the hot spots on the Internet, quickly attracting as many as 100,000 visitors daily. It's not hard to see why. For three generations of men, the world-famous *Playboy* brand name has been synonymous with sexy. And the magazine's target audience meshed perfectly with the predominant demographic of early Web users: young, upscale men who had trouble getting dates in college.

At one point, the *Playboy* site presented Web surfers with a little piece of neon blue, underlined hypertext—*The Women of the Ivy League*—that seemed to ensnare eyeballs as if they were fat, juicy flies caught in an actual spider's web. *Playboy* was enticing men to peer into the dorm rooms of the nation's elite universities and say: "Hello! What's *your* major?" Faced with this situation, most big, dumb American males would do the same thing: double-click.

But while *Playboy* has succeeded in collecting the only rare commodity on the Web—namely, the short attention spans of users—lots of eyeballs doesn't necessarily translate into success. Building a long-term business on the Web is done not just by momentarily *grabbing* our attention, but also by *sustaining* it with something of unique value.

And this is where *Playboy* has so far failed. The Ivy League feature on the Web, for instance, began with a color photo of Yale University coeds streaking across a quad with cryptic messages painted on their bodies. The accompanying text—written in *Playboy*'s typical glib style—mentioned that these naked Yalies were protesting *Playboy*'s presence on campus. Not only was it disappointing to find out this was the only photo available from the full print magazine layout, but there

was no information about the story behind all these behinds. What was
the logic of this demonstration? What specifically did these protesters
object to? It couldn't be the nudity. Even more pressing: Why would
anyone with a 1450 on the SATs and the brightest of futures want this
kind of exposure in the first place? Instead of answers, all visitors got
was the teaser photo, tidbits from an article, and a clear message: Go
buy our magazine!

There lies the problem: *Playboy's* Web site is mainly an advertisement for its print edition. "The magazine is the end-all and be-all," explains Eileen Kent, vice president of Playboy's New Media division,
who started up the Web site with a bare-bones staff of four people in
Chicago and rented space on several server computers in California.
Such costs, she says, "are justified as something that promotes the
magazine."

But if the Web is to fulfill its potential as the hottest new medium
since television and the hippest trend since rock 'n' roll, it has to stand
on its own. If Web pages are to become more than just the Pet Rock of
the '90s, browsing them has to be a satisfying, high-quality experience
in and of itself.

This is the challenge facing all content creators on the Web. Once a
site succeeds in hooking thousands, or even millions, of eyeballs, it
has to deliver something special. Something that causes people to return to the site again and again. Otherwise, it's just the digital equivalent of an accident on the side of the road. Everyone wants to see it as
they pass by, but the commitment ends there.

Kent says the *Playboy* site is updated twice per month. The average
visitor, she says, probably returns less often than that, although she admits she does not track such figures. Kent does know that the average
visitor spends eight to ten minutes there before moving on to another
site. Based on this information, it seems safe to say that a large percentage of visitors pop in for a visit, download a photo of the Playmate
of the month, wash their hands—and never go back.

Not only is this less than satisfying as a quality user experience, it isn't even a formula for making much money. The *Playboy* site was on pace to report more than $1 million in advertising revenue for 1996, according to Jupiter Communications, a New York research firm that tracks spending on Web ads. But some of that *reported* revenue may include ads that were really given away for free as an incentive to advertisers in *Playboy*'s print editions, as Kent has admitted to doing in the past. *Playboy* won't release the profit-and-loss figures for its Web site. But with a staff that has grown to eight full-time employees plus a hefty technology budget, the revenue doesn't seem enough to keep up with the costs of running the site.

A SENSE OF COMMUNITY

Contrast the *Playboy* site with a site called Bianca's Smut Shack. Upon entering, the visitor chooses a handle, or online name, and is presented with a hand-drawn floor map of an urban apartment. Click on any of the rooms and you become part of the intimate activities in that area, including ongoing bulletin board discussions and chat sessions with other people hanging out there at that moment. In the kitchen, for instance, people enter recipes in the cookbook. In the living room, they post erotic poetry. And in the bedroom, visitors log the dreams they had last night into Bianca's dream book—all for other visitors to read and comment on. Many of these dreams are so explicit, so personal, and so taboo that even the most jaded Freudian psychiatrist might blush.

The idea of the Smut Shack comes from the real-life comings and goings of a bunch of slackers in a bohemian apartment in Chicago. It draws its name from a New Age free spirit in her fifties since named Bianca, who used to drop by the apartment unannounced to spend a few nights. In real life, no one seemed to know her real name. She was last known to be trekking in Nepal.

The site first appeared in early 1994, making it among the Web's first 500 content creations. It is developed and run by David Thau, Chris "Freeform" Miller, and Jill Atkinson, friends who used to hang around that fabled Chicago apartment. They then moved to San Francisco and took day jobs at Hotwired, running the Smut Shack after hours. "The Shack is a place for free speech and dialogue," Thau says. "People drop in and leave things behind. It's not intended as orgy central. Actually, Bianca was known to be celibate. The truth is that it became more and more smutty as more people visited."

As the third most visited adult-oriented site (after *Playboy* and *Penthouse*), the Smut Shack typically draws only about a quarter of the number of visitors that go to the *Playboy* site every day. But here is why it should be considered more successful: The average visitor comes by ten times per month and spends an average of an hour each time, according to the log files maintained by the site's host computer. "Some people come back every day," says Thau. "The sense of community in the shack is very important to us." People who meet there have thrown Smut Shack parties in several U.S. cities as well as in Scotland and England. A few couples who have met in the Shack have been married. At least one of those couples, says Thau, had a baby.

This is one of the most surprising facets of the Web: People are looking for more than just information when they go online. They treat the Web as a place in which they can interact with other people. The most effective Web sites are not just billboards on the side of the road. They are more like a place where everybody knows your name—even if it's not your real name. The information, or content, can become the centerpiece of their conversations. But it's the total experience that compels people to return to that place again and again. The concept of community is one of the main themes that recurs in Webonomics.

The Smut Shack obviously takes better advantage of this than *Playboy*. Whereas *Playboy* stormed the Web armed with one of the world's most well-known brand names (up there with Coca-Cola and McDonald's), Bianca's Smut Shack had to establish a brand identity and loyal following gradually. It has done so by projecting a casual, fun, witty, and erotic sensibility. Taking advantage of the unique attributes of the medium, the Smut Shack is built around the ability to let people interact with one another and contribute to the ambiance. The *Playboy* site, by contrast, is centered around viewing a few of the photos taken from the magazine. This is the difference between a site that was grown organically in the Web's own soil and one that was transplanted from another terrain entirely.

Whereas the *Playboy* site changes its content only rarely and allows for little visitor participation, the Smut Shack changes every time a new person visits, just as a party or discussion group does. At the *Playboy* site, visitors pretty much know what they will see and do beforehand. In the Smut Shack, it's always a surprise. Quite simply, the Smut Shack is a higher quality experience.

The loyalty of those who visit the Smut Shack may or may not translate into commercial success. The site has had mixed results attracting sponsors. "Most nonsmutty folks don't feel comfortable associating with something called the Smut Shack," says Thau. But in mid-1996, the Shack began a membership service, charging $10 per year for the ability to register a permanent online name, create your own home page, host your own chat area, log on to members-only areas. The Shack also brings in revenue by selling T-shirts, stickers, and other items, plus running a 900 number so its members can call one another on the phone anonymously. By exploiting all these ideas and technologies, the Smut Shack may become the first adult site to build a community and generate profits at the same time.

AN INTERACTIVE, NOT MASS, MEDIUM

Sex and smut are not the only reasons people visit the Web. Although naughty words consistently dominate the top ten lists of search terms, taken together they represent only a tiny portion—only about 2 to 3 percent—of what people search for on the Web. "The so-called for-

bidden words are what you'll find at the top of the list," says Alta
Vista's Monier. "But the total number of sex-related queries only
amount to a few percent. All the other queries are about people,
places, old cars, quilting clubs, et cetera—all of them also amounting
to tiny fractions of the total." In other words, people visit the Web for
every reason under the sun.

But no matter what any given Web site specializes in, this principle
will always hold true: The quantity of people visiting is far less important than the quality of their experience. Contrary to what some people
believe, the Web is not a *mass* medium. It's a niche medium, a personal
medium, and an interactive medium.

There may be tens of millions of people surfing the Web. But unlike
network television during prime time, you'll never find a significant
portion of them in any given place. With hundreds of thousands of Web
sites to choose from, none are going to dominate the digital landscape.
The name of the game for any content creator on the Web is to find a
unique niche, then use the interactive features of the Web to cater to a
very specific and loyal group of individuals. The actual size of the audience should be a secondary consideration.

This is especially true for markets in which there are hundreds of
well-known and not-so well-known brands vying for attention. News is
a perfect example. News of all kinds is one of the main magnets that
attracts people to the Web on a daily basis. Nearly every newspaper of
considerable size has responded accordingly, already launching a Web
site or planning to do so. Round-the-clock headline news, however,
has become an easy-to-come-by commodity, available from more online sources than you'd ever care to visit.

The news is everywhere these days. Major wire services such as the
Associated Press, Dow Jones, and Reuters used to be only available on
a subscription basis to newspapers, and TV and radio stations. Now,
these twenty-four-hour-per-day news services are available online to
consumers for free. One service, called PointCast, even dials and logs
onto the Web automatically for you every couple hours, retrieves

newswire copy, organizes it according to your preferences, and wraps it all up in a very friendly graphical user interface that acts as a substitute for your screen saver.

The pervasive nature of modern news is slowly changing the news business in a dramatic and irreversible way. For a glimpse of this, try this little experiment. On a weekday afternoon, check out PointCast or any other Web news service based on AP or Reuters feeds (or even the news section on America Online). Read the summary of the top stories of the day and scan the list of headlines for a few stories that have particular interest to you. Then, on your commute back from work, tune in to National Public Radio. When you get home, watch the evening news on one of the big three TV networks, CNN, MSNBC, or other TV news channel. Then, the next morning, look for the top national and international news in the front section of your local newspaper. Chances are, by the time you finish breakfast that morning, you will have digested the same news at least four times.

This exercise will also force you to think about how every well-known "retail" news organization adds value to the basic "wholesale" product put out by the wire services. On the Web, retail and wholesale news services exist side by side. No longer will people harbor the misconception that all the information delivered by their favorite news organization was gathered firsthand. "The mystique is taken away," says Andrew Nibley, editor of Reuters NewMedia and the person responsible for building the company's presence on the Web.

VALUE-ADDED NEWS

When your audience already knows what the wholesale news of the day is, it makes distinguishing your retail news source from the competition a harder task than ever. That's why any news outfit that wants to attract attention on the Web must go even further than they do with the product they distribute via its traditional channel. It must add something of significant value—something that gives their news product a clear edge over everyone else's.

In this respect, the term "value-added" has become the new mantra of the news and information business. "The news is omnipresent," writes Max Frankel, the former executive editor of the *New York Times*. "It's what you do with and around information that counts more and more."

USA Today has been struggling with this issue ever since it set foot on the Web. In April 1995, the national newspaper published by Gannett Inc., announced that it would begin providing software for people to access its new Web site, charging $12.95 per month for three hours of access to its online newspaper plus $2.50 for every hour after that. But after four months, it managed to attract only about 1,000 subscribers, a disastrous showing for a newspaper that has a daily print circulation of nearly two million.

Lorraine Cichowski, vice president and general manager of the Web service, says the paper's first mistake was the "unnecessary" move into the Internet access business, a market well served by America Online, Prodigy, CompuServe, Microsoft, Netcom, and others. The second mistake was overestimating the value of its basic news product and charging a subscription fee in the first place. So, starting in August 1995, *USA Today* began phasing out its software business and made its Web site free.

That move, of course, immediately boosted the quantity of people who visited the site. By the end of the year, 80,000 people were visiting daily. Of course, these were not the same 80,000 people every day. Since visitors were not required to register their names and enter a password, the paper had no idea whether it was attracting a high percentage of repeat customers or just large groups of curiosity seekers who would visit once and never return. Probably, it was a mixture of both. But it doesn't really matter, because this is a clear case of a Web site that falls short when it comes to the quality of experience.

Anyone who checks the wholesale news several times per day on the

Web or on an online service, can see immediately that *USA Today* does not add enough value to the basic news. To understand why this is so, we have to go back and examine the original value proposition of *USA Today.*

For years, *USA Today* was considered an inside joke in the publishing world. When it sprang up in 1981, the idea of putting out a national newspaper in a country as big as the United States was considered absurd. Until then, all general-interest newspapers had been local. Even the *New York Times* considered itself a local paper at heart and still does.

When readers and news professionals are asked in surveys what they think is the most important part of the paper, the vast majority always say local news. A 1996 survey by *Presstime* magazine showed that 100 percent of the 318 publishers and editors surveyed ranked local news as having "high or very high" appeal to their readers. National news was ranked second, right? No, number two, believe it or not, was obituaries (another form of local news). National news ranked *seventh,* behind local news, obituaries, classified advertising, display advertising, sports, and entertainment. In the world of newspapers, the chief value-added news has always been local content. For national and international news, in fact, many papers simply rewrite or reprint whatever is on the newswire.

USA Today had a different idea. Its colorful design, bite-size graphics, and national, one-product-fits-all philosophy may have earned it the derisive nickname "McPaper." Yet it became one of the most talked about, quoted, imitated, and bestselling papers in the country, surpassing the *New York Times,* the *Washington Post,* and the *Los Angeles Times* in circulation and moving within striking distance of the *Wall Street Journal* for the top spot. *USA Today* showed that there was indeed a market for a national newspaper. Of course, Gannett paid a heavy price for that. The paper was awash in red ink, losing money every year until 1993.

Unfortunately, the hefty investment put into *USA Today* did not translate into an advantage on the Web. A big part of the reason that

the paper was not profitable for twelve years had to do with the enormous levels of spending required to secure national, daily distribution
for a very expensive, full-color news product. No other paper had tried
to use so much color, which is far more costly than black and white.
And no other general-interest newspaper had tried to make itself available virtually everywhere—on street corner vending machines in all
big cities, on newsstands everywhere, at hotels, in airports. This way,
the paper could tap into the large numbers of business people who
were traveling and wanted a familiar read. "It's a business travel audience," says Cichowski. "It matches the Web perfectly."

On the Web, however, everyone has national distribution. In fact,
everyone has international distribution. Also, everyone can publish in
full color at only a marginally higher cost than black and white.
There's no expensive ink to buy, just minor design costs. With those
two advantages rendered moot on the Web, *USA Today* has been left to
grapple with the basic problem: How can it use this new medium to
add value to the news?

For an example of a newspaper that has done this extraordinarily
well, point your browser at the *San Jose Mercury News* site. In a sense,
this paper lucked out. It happens to be the local newspaper in a region
that the global high-tech industry calls home. Apple Computer, Intel,
and Hewlett-Packard are headquartered here, as are many of the
world's other best-known hardware, software, and telecommunications
companies. The industry's venture capital community is based here, as
are countless promising start-ups.

The *Mercury News* has capitalized on this natural advantage. The tag
line for the paper's Mercury Center site on the Web became "News and
Information for the Silicon Valley Community." Someone who lives
3,000 miles away from San Jose can't get the print edition of "the
Merc." But on the Web, those readers can feel part of that community,
getting news and the inside poop on an industry that interests them—
all prepared by a team of reporters who live there. Here's a case where
simply being on the Web brought potential exposure to a new audience.

Intensively covering a specific topic and delivering it to an audience that you couldn't reach before is just one way to use the Web to add value to the news. An even more sophisticated way is by creating a value-added service that customizes the news for each individual.

The Mercury Center has done that as well. At the site, visitors can subscribe to a service called NewsHound by filling out a simple form indicating a specific topic of interest—be it marine biology, baseball, or microbreweries. You E-mail the form to the *Mercury News,* where a news-filtering program will search thousands of stories from the paper and wire services, selecting the stories that meet your criteria. You can fine-tune the criteria whenever you want. Every hour, the NewsHound sends whatever it fetches right to your electronic mail address. Your hourly report can be called "News of the Web," for instance, providing you with just that. A custom news service such as this doesn't replace the need for a general-interest newspaper. But it can add value to any reader's daily news diet.

USA Today's tag line is: "Your News. When You Want It." It promises the right thing, but doesn't quite deliver. There's little on the *USA Today* Web site that you can't get elsewhere. And the initial versions of the Web site contained nothing that let readers customize the delivery of the news to their individual tastes and interests.

By offering value-added services, one might think that the *Mercury News* would be attracting many more visitors than *USA Today,* right? Well, as you may have guessed by now, that's not the case. *USA Today* attracts ten times the Web audience of the Mercury Center. But the smaller audience at the Mercury Center simply has a better browsing experience. What's the proof? The Mercury Center was selected as the best newspaper Web site by *Editor & Publisher,* an industry magazine. And NewsHound won the award for best original feature on a Web site.

More tangible proof lies in the fact that many Web surfers are actually paying for the Mercury Center. In April 1995, the company began charging $4.95 per month for subscriptions to its Web site. (Current subscribers to the daily print edition only have to pay $1 per month.) Some content, such as daily news summaries and classified ads, are still free to everyone, regardless of whether they pay. But for those who do sign up, their monthly fee buys them access to special breaking news stories during the day, plus the paper's comics page and unlimited access to ten years of the paper's archives. Subscribers also get the special Web-only features such as daily reports from industry conferences and other special-interest items. And for paid subscribers, the service is free of ads.

Barry Parr, product development manager for the site, says the Mercury Center attracted several thousand paying subscribers within the first few months of deciding to charge—not a bad start for a regional paper with a daily circulation of 300,000. In addition, several thousand other subscribers pay a separate $7.95 per month for the use of NewsHound. By selling value-added services along with news, the *Mercury News* has been able to make its Web site a profit center rather than just a promotional vehicle for its print product.

The Mercury Center has succeeded not by looking to maximize the number of visitors as much as it is looking to solidify its bond with its most loyal readers and obtain some loyal new ones outside its traditional customer base. That is what all Web sites should be doing.

DECONSTRUCTION

You can already see it happening right before your eyes. Once they enter the Web economy, all magazines and newspapers that you can hold in your hands *deconstruct*—in the true sense of the word. They lose their unity. They break up or decompose into their constituent elements. No longer is the editorial product a cohesive package tightly controlled by a team of editors. Once on the Web, the editors must relinquish some of that control to the readers, who play a big part in reinventing and reinterpreting how that information is seen. Instead of flipping through pages in a linear fashion, readers may pick and choose from menus of stories, look up stock quotes, search databases of classified ads, and have conversations with editors and other read-ers. They may never even see what the editors deem the top story of the day.

For a time, the term "newspaper" and "magazine" will act as re-minders, as familiar metaphors that represent something from the old media. These words will enable us to compare how the interactive ex-perience differs from the ink-on-paper experience. But as these media assets deconstruct in the Web economy, such words will eventually give way to new ones. What we are left with is a participatory experi-ence that could in some ways be more powerful, more informative, and more compelling than the original editorial product.

Just because publications deconstruct when they enter Web space doesn't mean they will disappear in physical space. Paper publications in most cases will still exist—if they are able to withstand a new source of competition for their readers' attention. A deconstructed newspaper or magazine on the Web won't so much replace the paper product but ideally add to the relationship that the overall brand has with its customers.

Throughout history, new media have rarely supplanted old media entirely; they just forced change upon them. "No new medium ever completely replaces another," says Mark Kvamme (pron. *Quah-me*), CEO of interactive ad agency CKS Group. "Even cave paintings haven't gone away—we just call them graffiti."

When evening TV news programs burst onto the scene after World War II, many newspaper companies were eventually forced to shut down their afternoon editions. But instead of withering away, the smart publishers shifted their resources to the morning editions. The best musical recordings of the past weren't forgotten when digital technol-ogy came along; yesterday's LPs and eight-track tapes were just rere-leased on compact disc. Multimedia CD-ROMs have largely replaced unwieldy shelf-loads of encyclopedias and other big reference books, but smart book publishers have been learning to capitalize on this new technology, not ignore it at their own peril.

Books, newspapers, radio, motion pictures, broadcast television, cable television, desktop publishing—all of these media forms are going strong even though they have had to struggle to find their place in an ever-changing media mix.

No doubt, forced change can be disconcerting for traditional-minded publishers. But the smart brand-name publications are now aggressively using their print products as launching pads for new interactive services. *Business Week*, for instance, uses the magazine to advertise an online computer-buying guide and live chat sessions about timely topics, hosted by its editors. The *Wall Street Journal* publishes a growing "directory of services" in the paper every day. Subscribers can order news products such as Dow Jones News Retrieval, the Personal Journal, and of course the Interactive Edition site on the Web.

The *Journal*'s Interactive Edition in particular has extended the *Journal*'s brand into cyberspace in a powerful way. Not only did more than 650,000 readers register their names and E-mail addresses at the site during its free trial period from April to September 1996, but more than 50,000 people were actually paying for the service by the beginning of 1997. Again, that sheer number is not all that impressive. At $49 per year (or $29 for current print subscribers), such fees promise to bring in only a tiny portion of the *Journal*'s overall revenue stream—for now at least. But that small core of online readers are apt to be the paper's best targets for future value-added services that can bring in even more revenue.

In the news business, value-added products must deliver customized information to readers throughout the day, not just an online version of the paper product. Rather than cannibalizing its existing business, these types of services entice consumers to spend more time interacting with the brand name they have come to trust. Rather than boost market share, these interactive products boost "mindshare" among a group of ultraimportant customers.

DECIDING WHAT TO CHARGE FOR

These new interactive services must eventually become profitable businesses in their own right. Otherwise, they just drain dollars and creative energy from the original franchise. Here's where content creators must stay focused on the idea of creating a unique, quality experience. Putting the full text online for free, like many publications have done, is just a starting point. It might initially attract lots of Web surfers, but it is not a recipe for profitability.

Of course, there's nothing specifically *wrong* with attracting large numbers of visitors. But one of the most common misconceptions about the Web is that sheer numbers are proof that your site is successful—that all you have to do is run up big numbers, then sell advertising space on your site to marketers who want to reach your audience. Advertising certainly has its place on the Web. (We will discuss advertising beginning in the next chapter.) But reliance on sheer audience size is a recipe for success on *television,* not the Web. For content creators, the top priority must be making sure that the people who visit your site are satisfied enough to return again and again.

In addition to the *Wall Street Journal,* there are a select few content sites on the Web that actually manage to do both—attract a large audience and provide a high-quality, interactive experience to a core group of consumers. One of them is ESPN SportsZone. Since it went live in the spring of 1995, SportsZone has been right up there with *Playboy* among the most heavily traveled sites on the Web, quickly building up to an audience size of about 100,000 people every day. Developed by Starwave Corp., Microsoft cofounder Paul Allen's Seattle-based start-up, the site operates under a partnership with the ESPN sports cable channel, which is owned by Disney/ABC.

In sports, as in all other content categories, the process of adding value begins with knowing your market. Mike Slade, the CEO of Starwave, was a sportswriter for his college newspaper. He knows firsthand that sports fans are information junkies. Slade himself used to spend long nights pouring over scores, standings, and statistics spewing from the AP machine. But he could only provide a small sliver of that information in the next edition of the paper.

Sports fans always want more. When the typical baseball, football, hockey, or basketball devotee gets the morning paper, he pours over the sports pages as if he were an archaeologist inspecting a fossil, looking for every nuance. The millions of fans managing fantasy teams in a Rotisserie or Fantasy league are even more fanatical. To these people, the typical newspaper sports section is "an increasingly anachronistic subset of the total sports news," says Slade.

It wasn't until the advent of online services in general and the World Wide Web in particular that it became possible to give sports fans the ability to satisfy their bottomless hunger for information. Whereas newspapers only devote a few pages to sports and focus on the local teams, the SportsZone always offers the equivalent of 10,000 pages of continually updated data on every game, team, and player. Not only can baseball fans examine every box score, but they can look up scouting reports on minor league prospects. Basketball fans can even look up "game-flow diagrams," which graphically chart the shifts in the game's momentum over time. As the Web gets faster, the SportsZone plans to add more and more video highlights on demand, clipped from ESPN programs.

All of this stuff is free and supported by advertising. What Slade decided to charge for are two things: First, access to daily reports from very opinionated sports columnists with loyal followings. These columnists offer insights and context that can't be found in straight-forward game summaries and box scores. And second, the site charges membership fees for online Rotisserie leagues, in which the computer organizes daily sports data, compiles it, and presents detailed, customized reports telling individuals exactly how their handpicked team is doing. "We do all the paperwork," the Web site announces. In a sense, all the massive amounts of free information on the SportsZone site acts as an advertisement to draw some people into the paid areas of the site.

The end result is a two-tiered Web site. On one level, anyone with access to the Web can visit SportsZone for free. Meanwhile, a much smaller core of users pay $4.95 per month. They tune in more frequently and spend much more time per visit. Paying members have been growing into a sizable group—about 140,000 by mid-1996. Starwave predicts that by 1998 membership will surpass the three million subscription base of *Sports Illustrated* magazine.

Which set of visitors is more important? Tom Phillips, a vice president at Starwave, maintains that both groups are equal in his eyes. "We have to be indifferent as to whether you subscribe or not," Phillips says. "We're happy to have you either way."

That may be true when it comes to packaging a mass audience for advertisers. But in terms of forging a relationship between the content creator and the consumer, the paid visitors clearly should be top priority. Not only do they provide a reliable revenue stream, but when they subscribe they often provide key information that can give you a picture of what types of people are interested in your site. Forging an ongoing relationship with each of these loyal consumers is what doing business on the Web is all about.

One of the chief competitors to SportsZone, a sports Web site called SportsLine, takes a decidedly more aggressive approach to courting paid subscribers. Like SportsZone, SportsLine has a two-tiered service. SportsZone places a little ticket symbol next to the articles that are for subscribers only; SportsLine uses red stars to do the same. But SportsLine simply uses the red star more often, placing even a higher percentage of its content in the subscriber-only category.

Deciding what to charge for and what to give away for free is not easy. If you charge for too many things, it will drive away first-time visitors who want to sample your stuff to see how good it is. If you charge for too few things, you risk failing to attract enough subscribers to financially support your Web venture. The whole process is sort of like one of those summer evening carnivals on the boardwalk. If the band playing for free isn't good enough, people might not stick around to try those knock-the-pins-over-and-win-a-teddy-bear games for $1—or

buy some fried dough. If there are too many free games and food samples, the people charging won't make any money. And if you charged
admission to attend the carnival in the first place, it might deter people from coming at all.

The main goal is to form a lasting bond with individual consumers.
Charging a subscription for some of your content is not a prerequisite
to forging such a bond, but it serves as tangible proof that you are providing people with a quality Web experience. Even the $1 that the
Mercury News charges for print subscribers helps seal an important
part of the relationship between consumer and content creator. As soon
as a consumer pays for a service, she now has an incentive to use it as
often as possible. The question lies not so much in how much you
charge, but *what you charge for.*

Here is where the classic example of Mr. Gillette giving away his razors and charging for the blades offers little guidance. On the Web, no
one knows what are the razors and what are the blades. Each business
will have to decide for itself which works best. Early pioneers in this
area have the opportunity to set the trend for their entire industry.

CHURCH AND STATE

This tug-of-war over what you should charge for has been the subject
of many ongoing, behind-the-scenes battles at media giants. Take
Time Warner, for instance. By virtue of the sheer weight of its content,
Time Warner's Pathfinder site quickly became one of the most popular
sites on the Web after its debut in October 1994. The Pathfinder site
was conceived as an umbrella for dozens of online services from all
parts of the sprawling Time Warner entertainment and information
conglomerate—including the well-known magazines such as *Time,*
People, Sports Illustrated, Fortune, and *Entertainment Weekly.* In just
magazines alone, Time Warner was offering each consumer who visited
$150 per month worth of free reading.

The editorial side of the company ("the church") argued that readers should be picking up part of the tab for Pathfinder, while the business side of the company ("the state") argued that the service should rely only on advertising to support the venture.

Time magazine veteran Walter Isaacson, who was editor of the company's New Media division from 1993 through 1995, argues that information that people pay for is inherently more credible. "If a giveaway paper lands on your lawn next to the newspaper you pay for, you'll turn to the one you subscribe to for information," Isaacson says. It's just plain dangerous for a journalistic organization to rely solely on sponsors for its livelihood, Isaacson adds. It removes the direct economic bond that journalists have with their readers. When that bond is not there, he implies, all hell could break loose: Publishers could decide to let the line between church and state wither. They could begin selling out the editorial process to please advertisers, just like many publishers of free magazines and producers of infomercials already do.

Michael Kinsley, editor of *Slate*, Microsoft's Webzine has towed the same line. "Self-supporting journalism is freer journalism," Kinsley wrote in *Slate*'s inaugural issue. "Depending completely on advertising wouldn't be healthy, even if it were possible." But alas, he ate his words months later when Microsoft dropped plans to levy a $19.95 subscription fee. "We chickened out," Kinsley lamented.

The subtext is this: In a society in which many people cannot distinguish between fact and fiction, between reality and manufactured pseudoreality, the interest of advertisers cannot gain the upper hand. Would you want to learn about Medicare, for instance, on a Web site sponsored by a drug company—or by the Republican National Committee? "Not everything should be sponsored and free," Isaacson says. "I don't want to let the Web degenerate to that."

The problem that Time Warner faced is that much of its print content simply didn't work well on the Web. "I'm a subscriber to the print version of *Entertainment Weekly,* and I love reading it," comments Andrew Anker, president of Hotwired. "But you couldn't pay me to read

it online." (At least not until Internet connectivity is available in bath-
rooms.)

So the classic argument about subscription fees versus advertising
was besides the point. First, you need something for which people are
going to pay. Like many publishing enterprises, Time Warner has been
learning that what makes a quality reading experience doesn't necessarily make for a quality Web experience. Some of the very content
from which Time Warner makes millions in other media can't even be
given away on the Web.

The business model was out of whack. Pathfinder managed to generate about $2 million in advertising revenue in the second half of
1995, roughly its first six months selling ads. That was more than any
other content site on the Web. But the cost of paying a staff of more
than seventy people plus expenditures on server computers and other
technology put the venture in the red. Indeed, industry reports had
Time Warner losing close to $1 million per month on Pathfinder
throughout that period.

These mounting losses sent the company down a path toward developing value-added services for which consumers would shell out
money. People may not pay to read all those magazines online, but perhaps they would pay for a simple, personalized news service in which
they could custom-configure their own magazine that draws content
from dozens of Time Warner properties.

Perhaps readers of Time Warner's *Southern Living* magazine would
pay to experiment with some of the magazine's landscaping tips, creating their own virtual garden by using their mouse to manipulate on-
screen graphics, then show off their creations to other online
gardeners. Like Bianca's Smut Shack, the Virtual Garden could be a
place where like-minded people congregated whenever they logged
onto the Web. They would come back to the site again and again to
check the status of something they put in motion the last time they
were there.

What it all came down to at Time Warner was using the interactive features of the Web to deliver personalized media. Here's how Isaacson sums it up: "It's not mass media; it's personal. Products can have a broad reach but a very personal touch."

THE PATH TO PROFITABILITY

Often times, the interactive services that draw the most attention from Web surfers aren't at all the kind of stuff that reporters and editors are used to creating.

The *Boston Globe,* for instance, realized this early on when it decided to make its Boston.com site not just an online newspaper but rather a wide-ranging, citywide information service and online meeting place that draws on the resources of other media institutions in the region. One of the most popular features on Boston.com is a service to look up recent home sales as well as new homes on the market. Is this what reporters would consider news? No, but if you are looking for a home or just curious about the selling prices in your neighborhood, this is value-added information. It's also a way of generating revenue. While basic listing information is free, full property reports cost between $2 and $10 per listing.

If brand-name media institutions fail to capitalize on these opportunities, organically grown information services will be there to take these emerging markets away from them. Just consider Fish Wrap, an organically grown interactive news environment for students at the Massachusetts Institute of Technology. Many MIT students have little inclination to read the *Globe,* as many of them didn't grow up in the Boston area. Fish Wrap takes that into account. Not only does it sport a great tongue-in-cheek name, but this Web site packages the commodity wire service news in unique ways. Readers organize all that news into sections based on their personal preferences. If you are from Phoenix, for instance, you can create a section for stories about and from your hometown.

The most popular features involve new ways to cater to these personal preferences. The weather report will compare the forecast for Boston with that of your hometown. If you are from Calgary, it may tell you that Saturday will be unseasonably warm. If you are from Miami, it will tell you that the same weather is unseasonably cold. Instead of one "Dear Abby" for everyone, subscribers can select from several advice columnists. The "Ask Angela" column, for instance, is written by an MIT psychology major. She tailors her advice to her audience and gets all her questions via E-mail from this select group. There is a "graffiti board" feature that lets students express their opinions on very local issues such as: "Less than 10 percent of faculty are members of minorities. Is this a problem?" or simply: "What is the geekiest thing you've ever done?"

Like traditional newspapers, Fish Wrap does have a "page one." But it takes a different tack on who decides which stories should appear there. Instead of a team of editors making those decisions, the readers recommend their favorite stories from their personal-interest sections. These recommendations are tallied as votes. All stories can be voted on up to two days after they go online. Sometimes, this community has odd choices as to what it considers newsworthy. One day recently, the story with the most votes was a commentary entitled: "IBM foolishly wasted the potential of OS/2." It's not exactly something that would appear above the fold in the *New York Times*.

International news stories on the Fish Wrap site provide personalized context to help readers understand far-off events. If there is a flood in Zaire, the story will say the water has covered an area about the size of Massachusetts. Instead of a news story stating that forest fires in Brazil burned x-number of acres, the story could say it destroyed the equivalent of the inside Route 128 belt around Boston. By adding a local perspective to foreign events, such news can have a bigger impact. It hits home, so to speak.

Another organically grown news service is run by a start-up called Individual Inc., the Burlington, Massachusetts, company that runs a

Web site called NewsPage. Visitors fill out an electronic form in which they choose among 850 very specific business news topics—from genetic research to network security to groupware. After receiving the profile of a certain user's interests, Individual's software scans a stream of more than 20,000 incoming stories from 2,000 daily and weekly publications every evening and provides a customized news digest to each user every morning. In just its first two months in business, NewsPage attracted an impressive 50,000 users who pay at least $2.95 per month. Subscription fees make up one-third of the site's revenue. The other two-thirds comes from advertising.

It's quite an honor to become one of the sites for which a Web surfer will actually pay—for the simple reason that it doesn't happen all that often. In a Web economy flooded with free information, most users will tend to treat information charges as damage, and route around them. In this sense, the Web is like cable TV: People will pay for delivery of the medium itself, but will pay extra for only one, two, maybe three or four premium channels, if any.

But in terms of the relationship that consumers have with content, the Web differs from cable TV in more significant ways. Cable channels such as MTV, C-SPAN, and E! all receive a portion of the fees that subscribers pay to their local cable company. While that only amounts to a few pennies tossed to each channel from each subscriber's typical monthly bill of $25 to $35, those pennies add up rather quickly for channels that reach tens of millions of homes.

People who surf the Web also pay a monthly subscription fee—to their Internet access provider. But unlike a local cable company, the Internet access provider typically doesn't pay royalties to any individual content providers. On the Web, individual consumers decide for themselves what "channels" they want. Often, they store their channel choices as "bookmarks" in their Web browser program, which enables them to visit their favorite sites by clicking the mouse on any of the bookmark entries.

A recent survey shows that the average Web surfer keeps about forty different bookmarks. That number is likely to rise, if only slightly, as people discover more and more Web sites that interest them. Of course, people also periodically delete those sites that no longer merit their attention. The point is that the Web is a customized medium, and it's the customers who do the customizing. The chances that two people would have the same set of bookmarks is very slim—even if those two people had the same demographics. It's possible for Internet access providers to set up cablelike plans in the future (a package of ten value-added sites could be sold for a $5 per month premium fee). But most likely, Web sites will largely have to fend for themselves.

To stay viable, a Web site must strike an individual bargain with each Web surfer. The hypercompetition for both the attention and the dollars of consumers will force every successful content creator to abandon the fight to obtain the most visitors. Instead, the battle clearly must be fought on the basis of providing a quality experience tailored to each individual's taste. This makes the Web the ultimate in personalized media.

Can these personal, value-added services be considered journalism? Probably not, at least not in the traditional sense. But the plain truth is that newspapers and magazines and TV news programs have *never* made their money by providing the public with journalism—at least not directly. As one newspaper publisher told me: "We don't make money selling information. In fact, we lose money delivering the paper to people. We make our money by selling our audience to advertisers." For content creators who cannot or do not desire to rely solely on advertising revenue for their livelihood, the invention of new value-added services offers the best path to profitability.

<Chapter Summary>
• Building a long-term business on the Web is done not just by momentarily *grabbing* people's attention, but also by *sustaining* it with something of unique value, something that causes people to return to your site again and again.
• Don't just supply information electronically; create an online *community* where people with similar interests want to congregate and interact with one another.
• Although great masses of people use it, the Web is *not a mass medium* and never will be. It's an *interactive* medium, a *niche* medium, and ultimately a *personal* medium in which every user's experience is different than every other's.
• Online publications won't replace paper ones, as history shows that new media rarely displace old. Editors must *reinvent* their publications in cyberspace, creating a participatory experience that builds on the relationship the overall brand has with its readers.
• Ultimately, news and information sites will achieve profitability not by relying on selling advertising or by collecting subscription fees, but by inventing and charging for new *value-added services,* such as specialized delivery of knowledge, advice, or wisdom.

<CHAPTER TWO>

Marketers Shouldn't Be on the Web for *Exposure*, but for *Results*

BROCHURE-WARE

Mass marketing won't work on the World Wide Web. The idea that marketers can burnish a brand image in the minds of millions is fine for a TV advertisement or a print campaign. But it's an unrealistic fantasy in this new medium. What the Web can accomplish for marketers is potentially even more powerful. Still, countless marketers have ignored what the Web can do well and mistakenly tried to use their Web site to do what they have always been doing—simultaneously shipping the same message to the masses.

Consider the case of Volvo. In the fall of 1994, Volvo Cars of North America became the first automaker to establish a Web presence and one of the first advertisers on popular content sites. In those early days of the Web, the most popular content creators, such as Hotwired, Time Warner's Pathfinder, ESPN SportsZone, and *Playboy*'s site, all began charging between $30,000 and $100,000 for a three-month placement of a logo or banner on their digital pages. These ads are also known as "links." Click on one of these buttons and your eyes are transported, or linked, to a promotional Web site running on some other computer somewhere else. After interacting with that advertisement, you will presumably link right back to where you were.

In buying banner advertisements on the Web, Volvo was hoping to enhance its brand image. And by attracting Web surfers to its site, the Swedish automaker also wanted to give people in the market for a luxury car a new information tool that would make them consider a Volvo more seriously, says Bob Austin, Volvo's director of U.S. marketing. He notes that only about 6 percent of the adult population has the money and inclination to buy an automobile costing at least $30,000. He saw those people as having a high overlap with the early Web surfers. "We know that our potential buyers are well-off and tend to be early adopters—people who enjoy technology," Austin says. So the company spent about $100,000 developing and advertising what started out as essentially just an electronic brochure.

Not only did the Volvo site fail to lead to many, if any, sales, but it actually caused unintended problems. The only truly interactive part of the site was the ability to send E-mail to Volvo's U.S. headquarters in New Jersey. "People would occasionally write things like: 'Nice Web site, but the sun roof on my 850 leaks,' " Austin says. Many state lemon laws require responses to such complaints within a few weeks, otherwise the manufacturer has to take the car back. Since Volvo failed to staff the site with people who were qualified to respond to such complaints, the Web site became a tool not to *increase* sales but a potential way to *damage* them. So the E-mail feature had to be shut down within a few weeks.

With that bitter experience in hand, Volvo decided to pull back all its Web advertising and simply promote the site in its own TV and print ads. Austin says he just wasn't getting value for the money spent, especially since the content sites weren't able to provide hard numbers about who exactly they were linking to his site. "I'm not comfortable throwing more money at advertising the site," he says. "We're not here to sell Web sites. Web sites should be here to sell cars."

Volvo made two crucial mistakes. The first foible was in treating consumers on the Web as a distinct demographic group in and of itself. Back then, that was understandable. It's true that the early Web surfers tended to be upscale, well-educated, techno-savvy males. Although it may always tilt to that core audience, the Web is more and more coming to resemble a cross section of the population at large. As bigger crowds of people stream into cyberspace every day, the trick for marketers will be to pluck their best and most likely customers from that pool—not indiscriminately trying in vain to reach all of them.

The second, much bigger mistake was failing to take advantage of the unique attributes of the Web. Providing potential customers with an electronic rendition of a brochure—brochure-ware—is of little value when it's faster and easier to flip through one made of paper. As a result, Volvo was not able to forge relationships with individual consumers. The only method Volvo had for trading information with consumers was the nonfunctional E-mail feature. The worst thing you can do is suggest that you're willing to communicate with customers and then not have the capacity to respond.

LINK AND THINK

At bottom, the Web represents a back-to-basics approach for marketers. Picture the process of prospecting for customers as a giant funnel. Traditional mass-market advertising on TV and radio as well as in national newspapers and magazines work at or near the wide mouth of the funnel. No ad on a Web site will ever provide the mass exposure of those media. But where the Web can work its wonders, however, is at the bottom, or spout, of the funnel, capturing individual drops of business. "The most important thing the Web can deliver is a fully qualified lead or customer," says Emily Green, an analyst with Forrester Research Inc., who studies Web marketing.

Rich Everett, manager of interactive communications for Chrysler Corporation, puts it this way: He says there are four steps to landing a customer—tell, sell, link, and think. A traditional ad, he says, will "tell" you that a product exists and "sell" you on its benefits. The Web, however, must pick up where traditional ads leave off. If Chrysler does its job right on the Web, he says, it will "link" qualified and interested buyers into a virtual showroom and give them enough information and interactive tools to "think" whether they are actually going to purchase the car.

"On the Web," Everett declares, "everything we knew about advertising is out the window."

Advertising in the mass media is based on "impressions," a nebulous term for the marketing messages that get imprinted in the public's mind. Advertising agencies measure impressions in "gross ratings points." One gross ratings point on television means that you got your message into approximately one million households.

McDonald's, for instance, budgeted 30,000 gross ratings points for a recent fiscal year. That multiplies out to 30 billion impressions annually. With about 100 million households in the United States, that averages out to 300 impressions per household each year, or nearly one per day. No wonder that McDonald's has the slogan "Have you had your break today?" The fast-food giant is quite literally reminding every TV watcher to eat at McDonald's daily. The company pays a half-billion dollars per year in the United States for these little reminders.

The Web will never enable a marketer to achieve this kind of exposure. Never. There are simply too many Web sites, making it impossible to predict where Web surfers will go in any given session. Even if a mass marketer such as McDonald's bought advertising space on the most popular 100 sites, it still might miss two-thirds of the audience in a given day. Most importantly, an advertisement on a popular Web site—say, *USA Today*—usually consists of a banner that can only present a fairly small graphic or a simple message.

A banner is not as powerful as a TV ad. Let's say the McDonald's banner said: HAVE YOU HAD YOUR BREAK TODAY? It wouldn't be using full-screen graphics, audio, or other rich forms of communication to extol the satisfying experience of driving through or entering a McDonald's restaurant, where happy people eat happy meals. For that kind of presentation, the Web surfer would have to click on the banner and link over to the McDonald's Web site. But a banner ad will typically entice only about 2 to 5 percent of the people who see it to click on it. At best, even the most free-spending mass marketer could only hope to reach a small fraction of Web surfers.

This is why marketers on the Web must shift their basic objective and adhere to the second principle of Webonomics: Marketers shouldn't be on the Web for *exposure*, but for *results*.

To appreciate the difference between exposure and results, consider a brand name such as Prudential. Everyone alive today grew up with mass-exposure advertising pioneered by this and a handful of other American companies. In 1896, J. Walter Thompson, one of the first advertising agencies, created one of the first national, brand-image print advertisement campaigns when it appropriated the rock of Gibraltar symbol for the Prudential Life Insurance Company. This brand identity, complete with the "get a piece of the rock" tag line later popularized in TV commercials, has endured for a century. In fact, the corporate logo is still based on the same rock.

But when the investments arm of the company, Prudential Securities, embraced the Web exactly 100 years later, it smartly realized that putting up banners telling people to get a piece of the rock wouldn't work on its own. Today's sophisticated consumer recognizes a corporate image for what it is: a symbol that means something only if the company lives up to what it promises.

There has to be a compelling reason people would come to any marketer's Web site in the first place, then interact with the company, and finally return to the site again and again. So, Prudential created one of the first financial Web sites in which existing customers could instantly look up their account balances, perform transactions on their portfolio, and send E-mail to their personal financial advisor—and expect an answer.

This type of service-based marketing represents the Web at its most powerful. With access to a Web service like this, Prudential's existing customers now have a rock-solid reason for remaining loyal. And potential new customers who surf the Web have a rationale for signing up for the company's services. Prudential will continue to use *mass media* for reaffirming its brand image—an image, incidentally, that was tarnished by a major financial scandal in the early 1990s.

The company looked to the Web not for mass exposure, but for specific results—getting and retaining customers. While other financial firms were still in the stage of simply providing online versions of the brochures that they typically mail to clients and prospects, Prudential distinguished itself by providing individuals with custom access to their own information. The best ads on the Web don't tell you only about the company and its products; they also tell you about yourself.

Providing a valuable service that keeps your customers loyal is just one type of result that the Web can deliver. Getting highly interested consumers to spend time learning about a new product, such as a new car model, is also valuable to a marketer. Collecting psychographic, or consumer psychology, information from a person using or considering your product is another type of result. And, of course, actually taking orders and selling your product over the Web is the ultimate end.

ALL EYEBALLS AREN'T CREATED EQUAL

To say that this second principle challenges the fundamental worldview of the advertising industry would be a tremendous understatement. Traditionally, advertisers purchase impressions based on how many people *might* see the ad. Advertisers compare the cost of buying print pages and broadcast time based on the amount of money it takes to reach a thousand consumers. This ratio, the cost per thousand (confusingly shortened to CPM—the M being the Roman numeral for thousand), is ingrained into the consciousness of every advertising industry executive. The television industry uses Nielsen ratings to set ad prices, and the publishing industry uses audited circulation figures.

In this model, a network television show will typically have a CPM of about $5. A typical newspaper or magazine would be priced at around $40 to $60, since they provide a smaller but more targeted geographic or demographic segment of the mass audience.

In the early days of the Web, content sites didn't know what to charge for banner advertisements. So they arbitrarily settled on a $75 to $100 CPM on the theory that a Web site can provide an even more targeted audience than a special-interest magazine.

Those were the official prices at least. The little-kept secret was that few advertisers were paying the prices published on the official advertising rate cards. "There are rate cards, but nobody pays the official rate," says Mary Lou Floyd, business manager for AT&T's promotional Web site. "Some are terribly unrealistic, so you go in and do heavy negotiating."

Although advertisers are generally comfortable paying for potential exposure for a certain number of eyeballs, getting into the whole CPM mind-set on the Web was a big mistake for everyone involved. Since the medium was new and no one could even prove that they were indeed attracting the number of visitors that they had claimed, few advertisers were confident in the value they were getting for their money.

The CPM model should be moot here. The Web should not be just another way of selling exposure to large numbers of eyeballs. This new medium wouldn't be such a big deal if it were just a slightly more targeted way of reaching an audience with an advertising message. Rather, the Web represents a fundamentally new way of approaching the task of marketing.

Even though logic dictates that exposure should take a back seat to results, countless businesses piling on the Web have been putting their priorities precisely in reverse.

PC Meter, a Nielsen-like ratings service for the Web, has been preying on this fundamental misunderstanding. Whereas the A. C. Nielsen Company recruits a sample of TV watchers and then installs an electronic device in their sets to track viewing habits, PC Meter uses special software to do the same for personal computers. National Purchase Diary (NPD), a Port Washington, New York, consumer research company, installs this piece of software on a sample of computers to track surfing habits. By the summer of 1996, NPD had installed the PC Meter software on a sample of 10,000 home computers throughout the United States.

How do they get people to agree to such monitoring? "We tell people that their contribution is important and that we appreciate it," says Steve Coffey, a former vice president of data collection at A. C. Nielsen who now runs NPD's PC Meter project. There is also a nominal reward, such as an appliance, a radio, a crystal vase, or a coffee mug. "And we guard your privacy," Coffey says. "You show me that you're going to HotSex.com and no one will know. Not your boss, your wife, your girlfriend, not even HotSex.com."

What does NPD do with all the data it collects? It compiles it into lists of top-rated Web sites. The data are broken down into categories—which sites scored the highest among females as opposed to males, for instance, or how competing news sites, shopping sites, adult sites, search engines, and so on stacked up against one another. Then NPD sells that data to advertising agencies, media planners, hardware and software makers, and Web site developers.

The top-rated Web sites have been the search engines such as Yahoo!, Lycos, Alta Vista, and InfoSeek, as well as the default home pages of browser programs from Netscape, Microsoft, America Online, and CompuServe. These are the places that capture the highest share of attention. Sites such as these have been garnering "reach ratings" that range from ten to as high as thirty-eight, meaning that 10 to 38 percent of Web surfers were visiting these sites at least once per monthly rating period. And in turn, these are the sites that have been capturing the lion's share of advertising dollars.

The problem with these sites, however, is that they are like billboards around airports. Lots of people will pass by but very few will take the time to notice them. Ad banners at these sites tend to get very low "click-thru" rates, meaning only a tiny percentage of surfers— typically fewer than 1 percent—will click on the banner and visit the marketer's Web site.

The next tier of sites, from the Web's most popular content creators, have been receiving PC Meter reach ratings that range from one to six. Pathfinder, C/Net, Disney, ZD Net, *USA Today,* ESPN SportsZone, Dilbert, *Playboy,* Hotwired, the *Wall Street Journal,* and CNN's Web site have all been in this range.

But if you consider advertising on these sites from a mass-marketing perspective, the numbers aren't very compelling. Let's say twenty million people surf the Web in a given month. A content site with a five rating will be viewed by one million people (20,000,000 × .05). If you want to reach one million people with a marketing message, you're better off paying the often lower CPM rates for radio, newspapers, magazines, or TV. Those media all provide a much richer format for a marketing message than a simple two- by four-inch Web banner on someone's computer screen—even if you consider that it's now possible to animate those banner ads with moving graphics.

The Web does its magic when a consumer actually clicks on the banner. Research shows that only about 2 to 5 percent of the people who see a banner on a content site will actually do this. So, instead of a million people, you are really getting about 25,000. If these 25,000 people are excellent prospects for your product or service, the money you have spent on advertising has been well worth it. If not, if these 25,000 folks are just curiosity seekers who happened to stumble upon your banner, then you've wasted your money.

Many marketers have already caught on to this very crucial fact. To see how this is shaking out, take a look at the ratings data compiled by Internet Profiles Corp., or I/PRO. Based in San Francisco, I/PRO installs software on dozens of client companies that have built Web sites. The software monitors the internal log files being generated on the server computers that run these Web sites. Whereas PC Meter monitors what individual PC owners do, I/PRO monitors the usage patterns of the Web sites themselves.

After studying the actual usage data at more than seventy-five content sites that subscribe to its ratings service, I/PRO concluded that the relationship between traffic on a site and advertising rates is "weak at best," says Bob Ivins, I/PRO's vice president of market research. In fact, rates have jumped all over the map.

Playboy, for instance, has been charging $7.50 to $10 per thousand impressions. Netscape, has been charging a CPM of about $20. Pathfinder has been asking for $75 and Hotwired claims $150. How could there be such a big difference in the cost it takes to put your banner before a thousand sets of eyeballs?

The logic can't be explained in terms of numbers. Thus, there is something more going on here. All eyeballs aren't created equal. Depending on what your product or service is, one set is obviously more valuable than another. Many marketers have been discovering that quality of experience is more important than quantity of visitors. A Web surfer who spends time returning to his favorite content site again and again is going to be more receptive than someone who visits just once and never returns. These repeat customers will be more likely to click through to your promotional site. Once these qualified and interested consumers are at your door, results can follow.

REGAINING CONTROL

The distinguishing factor between one-way media and two-way, or interactive media, is the simple matter of control. In traditional media, advertising is *intrusive.* The marketer purchases space and has complete control over what goes in that space. The viewer or reader has to look at that ad as the marketer intended it. The only recourse is turning the page or changing the channel. As a result, the advertisers can say whatever they want. And they sometimes take this paid-for privilege to absurd heights. Does anybody honestly believe, for instance, that drinking Slim-Fast shakes twice a day amounts to "balanced nutrition for a healthy life," as the company's slogan says? Probably not. But if you repeat it often enough using an emotional rather than a rational appeal, you end up with a brand image.

The rule of thumb on Madison Avenue is that the average consumer is bombarded with 3,000 advertising messages per day. You might read the morning paper, see billboards, and listen to the radio on the way to work (or glance at the ads in the subway train). Later, you might flip through a magazine at lunchtime, then come home and sift through marketing pitches in the mail and finally watch several hours of television in the evening. With logos and messages emblazoned on our T-shirts, sneakers, and jeans, we have all become walking advertisements. And we have little or no control over which ads come at us. That we are immersed in commercialism from the time we wake up to the time we go to sleep is now a simple fact of life. If advertisers could find a way to sponsor our dreams—or better yet insert subtle product placements—they would undoubtedly do so.

For many people, the initial response to all the marketing now happening on the Web might be: "Oh, great, I can't even get away from ads when I'm on my own personal computer."

But here is where the relationship between marketer and consumer gets flipped on its head. On the Web, people obtain complete control over what messages they choose to interact with and how they interact with those messages.

When this happens, the familiar notion of an advertisement or a commercial *deconstructs*. Like the concept of a newspaper or a magazine, ads as we know them will not exist in the Web economy. When marketers and their advertising agencies fully realize that they must relinquish absolute control over the message that they are communicating to the public, then the game changes forever. As the users exert their free will, an advertisement morphs into an interactive marketing experience in which the consumer and marketer have a more balanced, peer-to-peer relationship. The term "advertisement" becomes just a metaphor, just a way to compare what we are now doing to something that we already know too well.

Nicholas Negroponte, the director of MIT's Media Laboratory, calls this the difference between *pushing* and *pulling*. Old media push messages at us. In the new media, we pull the information. Consumers on the Web actively seek information from the marketer. Getting your message out to an individual requires that individual's consent. If a consumer is in the market for a new home, for instance, she might at some point go to a Web directory, look up Web sites run by mortgage companies, and research the latest deals and prices. If a marketer wants to send a message to that consumer during this process, he must provide some sort of service that would be of use to the consumer.

People, of course, do this all the time—looking up companies in the Yellow Pages, for instance, and contacting companies individually. But in the Web economy, this process can be far better for both the consumer and the marketer. Never before have consumers been able to go to one place—their computer—to seek out information from a wide variety of companies. And never before has marketing and customer service been so cohesively coordinated as part of a single, information-rich, interactive experience.

These distinctions mean that marketing on the Web is of a fundamentally different nature. Consumers on the Web won't sit through an intrusive ad—because they don't face that choice. It's not a case of *opting out* (flipping the page, changing the channel) but rather a case of *opting in* (choosing to view the marketing site in the first place).

As a result of this shift in the balance of power, the Web often serves as a great bullshit detector. "Conning the customer won't work when people regain control," a new media research specialist at a global advertising conglomerate told me. "The whole language of branding dissolves in the new media. The logic behind brand differentiation disappears. The new generation of consumers are more sophisticated. Consumers see right through what advertisers are trying to manipulate them into doing. Most people in advertising don't understand that. Advertisers have been getting away with murder."

DIMINISHING RETURNS

The old joke is that advertisers waste exactly half their money. Only they don't know which half. Marketers can develop an unscientific hunch whether their ads are working or not. They can commission studies to sample public reaction. But they can never really *know* whether their ads are effective. They spend their money, and if they like their business, then all is well. Mass marketers usually have no idea whether they can achieve even better results for half the price.

For decades, this uncertainty was the nature of the business. The process of impressing a brand image on the public mind began with hiring an advertising agency. The creative people at that agency would try to come up with a spectacularly catchy campaign, one that would form an indelible impression in the minds of all those who could manage to muster up a few brain waves. Campaigns such as "You asked for it. You got it. Toyota!" are like that. Once in a while the slogan would become part of the vernacular, remaining in the collective conscience of society for generations. AT&T's "reach out and touch someone" campaign dates back to 1908, and it still rings a bell.

With this formula, advertising swelled into a multihundred-billion-dollar industry worldwide. The agencies prospered by taking a 15 percent commission off of all media purchases in radio, TV, magazines, newspapers, and outdoor ads. An agency that created a successful brand campaign could live off those commissions for years and years, just placing the ads where they thought they might work best. Agencies also developed extensive research tools, such as focus groups, which inevitably yielded results showing that all this spending was justified—that advertising is indeed effective. And who could argue? "Frankly," says one executive at a major advertising agency, "it was an extremely generous income stream for very little work."

As the twentieth century races to its close, it's clear that this form of mass marketing has already reached its zenith. It will never, ever go away—not so long as there are mass media. But there are four main reasons why its dominance is already diminishing. Call it the Four C's: clutter, clicking, cynicism, and competition.

There's simply too much *clutter.* When someone is bombarded with 3,000 marketing messages per day, the impact of adding an additional message to the mix is often minimal. To stand out above the din, marketers have had to spend higher and higher amounts on more outrageous ads, with more sex and more special effects—and they've had to repeat those ads more often. The result is escalating spending with only marginal results. This is the very definition of the law of diminishing returns.

Since the advent of the TV remote control and fifty-plus channel cable systems in the 1980s, people have been *clicking* around the dial during commercials to zap unwanted ads. Some studies have shown that few people channel surf, while others have shown that it's widespread. It's safe to say that some people are avoiding some commercials some of the time. That's got to make TV advertising at least marginally less effective than it once was.

People who have grown up immersed in commercialism now see it for what it is. Study after study has shown that citizens are exhibiting all-time high levels of *cynicism* toward everything in public life, including the political process, the judicial system, the mass media, and advertising. People simply no longer believe what advertisers claim to be true.

Finally, there's *competition.* Beginning in the 1980s, the insurgent direct-marketing industry diverted billions away from mass marketing, as sellers of certain types of products sought a cut-to-the-chase way of reaching their most likely customers. In addition, cable TV hacked away at the dominance of network TV ratings. Now, the Web is shaping up to be an even more powerful source of competition, literally prying away eyeballs from TV screens altogether. Kids with PCs at home are already spending as much or more time on their computers than they are watching television.

The net result is that people are spending less and less time with mass media. Thus, it becomes more and more expensive to reach the mass audience when it does tune in. The major broadcast networks are reporting lower overall ratings, yet they boosted their overall CPM rates up 12 percent for the 1996–97 season. "The advertisers are actually paying more to get less," Jamie Keller, head of the upstart WB network, told the *Wall Street Journal.*

The Four C's have already been putting a squeeze on the advertising industrial complex, known for its gleaming corporate offices along New York's Madison and Lexington avenues. Average agency commissions have been negotiated down to 8 to 12 percent. "Don't even mention the 15 percent figure to them," an industry consultant told me. "They get too depressed." And the concept of a sole "agency of record"—a single firm in charge of creating and executing a uniform brand image campaign for all media in all parts of the world—has been blown apart. Marketers now typically assign new creative work to one firm, but then hire lots of specialty agencies to execute mini-campaigns in different types of media and in different regions.

The bottom line is that advertising agencies are now working harder for less money. Mass-market advertisements are still sometimes effective, but they are experiencing a wicked case of diminishing return on investment. And the Web is accelerating this trend dramatically.

A NEW PSYCHOLOGY

Advertising, it has been said, is all about unleashing desire. An effective advertisement will make you yearn for something that you previously didn't know you needed. Ad men, John Kenneth Galbraith wrote in his 1958 book, *The Affluent Society,* "are effective only with those who . . . do not already know what they want. In this state alone, men are open to persuasion."

Consider cigarette ads. The FCC banned them from the airwaves in the early 1970s precisely because these commercials were able to convince people that cigarettes, although dangerous, are glamorous. Print ads for cigarettes have a similar effect, even though they may not be as potent. The Marlboro Man is still one of the world's most recognizable characters. The vision of a cowboy riding his horse through a shallow lake as the setting sun bounces off the pale mountains is alluring. The "Come to Marlboro Country" campaign works through enticement, identification, and association. The "information" in the ad—the Surgeon General's warning—can't match the power of the image.

This might be an extreme example. But almost all ads in intrusive, one-way media employ a similar psychology.

The Web calls for a new psychology, a new way of enticing people to buy things. It has to be a psychology based less on manipulation and more on peer-to-peer negotiation. Yet it is a psychology nonetheless. All marketers must keep generating new demand for their product, not just rely on the few customers who might already be predisposed to buying it.

On the Web, powerful imagery that tunnels into the subconscious of consumers doesn't work all that well. The goal shouldn't be to shout your message repeatedly in their faces but to identify and respond to their needs. Mass-media advertisements usually go too far over the line, trying to get you to want something before knowing whether you are open to such a pitch. An effective marketing site on the Web will play to the other side of the line. It all begins with the needs. So instead of extending the old psychology based on unleashing desire, marketers on the Web must get down to the more mundane chore of assessing needs and responding to them.

This is how it may work. You may *need* a car. But how does a marketer get you to *want* a Ford Taurus? Every car company has a Web site, but which car company has the best Web site to convert your need for a car into a desire for a certain car?

One site might do it by asking you about your lifestyle. If you are a young single man, and you prefer a sporty vehicle, a Honda site might suggest a Prelude rather than an Accord. By responding to your particular need, this site might have an edge over the others. A good car site should also tell you how much you can afford in monthly payments and compare leasing deals to buying.

The Ford site, for instance, has a financial planner feature that does just that. If you enter your income and monthly expenses, it will come back at you with a number. If it turns out that you can afford a $255 monthly payment, that becomes the all-important number when shopping around. You may feel good about a company that helped you determine that figure. An auto company's Web site should also allow you to choose from the menus of options that you might like. When this process is done, the site should be able to custom-configure a car for you and give you an invoice that you can print out and take to the dealer nearest you.

This process is known as "needs gratification." Advertising generally has done very little in this realm. This is not to say that the traditional role of unleashing desire goes away. It just ceases to be the all-dominant form of marketing. The most successful marketers in the future will do both: use mass media to unleash desire and use the Web and other interactive media to finish the job by responding to those needs and desires.

ADVERTISING THE ADVERTISING

Marketers must have some way of telling the world about their Web site. If people don't know about it, they won't ever go there. This prompts the philosophical question: If you put up a Web site that nobody visits, does it exist?

There are four main ways to promote a Web site. First, a marketer can mention it in its traditional print and TV advertisements as well as its brochures, mailings, and other promotional materials. This tactic has only a tiny incremental cost. And it performs the job of inviting customers already receiving your marketing message to interact further with your company. Already, this tactic has become pervasive, and it should be mandatory for most marketers. Of course, putting a Web address on your TV ads may not be as effective as you might think: People often totally forget the commercials they've seen. If they haven't written it down or made a mental note, they won't necessarily remember your URL the next time they start surfing the Web.

The second way of promoting your site is by garnering press attention. As anyone who reads newspapers or magazines knows, there has been an explosion of coverage about information technology over the past few years. Every major print and television news outlet now has at least one cyberspace beat reporter. Of course, getting "free" media is rarely free. Often, you have to hire a PR firm to get the word out. But the opportunities are great. When Holiday Inn announced its Web site in 1995, it received more press attention than any other event in the company's history, by a two to one margin, says Les Ottolenghi, director of emerging technologies for the hotel chain.

The third way is by trading hyperlinks with other sites on the Web. There are countless opportunities for this. A clothing retailer might have an online catalog on the Web that links to a central "catalog of catalogs" site in return for a listing and hyperlink back to that site. Sometimes, you won't even have to provide anything in return. If someone really digs a Web site, they will often provide a hyperlink to it on their own site just for fun. To gauge how popular your site is among builders of other sites, there are software packages now— called spiders—that crawl around the Web measuring how many other documents have hyperlinks that point to yours.

This is just one reason why the Web serves as the ultimate word-of-mouth medium. If your site is a hit, visitors will tell two friends, who will tell two friends, and so on and so on and so on—via E-mail, hyperlinks, or good old-fashioned conversation.

The fourth and most complicated way, of course, is by purchasing banner advertisements and hyperlinks on the most popular sites. This is the area that received the most attention in the early days of the

Web. But it is only part of a mix of promotional tools. As marketers explore all these options, they will generally become more and more demanding when it comes to paying for Web advertisements.

As an example of this, consider IBM. Mary Ann Campanetto, IBM's director of digital publishing and advertising, says the Web has become the biggest topic at all the company's internal meetings. She adds that the Web is "a defining medium for IBM." Harkening back to Marshall McLuhan's medium-is-the-massage credo, IBM believes that "where we advertise is as important as what we say," she says.

With this kind of heightened importance attached to its Web presence, IBM has become ultrapicky as to which content sites they choose to place banner ads, as well as how they pay for them and what they expect for their money. As such, the company has developed a list of guidelines:

1. Sponsor only the most compelling content.
2. Purchase direct links to IBM's Web sites, not just a banner.
3. Request editorial synergy and support, including host-site promotion to drive traffic to IBM's site. (In other words, IBM would like articles that mention IBM and provide an embedded link to IBM's site. This demand creates a vexing problem for editors. "As an editor, you have to drive people off of your editorial content to make money," says Denise Caruso, a columnist for the *New York Times.* "What does this do to our credibility?")
4. Seek to be the exclusive information-technology sponsor of any site.
5. Negotiate preferred positioning on the pages.
6. Demand minimum page view CPM guarantees. (In other words, if the content doesn't get a certain amount of traffic, IBM doesn't pay the preset price.)
7. Require third-party measurement and auditing, verifying audience size.

8. Obtain free trial ads before agreeing to paid ads.
9. Request combined contracts with existing media. (Content creators such as Time Warner claim that they do not throw in free or heavily discounted Web ads for its current TV or magazine advertisers, but companies such as IBM continue to demand such deals.)
10. Get short-term exit clauses (in case the site turns out to be a dog).

In general, the bigger an advertiser you are, the more clout and leverage you have to negotiate these kinds of terms. That's why it makes sense that the biggest advertiser in the United States, Procter & Gamble, was the first to strike a breakthrough agreement when it began advertising on the World Wide Web in 1996. P&G spends more than $3.3 billion per year on advertising and has products that account for more than one-third of all U.S. retail sales in coffee, diapers, detergents, fabric softeners, facial and bathroom tissue, sanitary products, paper towels, shampoo, and toothpaste.

When the Cincinnati-based company descended onto the Web economy, it wanted to do it on its own terms. Instead of paying a CPM rate to reach X-thousand eyeballs with a banner ad, P&G signed a deal with the popular Yahoo! search service to pay only for what's known as "click-thru's." A click-thru happens when a consumer sees the banner ad and decides to actually click on it and visit the marketer's site. If only 2 percent of the people who see a banner actually do this, the advertisers would only pay for every thousand of *those* users.

By purchasing ads this way, marketers cut to the chase: Instead of fighting a futile battle for mass exposure, they are paying for results—real customers who are interested enough to pay a visit. When click-thru's instead of CPM become the measure, the marketer and the content creator share the risks and rewards of this new medium equally. The ads become like salesmen working on commission.

"It's the right idea," says Andrew Anker, president of Hotwired,

< W E B O N O M I C S >

"but it's the wrong implementation." He objects to advertisers paying only for click-thru's because whether or not a user clicks on a banner is highly dependent on what the banner says and looks like. Creating an enticing banner is the job of the creative department of an ad agency. "It's asking us to pay for the success or failure of their advertising." A better way of encouraging result-oriented advertising would be if a compromise was struck: A low CPM rate supplemented by click-thru incentive clauses.

This form of marketing might have a familiar ring to it. When you talk about highly targeted sales pitches, 2 to 5 percent response rates and a result-driven philosophy, what you have is a form of direct-response marketing, known to most of the world as the junk mail business.

But luring people to your Web site for product information and a potential purchase is different from junk mail in two important respects. The first has to do with the costs involved. Because it involves the postal system, direct-response marketing is the most expensive type of marketing of them all. While mass media typically have CPM ratios of about $50 or under, a direct-mail campaign can easily cost $500 for every thousand people to which a letter or sale brochure is sent.

In comparison, the economics of the Web become more and more compelling as the price of paper and postage increases. On the Web, almost the entire marketing investment can be seen as a "capital" expenditure, like a building. In other words, once you make the investment and build the Web site, you don't have to spend much more if an extra 100,000 people visit the site. In direct mail, by contrast, you must spend an average of 50 to 75¢ extra for every extra person that you want to reach with your message. And after most of these prospects throw your letter or brochure in the trash, you have nothing left. In this sense, direct mail is a "consumable" cost.

The other way the Web differs from junk mail is that consumers decide to visit a Web site, whereas they have little control over which marketing pitches they receive in the mail. For a marketer, this is both an advantage and a disadvantage. Marketers know that the people who voluntarily come to their site are good prospects, yet they don't have as much control over who those people are as they would in generating a direct-mail list.

That's why marketers on the Web have to be ultrastrategic as to how they generate traffic to their site. Campanetto, of IBM, says she's not satisfied with 2 to 5 percent click-thru rates when placing a banner and hyperlink at a content site. She believes that you can greatly increase that percentage just by putting something compelling into your banner ad. "If you have something provocative, it jumps," she says.

Campanetto points to special events as a way of generating interest. When IBM sponsored play-by-play, live coverage of the Gary Kasparov versus Deep Blue chess match in 1995, millions of people streamed to that Web site to track the moves of the human and the computer, all the while receiving running expert commentary. (In a surprisingly close series, the human prevailed.) The IBM ads on that site generated click-thru rates of 30 percent. Three out of every ten people who came for the chess coverage also interacted with IBM ads for PCs, software, and network services.

A CALL TO ARMS

For the advertising industry, the Web simultaneously poses the biggest challenge and the biggest opportunity in a long time. So far, the prognosis isn't good. According to a study by Forrester, advertising agencies created and implemented only 26 percent of consumer brand Web sites. Meanwhile, 51 percent of marketers created their sites by contracting the work out to specialty Web site development shops and Internet service providers. The final 25 percent, including major brands such as Holiday Inn, did the work themselves in-house.

The economics of developing a marketing campaign on the Web doesn't favor the traditional advertising agency. Witness a typical thirty-second television commercial, which is not all that expensive to produce—on the order of about $50,000. However, buying time on local TV stations and national networks can cost on the order of $50 million for a major campaign.

On the Web, not only are the overall costs much lower, but they shift away from placement and toward production. A state-of-the-art corporate Web site that provides real service and value to consumers can cost upward of $5 million, if you include the staff it takes not only to develop it but also to run it for the first couple years. But spreading the word on the Web is relatively inexpensive. For about $500,000 total, you can buy banners and hyperlinks on several major search services and content sites for those couple years.

Advertising agencies traditionally have made their money not from their creative services. Rather, they get paid when they place the ads—making a 15 percent commission (now 8 to 12 percent) on all media purchases. You can see how this model falls apart when you try to apply it to the Web. When media purchases become only a small fraction of the overall marketing expense, commissions become minuscule.

With this shift from mass-media placement to digital media production, advertising agencies that want to play in the Web economy must shift what they do. No one expects them to miraculously turn into software development companies overnight. Rather, the traditional advertising agency must transform itself into a media-advising agency. These firms must become expert on all media and advise their clients as to the best strategy and tactics for both mass media and interactive media. Yes, they still must be able to create catchy jingles, sexy visuals, and snappy slogans. But when their client needs off-the-shelf software or software development services, the media-advising agency must also know where to get the best stuff and how it works.

And so the Web is a call to arms: The media landscape is more complex than ever, with more ways to get a message out and more ways to connect with individual consumers than ever before. Media-advising agencies should be expert not only in quantitative measures such as CPM but the more important qualitative knowledge of which Web sites work best for what purpose.

With the commission structure out the window, the media-advising agency must be able to provide its creative talents on a fee-for-service basis and perhaps provide its media expertise on a retainer basis or a per-hour basis—like a consulting firm. Some marketers may even force the media-advising agency to share their risks. If an interactive media campaign doesn't lead to measurable results, then the agency gets paid very little. If it does, it gets paid a lot. This may not always be an easy, enjoyable transition to make. But looking like a big old dinosaur can't be much fun, either.

Most important, the ad agencies of the future must know how to forge new and closer relationships between marketers and consumer. The Web makes the marketing process a much more collaborative one. "If we do our job right, the consumer can choose when, where, and in what order he or she wishes to access elements of persuasion," says Michael Bungey, chairman and CEO of Bates Worldwide, a top New York ad agency. "Each message becomes utterly individual and unique. In truth, the only place our brand message exists in its totality is in the mind of the creative consumer."

<Chapter Summary>
• The Web must pick up where traditional advertising leaves off. Whereas mass-media ads *tell* you that a product exists and *sell* you on its benefits, a Web ad must *link* you to in-depth product information and prompt you to *think* about actually making the purchase.
• Like a human salesperson, a marketer's Web site must achieve results—by learning about a customer's *preferences*, providing *service*, retaining *loyalty*, and ultimately landing future *sales*.
• Mass media *push* messages at us by intruding on our time and space. In the new media, we *pull* the information. Consumers on the Web actively seek information from the marketer. Getting your message out to an individual requires that individual's consent.
• The old model of pricing and selling advertising should not apply to the Web. All eyeballs aren't created equal. Instead of purchasing exposure via the standard cost per thousand (CPM) ratio, marketers should work at attracting smaller numbers of qualified and interested consumers.
• There are four reasons why the total dominance of mass-media advertising is diminishing. Call it the Four C's: *clutter* (too many ads coming at us), *clicking* (the ability to channel surf during commercials), *cynicism* (people no longer believe what the ads say), and *competition* (first from direct marketing and now from interactive media).
• There are four main ways to promote a marketing site: by mentioning the address in print and TV ads, by garnering press attention, by trading "hyperlinks" with other Web sites—thus building "electronic word-of-mouth," and finally by purchasing banner placements on popular content sites.

CHAPTER THREE

Consumers Must Be Compensated for Disclosing Data About Themselves

Surfing the World Wide Web can pretty much be an anonymous activity. The famed *New Yorker* cartoon about how on the Internet nobody knows you're a dog still holds true. That is, unless you happen to tell others that you're a dog, along with what backyard your doghouse is in, plus what kind of leash you wear and what flavor Milk-Bone you prefer and why. When you disclose this data, others on the Net will consider you a very valuable dog indeed. But there has to be a damn good reason you are going to strip off your anonymity and reveal your innermost information.

Yes, information privacy is a huge concern. But many consumers are beyond worrying about whether Big Brother and the data spies are invading their personal infosphere. They're willing to make a trade-off—if the deal is a good one. To a marketer, of course, information about who you are and your usage of a product can make all the difference in the world. "If you tell me that your mini-van is five years old," says Rich Everett, manager of interactive communications for Chrysler Corporation, "I want to get an attractive lease rate to you immediately."

To obtain information about customer satisfaction and purchasing plans, Chrysler at one point sent an E-mail message to 200,000 Chrysler owners, many of whom gave their Internet address to Chrysler over the Web. The message offered free wiper blades to those who opted in and agreed to disclose what was on their minds. The response rate was only in the 6 to 8 percent range. But that's much better than a typical direct-mail campaign. And because it doesn't use paper and postage, it's a much cheaper and faster way to engage customers in direct response.

Of course, getting people to feed this kind of data into a corporate computer on some far-off network is a tricky challenge to say the least. "It's a big problem," says Mary Lou Floyd, business manager of AT&T's promotional Web site. "You need to require people to register their name and other information at your site to know who they are. But once you require registration, you might lose them altogether."

Mandatory registration is what Saatchi & Saatchi researchers call a "flow breaker." It interrupts the path of least resistance that Web surfers often find themselves taking. By requiring consumers to disclose their data as the price of entry into a site, you put up a barrier that causes some consumers to take a detour around it. Better to give them a no-hassle taste first, then entice them to tell all about themselves later. The key at that point is to provide enough value in return for information so that consumers gladly enter into the bargain.

DISCLOSING DATA TO CONTENT CREATORS

One of the first Web sites to grapple with the principle of compensating consumers for disclosing data was Hotwired. Launched in the fall of 1994, Hotwired was not to be an online version of the *Wired* magazine, but rather an all-original brew of cheeky commentary, eye-popping, fluorescent graphics and interactive features. In keeping with the Internet's tradition of making information free, the publishers of Hotwired decided not to charge a subscription fee. Instead, it would make its money selling ads that hyperlinked consumers to the advertiser's own Web site.

In an attempt to tell its advertisers something about its audience and verify who was visiting, Hotwired had required all surfers to call up an electronic form and fill in their name and address, E-mail address, and answer a few questions about their interests. Within a few minutes, the system would E-mail back registration information. Then, every time visitors went to the site, they would enter their user ID and password.

Thus, the deal was struck: In exchange for their information, the surfers would receive "free" information and entertainment. By the middle of 1995, about 200,000 individuals were visiting Hotwired each month—an impressive figure, especially for a publication that had no printing or mailing costs. (*Wired* magazine itself, by contrast, was spending $1 million per month on production and distribution.)

But as more and more new sites cropped up on the Web—most not requiring registration—Hotwired found that many Web surfers were blowing by its service altogether. So in August 1995, Hotwired made registration optional. "At first, we were the only Web site doing media [content]," says Andrew Anker, president of Hotwired. "Then all of a sudden we saw lots of Web sites doing it. And we were missing the people who had passworditis. People were saying: 'Oh no, another site with another password.' "

In keeping with the principle of rewarding consumers for disclosing their information, Hotwired has made sure that those who do register receive real benefits. The software offers registered members customized views of the content by remembering preferences that users cite when enrolling. In addition, it remembers when registered users last visited and will place all the new content since that time under a special "What's New" section.

To make this trade-off even easier, Hotwired took advantage of a built-in feature of the Netscape browser called the "cookies" file. This file is created and maintained by the browser software—without the user's intervention and usually without the user's knowledge. Web sites that take advantage of this feature insert a cookie, or set of user identification codes, into that file. Then, the next time the user visits that site, it automatically checks out his cookie, telling the site who he is and that he's been here before. Registered members of Hotwired will have a cookie that automatically logs them in. This way, there is no longer a need to remember a password. "Membership should be easy, not hard," Anker says.

Anker says that the overall goal in the "quid pro quo" bargain is to build an intimate relationship with each member. "The more you tell us about yourself," he says, "the better we can serve you with customized content."

Content creators and marketers are in the same boat in this respect. Both must push the envelope on this third principle of Webonomics. On the Web, the amount of information that a consumer provides can be far greater than in any other medium. The consumer must give more. And in return, the consumer must get more.

An especially powerful deployment of this principle comes from a site called Firefly. Developed by Firefly Network Inc. (formerly Agents Inc.), a startup in Cambridge, Massachusetts, Firefly went online in early 1996, initially offering a music and movie recommendation service. To use the service, visitors must enter their age, gender, zip code, E-mail address, and then choose a user name.

Establishing a unique but anonymous identity for each user is vital because of the incredible amounts of information that the users supply. "We only know members by their handles, such as Purple Butterfly," says Pattie Maes, a professor at the MIT Media Laboratory who cofounded the company. This way, privacy is ensured at the same time that valuable and intimate data is collected.

In the movie-recommendation service, members begin by selecting from a list of eight categories of movies. If you choose "cult films," for instance, the software will come back with a list of ten or so films that you are to rate on a one to seven scale. You can select a seven rating if you think it's "the best," a neutral four rating if you've never seen the film, a one if you believe it's a real turkey—or any number in between those for finer distinctions.

After rating close to 100 cult films, from *The Terminator* to *Harold & Maude* to *Dead Poet's Society* to *Brazil* to *2001: A Space Odyssey,* the software on Firefly's server computers will sift through a massive database of correlations. People who tend to love *The Shining* may also love *Dawn of the Dead* but hate *The Lonely Guy.* People who love *Barton Fink* may also love *Bagdad Cafe* and hate *Tampopo.*

The more data Firefly collects from members, the more precise its correlations become. The site's objective is to convert your preferences into a short list of recommended movies—hopefully ones you haven't yet seen. When the list appears, you can print it out and take it to the video store. The music-recommendation service works in a similar fashion—only with recording artists instead of movie titles.

Firefly also stores and retrieves a cookie on your computer so that you are recognized the next time you visit. But it goes much further than that; the software remembers everything you tell it. The next time you log in and start rating more music or movies to generate a new list of recommendations, it can draw on the past knowledge to create a list even better suited to your tastes. Although taste is an elusive thing to measure, people are always looking for a person—be it an aunt, a friend, or a favorite movie reviewer—to act as an arbiter for them. Firefly aims to be that arbiter of opinion. Maes calls Firefly one example of a type of "intelligent agent," the category of artificial intelligence software in which she specializes at the Media Lab.

Not only does all this data collection have intrinsic value to the members of the service, but it has enormous economic value to record companies, music stores, movie studios, and advertising agencies. In fact, Firefly Network sells this very same data to those companies. Packaged in easy-to-read reports, the data help these companies predict what types of entertainment play best in which age groups and regions of the country. And it gives them a window into the minds of consumers that they might not be able to get elsewhere. As such, it helps entertainment companies better target their mass-media marketing efforts.

Selling information on its members' tastes accounts for one-third of the company's revenue. Firefly Network makes an additional one-third of its revenue from licensing out its proprietary database software and agents' technology to builders of other Web sites. Early licensees include Reuters NewMedia, Yahoo!, and ZD Net. The company makes the final one-third by selling advertising.

Unlike most other content creators supported by advertising, Firefly Network doesn't just sell banner ads that hyperlink to marketing sites. The Firefly site adds a whole new dimension to advertising. Firefly has the audacity to ask consumers to rate how effective the ads are. Every banner advertisement on the site displays its own seven-point scale. This is a fairly radical concept. Imagine if TV viewers were given a chance to press buttons on their remote to appraise the commercials they see. No doubt, lots of advertising agencies would get hit with some pretty sobering statistics. But most marketers would jump at the chance to get data like these.

While it's easy to see what's in it for the marketers, the obvious question is this: Why would a busy person spend time evaluating the ad messages coming his way? The answer also can be found in the third principle of Webonomics. "People like to contribute," Maes says, "especially if it will change things." And on Firefly, if a consumer rates the ads he sees, he will start receiving more customized and relevant ads in the future.

One early ad effort by Bantam Doubleday Dell, the publishers of this book, demonstrated how valuable this is. BDD placed an ad on Firefly for Al Franken's hit book *Rush Limbaugh Is a Big Fat Idiot and Other Observations.* In the month after it appeared, this was the most highly rated ad on the Firefly service. Not only did BDD learn that the ad was well-received but it learned what kinds of people liked it and what kinds of people didn't. The reports about the people who rated the ad revealed some interesting correlations: People who liked the ad tended to like U2 and other "alternative" rock groups. But the ad was absolutely despised by people who like country music.

On the Web, marketers must leverage this kind of information to better target their ads. Perhaps alternative rock fans could receive ads for nonfiction books written by liberal authors, while country music fans could receive ads for books by conservative authors.

That is exactly what advertisers on Firefly are doing. "Two people sitting side by side could be using the same part of the service and be seeing different ads," explains Doug Weaver, vice president of ad sales at Firefly Network. One advertiser, MCI's 1-800-Music Now mail-order service, placed ads based on musical taste. People who liked classic rock saw a banner that said USE WINDOWS TO BUY THE DOORS, while people who like alternative rock saw a banner that said: THERE ARE CRASH TEST DUMMIES ON THE INFO HIGHWAY.

Many people who visit the Firefly site consider it valuable to receive movie and music recommendations as well as targeted ads. But the most compelling reason for people to return and give out their personal information has to do with something even more powerful: the sense of community that surrounds Firefly. Like Bianca's Smut Shack in Chapter One, Firefly enables people to meet other people with similar sensibility.

Everyone who joins Firefly gets a simple but personal home page on the site. The page lists their handle, their age, and a collection of movies and recording artists that they like the most. Members can search among the hundreds of thousands of these member profiles to determine who has tastes most similar to them. Then, they can send that person a private E-mail message and start an online friendship that potentially could lead to something more.

Thus, the members of Firefly don't come just to search through the typical information and marketing material found on most Web sites. They come to make this very explicit trade-off. "You give us this information," Weaver says. "We'll give you these services and membership in a community where you can form relationships."

It may be too early to tell whether Firefly's business model is a formula for reaping large profits over the long term. But the site attracted 250,000 members in its first six months, plus an impressive array of investors who believe that profits will roll in. In its first wave of venture financing, Firefly Network raised $7.6 million from Dun & Bradstreet, Merrill Lynch, the Japanese publishing company Softbank, and other investors—in exchange for a portion of the company's equity.

DISCLOSING DATA TO MARKETERS

This trade-off of information and entertainment for valuable data is an especially powerful tool for marketers.

A simple example of this strategy is the Web site from Stolichnaya vodka, where visitors engage in activities such as stepping behind a fully stocked virtual bar. First, you select a name for your concoction, choose ingredients from on-screen menus, and mix your own drink—all the while learning about Stoli's many flavors of vodka.

Then, you submit your recipe along with your name and E-mail address. Your creation instantly appears with your name on a list along with drinks created by other visitors. Finally, you can browse the list and rate the drinks, using a system of one to three olives. On a recent visit, the top-rated drink was a turbocharged mixture called "Bartender, I'll Have What the Guy on the Floor Is Having." Other whimsical drink names have included "Aunt Olga's Spicy Tongue Kiss," and a wicked Bloody Mary takeoff called "My Chic Kremlin Cyber Solution."

Not only is this a fun way for consumers to spend time thinking about Stoli's products, but it's a good way for Stoli to learn the often unpredictable preferences of consumers—a key element in the psychographics of vodka usage.

Here we seem to have a great example of consumers providing valuable information about themselves. Except that the information being given to the Stoli site just sits there. "We're not using this information at all," says Bob Manni, group account director at Margeotes Fertitta & Partners, the New York ad agency that created Stoli's Web site. Why not? "Frankly, we just wanted to provide a place for people to have fun with the product. We didn't do this to collect data. We don't want to bother people."

Manni says that his agency was one of the first to recognize that the Web, with its upscale clientele, would be an ideal place to boost the image of its clients. So the agency set up an interactive division in 1994. The agency launched the Stoli site in March 1995. The idea was to extend Stoli's high-profile "Freedom of Vodka" print campaign to the Web.

To promote traffic to the site, Margeotes purchased hyperlink banners on popular content sites. For instance, it placed a hyperlink banner in the *Sports Illustrated* section of Time Warner's Pathfinder site during the month of the annual swimsuit issue. Guys who were checking out the bikini babes were presented with the option of clicking on a Stoli banner. A small percentage of them did so. And that was enough, says Manni, to double traffic to the Stoli site for a few weeks.

By mid-1996, the Stoli site was drawing several thousand visitors per week, says Manni. Yet he couldn't provide direct evidence that the site was generating new demand for Stoli's products. The total investment in the site, he says, was well under $1 million. For that money, Stoli's U.S. importer Carillon Importers got a very clever and well-designed Web site. But there didn't seem to be any radically new benefits for the marketer here. "We hope that when people go to buy vodka, they will select Stoli," Manni says. You could say that about a TV ad or a print ad, too.

By contrast, check out the site from the Jack Daniel Distillery. Launched in August 1995, the site offers up a tour of the small town of Lynchberg, Tennessee (population 361), the rugged nineteenth-century village where Jack Daniel first concocted his Old No. 7 Tennessee Sour Mash Whiskey. As the home of the oldest distillery in the United States, the place is steeped in history. "We offer people the Lynchberg experience," says Peggy Vessels, marketing communications manager for the brand.

Surfers can visit the general store, step into Mr. Jack's office, get a play-by-play of the eight-step distillation process, and learn fascinating, personal details about the legendary Jack Daniel. (Born in 1850, Jasper Newton Daniel was 5′ 2″ tall. He founded the distillery when he was thirteen years old. One day, after he couldn't open the safe in his office, he kicked it in frustration, broke his foot, and eventually died, in 1911, from the wound's infections.)

At the beginning of the tour, visitors are asked to sign the guest book. They simply provide their name, where they're from, plus a comment about the product or an opinion of how they liked the tour. In return for that information, consumers receive a personal E-mail message signed by a Jack Daniel employee responding specifically to their comment. And unlike the Stoli site, all the information that people enter is kept in a marketing database. Vessels says that this kind of correspondence is an extension of the relationship that the Jack Daniel brand has always had with its customers. The company averages 130,000 letters per year from loyal fans of the whiskey.

"Earning friendship," says Vessels, is what the company has been about for more than a century. When Mr. Jack was alive, customers would ride into town, throw down a few shots, have some conversation, and maybe purchase a few bottles to go. The company knew these customers personally. But beginning in the 1950s, when Jack Daniel's whiskey became a nationally advertised brand, sales grew dramatically and the company no longer could form individual relationships with a high percentage of its customers.

The Web is helping the company get back to those one-on-one marketing roots. And it's the customers' built-up loyalty to the brand that enables this. Like many well-known brands, Jack Daniel's whiskey has become part of the culture. People who drink it consider it part of their identity, and they want to associate themselves with the product. That's why Jack Daniel's T-shirts and other products—now available from a catalog that can be ordered online—have long been popular.

So, when Vessels and her small team of Webmasters began exploiting the information in the Web site's guest book, customers were not upset that their privacy was being invaded. In fact, it was just the opposite. "People really like to hear from us," says Vessels. "If people see our name on an envelope, they'll open it." And the same goes for E-mail. The company sends E-mail messages to inform customers of newly introduced products, such as a J.D. and Cola mixture or a new J.D. microbrew. It also sends messages to people who live near the locations of upcoming company-sponsored events, such as rock concerts in hip L.A. clubs or Jack Daniel's birthday events around the world every September.

The cost of developing the Web site for Jack Daniel was less than $100,000. The price tag was so low in part because the company didn't hire an advertising agency to do the work. The strategy and design was done in-house. Once the layout and features were designed, Vessels contracted out an independent Web site programming company to do the coding and technical work. Vessels also decided not to spend money advertising the site by buying banners on popular content sites. She figured that loyal customers would find the site by searching for it on their own, hearing about it from drinking buddies, or through free hyperlinks that fans of the site include on their own homegrown Web pages.

The precise return on Jack Daniel's modest investment on the Web is difficult to measure. But Vessels says the site acts as an inexpensive way to retain loyal customers and recruit new ones. The people who visit and receive E-mail from the company tend to tell other online friends about it. Thus, the company now has a powerful new way to enlist customers as marketing agents for the brand. "The Web is the ultimate word-of-mouth medium," says Vessels. "It's direct marketing, advertising, and public relations all rolled into one."

DISCLOSING DATA FOR DISCOUNTS

Perhaps the most obvious way to obtain data from consumers is this: Provide consumers with discounts on products that they want in return.

In the world of mass marketing, the most prevalent way to give discounts to shoppers is the century-old practice of circulating coupons. Marketers pay to have their coupons delivered in Sunday newspapers, in mass-mail packets, and in supermarket aisles. But just like all forms of mass marketing, couponing is experiencing a wicked case of diminishing returns. As consumers are faced with more and more marketing messages competing for their limited attention, they are paying less and less attention to coupons. The average household now receives about 3,000 coupons per year. But actual redemption has been on a steady decline, dropping to 2 percent in 1995. That's half the rate of 1980.

Although the majority of shoppers use coupons at least some of the time, more and more people have decided that it's not worth the effort. Think about the work it takes to sift through pages and pages of coupons in search of the few products that you want to buy. When you find one, you must clip it, search for the product in the aisles of a store, and then remember to hand the coupon to the checkout clerk. All for 25 to 50¢ off. Manufacturers, meanwhile, spend millions of dollars printing and distributing these coupons—only to have most get thrown in the garbage.

No wonder that consumer product giant Procter & Gamble has already cut its use of coupons in half and is test-marketing the idea of eliminating them entirely. At the same time, P&G is making a big push on the Web, which it sees as a more cost-effective medium. The overall goal of its latest marketing efforts is to boost sales while reducing spending on marketing to 20 percent of revenue, from the current level of 25 percent.

The biggest problem with coupons is that it's a one-way form of marketing. When a customer cashes in a paper coupon—say, for a jar of tomato sauce—the maker of the product has no way of knowing who that customer is or what their motivations are. Is this a loyal customer, or is this a new customer trying the product for the first time?

On the Web, the idea of trading discounts for data has been under-explored territory. One site, called H.O.T.! Coupons, is run by Money Mailers, the leading direct-mail coupon company. On the Web site, visitors type in their zip code to find a list of coupons that can be used in their region. If they find one that they like, say, for a Chinese restaurant or for a car wash, they print it out and use it just like any other coupon. But just because these coupon are online doesn't mean they're better. In fact, the process of searching for coupons that you want is even more time-consuming here. And it's still the same one-way process. The marketer doesn't get to learn anything about the consumer.

A few marketers, however, have gone further and taken advantage of the medium. The Web site for Ragu brand Italian food, for instance, will mail you paper discount coupons if you provide them with your name and address. And if you enter your E-mail address, Ragu will send you a message whenever a new feature is added to the Web site or whenever Ragu introduces a new product. In doing all this, Ragu has found a way to make the discount-coupon process interactive. In exchange for discounts, consumers are telling Ragu who they are.

The Ragu site also happens to be about more than discounts. The site also succeeds in creating a compelling Italian mystique around its products. Visitors enter a place called Mama's Cucina, where they can meet Mama and watch her present information about gourmet Italian cooking and culture. Visitors can learn to speak Italian and engage in fun activities. Of course, they also see ads for new flavors of Ragu pasta sauces. But the Ragu brand name has become something more here. Instead of a collection of products on a shelf, Ragu has become a community of interest for all things Italian.

The give-and-take process works best when the stakes are higher than just a modest discount off of a supermarket item. Remember, the more you give, the more you get. Consider the process of selling cars. Time Warner's Pathfinder site has drawn several major automakers as advertisers. So information about what kinds of cars its members drive and what their buying plans are is extremely valuable. Once it collects such data, Time Warner can provide that information to marketers to keep them committed to spending their advertising dollars on Pathfinder.

Recently, the site ran a promotion. "Talk to us about cars," it said. Consumers were asked to fill out a detailed thirty-question survey containing all the questions automakers need to know about demographics, expected price range, details on current car ownership, and so on. In exchange for that, the Pathfinder site promised that "five lucky winners will get a Pathfinder T-shirt." A chance to win a T-shirt? For most people, that's not going to be enough compensation. As consumers become more and more savvy about just how valuable their personal information really is, they'll want something more compelling in return for it.

In this respect, the Web represents an enormous shift in power to the consumer. When it comes to prospecting for car buyers, automakers will have to give up a lot more. Manufacturers have traditionally advertised rebates up to several thousand dollars for consumers who buy during a certain promotional period. Instead of or in addition to that, manufacturers could ask Web surfers to fill out a questionnaire about their car-buying plans and what they are looking for in a new vehicle. In return for that kind of detailed data, consumers could receive a $1,000 rebate upon the purchase of a new car—or a certificate for a free CD player. These offers can be issued as code numbers or certificates that can be printed out and taken directly to the dealer. This is the kind of bargain that will attract people.

Another trade-off that Web surfers will come to expect is free online time in exchange for their data. A marketer might agree to buy you a free hour—or even a free month—of surfing time in return for participating in a survey. Internet service providers themselves have a lot to gain from such deals. Suppose America Online signs a deal with a major advertiser who agrees to place banners on AOL's home page. Whenever a user clicks on the banner and visits the marketer's site, AOL's hourly billing meter immediately stops. In a sense, marketers would be picking up the tab.

This principle of exchange data for something of real value could even extend beyond online time to all kinds of technology. Marketers could provide consumers with software, for instance. Spend a half hour participating in an online focus group about banking and financial services and receive a free personal finance software package.

With these kinds of deals happening all over the Web, it was just a matter of time before some entrepreneurs cut to the chase. At least two start-up companies have launched schemes for paying customers directly for disclosing data and paying attention to advertisements on their special Web sites. First, Cybergold Inc., founded by Silicon Valley software veteran Nat Goldhaber, is inviting consumers to fill out a questionnaire. Once registered, they can view a list of advertisements. Next to each will be the image of a gold coin with a cash or coupon value.

By clicking on a coin, consumers will be hyperlinked to the ad. When they are finished interacting with it, the coupon value will be credited to their account. These coupons can be spent on merchandise, online connection time, and subscriptions to information and entertainment. Goldenhaber has already recruited automakers, book publishers, technology companies, and financial services firms that have agreed to pay consumers directly.

Another site, called GoldMail, offers a free electronic mail service supported by advertising. It has recruited companies such as Holiday Inn, Chevron, Iomega, and Spiegel. Users are asked to view ads to earn points that are redeemable for merchandise. While the concept is a good one, GoldMail's value proposition for consumers is often dubious. To earn the 80,000 points needed to buy a camcorder, for instance, a user must view 1,600 advertisements. That would take more than two hours per day for an entire month. If someone had that much time to kill, they probably wouldn't have much use for a camcorder; their life wouldn't be worth putting on videotape.

Consumers will decide which deals serve them best. They are waking up to the fact that their personal information should have a price tag—and a fairly high one at that. Once enough people are fully aware of this, marketing will never again be the same.

AND NOW, A WORD ABOUT PRIVACY

All this personal data floating around in cyberspace could be cause for alarm. Hysteria about information privacy has been growing ever since the advent of the personal computer. And it has reached fever pitch with the explosion of the Internet. Thousands of media reports have presented life in the information age as a stark trade-off: Things become more convenient and access to information expands, but people can easily find out really personal stuff about you.

By now, most consumers realize that the issue of information privacy is more a matter of thousands of Little Brother corporations collecting relatively trivial bits about you rather than an all-powerful Big Brother controlling your life. In fact, the government has had surprisingly little involvement in this issue. Information privacy is regulated by agencies such as the Federal Trade Commission, which makes sure, for instance, that companies that compile credit reports don't abuse the financial data that is kept on millions of citizens. But beyond that, the issue has been left to the devices of the free market.

Even if a consumer surfing the Web is tightfisted about giving out his personal information, some of it may leak out anyway. If you visit a Web page maintained by the Center for Media and Democracy, for instance, you'll find a public-service feature called "Who's Watching You and What Are You Telling Them?" This Washington research and lobbying group shows consumers that any Web site you visit can tell four basic facts about you whenever you log on: what type of browser software you have, what type of computer and operating system you're running, which Internet access company you subscribe to, and where that company is based.

To most people, this is not very important or private stuff. The far more personal information involves the data behind purchasing decisions. What mutual funds do I own? What kind of toothpaste does my family use? What kind of car do I drive? What size underwear do I wear? What porn sites do I visit? When am I going away on vacation and what hotel am I staying in?

But here is where free-market Webonomics works in favor of keeping that information under wraps. Consumers freely choose to provide their data to marketers in return for discounts or better service—or to content creators in return for free information and entertainment. But you don't have to play that game if it makes you uncomfortable.

Besides, that data should stay under wraps. Consumers are coming to insist that marketers don't resell their private data. When a consumer takes the time to form a relationship with a marketer and give her personal data in exchange for a service, she wants that data to be used only for the purpose it was intended. And if she finds out otherwise, she will likely terminate her relationship with that company and tell her friends to do likewise.

Many marketers already realize this. And they go out of their way to inform consumers that they will keep the data to themselves. When a visitor enters Mama's Cucina at the Ragu site, for instance, there is a notice that says MAMA KEEPS HER MOUTH SHUT above the area where people enter their name and E-mail address. In this sense, the power shifts from companies to consumers. The smartest marketers profit from protecting their customers' privacy, not violating it.

Indeed, the advertising industry has developed a set of goals for information privacy. An industry coalition called CASIE, formed in 1994 by two major advertising trade groups, is very specific as to how personal data should be handled. "We believe that if a marketer seeks personal information via interactive electronic communication, it ought to inform the consumer whether the information will be shared with others," states CASIE's 1996 position paper on privacy. "We also believe that before a marketer shares such personal information with others, the consumer ought to be offered an option to request that personal information not be shared. Upon receiving such a request, the marketer ought to keep such personal information confidential."

The aversion to corporate trafficking of personal data means that any proposed "Web-wide" registration system will meet with high resistance. Several start-up companies have come up with schemes that enable Web surfers to go to one central site, answer a series of questions about their demographics, and receive a single password that can be used at hundreds of marketing and content sites. "It's a hassle to fill forms and get a password every time you visit a new site," says Ariel Poler, president of San Francisco-based Internet Profiles Corp. (I/PRO).

To make things easier, Poler's idea is to entice consumers to come to his site, provide their names, postal address, E-mail address, then answer fifteen or so questions about their age, gender, marital status, what their income is, who they work for, what their title is. He would issue what he calls an I/Code to each consumer. Sites run by car manufacturers or publishing companies would subscribe to the I/Code service. Then, these businesses would simply ask consumers to provide their I/Code when logging in, thus saving people the trouble of answering the same questions over and over and having to remember many user IDs and passwords.

Obviously, if a system such as I/Code catches on, it would put the company that owned the system in an enviable position, sitting on a gold mine of data. But Poler admits that for such a system to succeed, it would require a critical mass of Web sites and consumers to accept this system. Due to the decentralized nature of the Web, that is highly unlikely to happen. The public simply doesn't want a Big Brother of the Web. They don't want all information about all people being sucked into one database. Indeed, lack of consumer acceptance of the plan finally caused I/PRO to eliminate its I/Code division, in the process laying off thirteen of its ninety-five employees in September 1996. Consumers have spoken on this issue: Centralized preregistration is simply a bad idea.

So is taking advantage of unsuspecting children. Marketers and content creators should refrain from collecting personal data on children who are not capable of making up their minds as to what is appropriate. What if Joe Camel goes on the Web and tries to forge relationships with kids? One can imagine kids telling cute cartoon characters anything they want to know.

Since it attracts so many kids, the Disney site has to be especially careful about such matters. When it was launched in the spring of 1996, Disney's site, for instance, had a guest book feature called—you guessed it—"Be Our Guest." The clock character from *Beauty and the Beast* welcomed kids to sign in and enter a contest for a valuable prize. Kids could provide their name, address, and other data for a chance to win a trip to Disneyland Paris. "Ten lucky kids will be chosen," the contest rules said.

The Center for Media Education, a Washington watchdog group, did a study on this phenomenon and found rampant buying and selling of information about children by direct marketers and information brokers. Just one company, Metromail, adds 67,000 names of kids and babies to its database every week. At the urging of such groups, several members of Congress sponsored a bill that would make it illegal to sell information on minors without parental consent.

The proposed law would also require list owners to disclose to parents what information they have on the children, as well as the source of the information and the intended use of the data. "The concern is that parents don't know that information they give about their kids for one purpose can wind up in a computer database used for another," said a spokeswoman for Rep. Bob Franks, (R-N.J.), the sponsor of the bill in the House.

All creators of Web sites should take privacy concerns seriously. To prevent a consumer backlash, Web sites that collect information from consumers should inform those consumers up front exactly how their data will be used. And if the information might be sold for another purpose—an unwise move, in most cases—that intention should be stated clearly and consumers should be given a chance to opt out. In the case of children, Web sites should adhere to the strictest standards about obtaining parental consent before obtaining any such data.

After basic guidelines such as these are met, free-market Webonomics can be put into action. The Web is all about individual freedom and personal control. As long as consumers are compensated for disclosing their data, as long as they are properly informed about how such data will be used, adults can decide for themselves what information they want to give out to whom.

<Chapter Summary>
• Consumers are concerned about data privacy but are resigned to the fact that they won't get it. They will trade valuable information about themselves—*if the deal is favorable.*
• Getting consumers to register their names and other data at a Web site requires something significant in return, such as personalized news, entertainment and advice, or membership in a compelling online community.
• Don't just collect personal information for your own purposes; *use it* in a way that provides the consumer with a tangible benefit.
• Instead of issuing coupons and not knowing anything about the consumers using them, marketers on the Web should provide discounts and rebates in exchange for vital demographic and psychographic information.
• There are *limits* to such data collection: Marketers must inform consumers whether they will be selling their data, then give consumers a chance to *opt out.* And they should refrain from soliciting children for information.

\<CHAPTER FOUR\>

Consumers Will Shop Online Only for *Information-Rich* Products

Information is what sells products on the Web. If the Web is good at anything, it's good at presenting tons of information and involving people in the process of sorting through it. Marketers must exploit this ability. As a result, the products that people will shop for and buy using their home computers are the ones that can be wrapped in sheaves of facts, news, knowledge, wisdom, and advice.

Think about books, music CDs, mutual funds, cars, consumer electronics, computers, software, travel packages, houses, and gift items. Such information-rich products are the ones that take time to contemplate. There are entire magazines and newspaper sections devoted to these "high-involvement" product categories. When deciding which of these products to buy, many consumers will do research, ask their friends for recommendations, even go to expositions to learn more about the products. These are the types of things people will actively shop for—and in many cases purchase—on the Web.

On the opposite end of the spectrum, information-poor products that you don't have to think about much are a tough sell. There are many well-known and well-advertised products that fall into the low-involvement camp: Think of most of the thousands of supermarket and drugstore items that shoppers pass in aisles regularly. Busy consumers may use the Web to enroll in a service that delivers a preselected load of supermarket items to their doors each week. But most people would lose the will to live if they found themselves sitting at their computers

and comparison shopping on Web sites dedicated, say, to Tide detergent or Right Guard deodorant. It's not worth spending time actively
seeking information about these products—simply because there isn't
much information to be had.

BACK-TO-BASICS RETAIL

The huge opportunity to sell information-rich goods on the Web arises
from an information gap in traditional retail.

Traditional, brick-and-mortar stores have had to cut back on informative customer service personnel in order to lower prices. In today's
cutthroat retail environment, such a scenario is nearly unavoidable. As
the most store-saturated, mall-jammed country on the planet, the
United States has about five billion square feet of retail space, according to the National Research Bureau. That's nearly twenty square feet
for every man, woman, and child in the country—enough to give every
person his or her private shopping aisle. This figure also represents a
jump of more than 50 percent, from thirteen feet per capita, in 1980.

As more and more stores spring up, the NRB data show profits per
square foot decreasing accordingly. It only makes sense: The glut of
stores has brought fierce competition and price slashing. This trend, of
course, favors the big chains, which can afford razor-thin profits and
make up for it in volume. Independent stores, meanwhile, have been
struggling, getting acquired, or declaring bankruptcy and closing
down.

The result is a retail landscape dominated by nationally run megastores such as Wal-Mart and Costco and "category killers" such as Staples, CompUSA, Barnes & Noble, and Circuit City. These stores stand
as monuments to low prices on high-volume products as the key to success. The people who manage these stores are often expert at maximizing profit per square foot. But they're generally not like the small
shopkeepers of yesteryear. Rarely do you find people in these stores

who have made knowledge of the products their life's work. Intimate customer service and product expertise has become part of retail history, something that only your grandparents would remember.

On the Web, retailers don't have to worry about profits per square foot. Real estate in the Web economy is not a scarce resource. Cyberspace is boundless, and it can be traversed in the click of a mouse. Misunderstand this and you will suffer the fate of the so-called cybermalls.

Almost all the attempts to create a group of stores "under one roof" have failed or are failing on the Web. One of the early ventures, marketplaceMCI, disappeared with nary a trace from the Web in mid-1996. This joint venture with Rupert Murdoch's News Corp. was a collection of more than thirty stores—including online renditions of Nordstrom's, OfficeMax, Omaha Steaks, and Lady Foot Locker—held together by a single graphical user interface. The cybermall failed to attract enough shoppers, despite MCI's expertise in communications networks and its heavy expenditures in TV advertising to promote it.

This dismal failure, however, did not deter IBM from launching a global cybermall called World Avenue. IBM is hoping to attract beginners in Internet commerce, companies that have yet to establish a Web presence. As the mall owner, IBM collects a $30,000 start-up fee from such merchants and $2,500 per month rent to offer a catalog of 300 items. IBM also takes 5 percent of all sales.

Thomas W. Patterson, IBM's chief strategist for electronic commerce, notes that all of these prices are negotiable. He says that World Avenue sold $5 million worth of merchandise in its first four months in business, via merchants such as the Limited Express and a small Colorado-based camera shop that's selling its wares all over the world. "We're not in it for short-term profit," Patterson says. His overall plan seems to be this: First, lock merchants into IBM's software and electronic commerce solutions. If they do leave the mall, he says, "we plan to transfer our processes back to them in house."

In the short term, IBM may succeed in drawing a few naive companies. But over the long run, the IBM venture, too, will fail as currently conceived. As soon as merchants become moderately successful, they would resent paying the 5 percent to IBM and would try to strike out on their own. The idea of renting retail space on the Web is silly at best. The concept of a mall is based on geography. On the Web, geography is rendered moot.

Despite its huge success on cable television, even the Home Shopping Network (HSN) fell flat on the Web with its Internet Shopping Network (ISN). On TV, of course, HSN generates demand for products by having attractive models and slick pitchmen hyping jewelry, the blouse du jour, or the latest "ab" machine in your face. When viewers become transfixed and begin yearning to achieve personal fulfillment through consumption, the TV models auction off the products until enough people impulsively start dialing their phones. Using this formula, home shopping over cable TV has grown into a $3 billion-plus industry since its beginning in the 1980s.

The Web is the opposite of the Home Shopping Network. Web surfers are in control of choosing which products appear before them. It's hard to pull off a hard sell this way. So, HSN's skills honed on cable TV aren't applicable on the Web. Originally set up as a full-fledged cybermall with stores in over a dozen categories, ISN eventually scaled back to offer only computers and software. For obvious reasons, computer products are so far the most popular items purchased on the Web. However, for the Web to become a major factor in retail, marketers must be able to sell a much broader range of products.

The competition in the Web retail economy is fierce. But success here is not a matter of maximizing your use of expensive real estate. Rather, it's a back-to-basics approach of knowing your customers and products thoroughly. Retailers must present detailed information about their products in an intelligent way. At the same time, they must cultivate and keep a flock of loyal customers. That's what small, independent stores have always done well. In this sense, the personally owned and operated stores of the past can be resurrected. Only now, instead of mom and pop, we have geek and nerd.

YOUR PERSONAL CONNOISSEUR

Perhaps no other retailer has better exploited the information-rich nature of the Web than an outfit called Virtual Vineyards. The idea for the company grew out of a conversation between two brothers-in-law in the summer of 1994. Napa Valley wine expert Peter Granoff was frustrated with trends in his industry. He'd seen distributors and retailers squeeze out hundreds of small but high-quality wineries at the same time that Americans were beginning to significantly increase their consumption. Liquor superstores were now dominating the landscape. Stores were growing larger and larger, becoming more and more impersonal, focusing on cutting prices, and stocking brands from the largest suppliers that could produce in great volume. In other words, it was becoming just like the rest of the retail industry.

Robert Olson, the husband of Granoff's sister, had just left a job selling software for Silicon Graphics and was in search of opportunities serving consumers over the Web. Granoff and Olson decided to combine their interests. The two figured that there must be a geographically scattered clientele that appreciates fine wines from small vineyards but has not found retailers in their local area who appreciate and stock those brands. They also figured that the Web was the perfect vehicle for attracting those customers.

Launched in January 1995, Virtual Vineyard was originally part of the Internet Shopping Network. Granoff and Olson were betting that the draw of that network would be worth the monthly fee that they paid in rent. But business, in fact, was so good that they soon decided to sever its relationship with ISN and venture out on their own. Throughout 1995, sales increased by an average of 20 percent month over month. The company reached the $1 million revenue mark in its first year. The site makes that money by taking a flat commission on every sale.

The secret of their success lies in the ability to convey specialized information. Granoff personally tastes hundreds of wines. He not only reviews, recommends, and categorizes each one, but he has set up an objective rating system in which each wine is given a one to seven grade in seven different categories—intensity, dryness, body, acidity, tannin, oak, and complexity. If he was the proprietor of a traditional store, people might come from miles around to get his opinion before they bought. However, he would have to endlessly repeat his wisdom hour after hour, day after day. The Web, by contrast, affords a chance to present all of this information in one place so that it is available for viewing at any time from anywhere.

The result is a value-added shopping experience that most consumers couldn't find otherwise. In a sense, Virtual Vineyards is a throwback to the days when shopkeepers would earn a special sort of trust among their customers. Before the advent of mass advertising, customers would rely on the store owner to tell them which products were worth buying. And before the proliferation of credit cards, shopkeepers would keep a tab in their ledger books—to be paid when the customer had the money. The practice of personally extending credit to customers will never return. Credit cards are here to stay (and are the payment method of choice at Virtual Vineyards). But the idea of having your own personal connoisseur is back with a vengeance.

At Virtual Vineyards, price isn't the all-important factor; trust is. Granoff may suggest that people in search of an excellent gift idea should spend $89.50 for a selection of three choice bottles of cabernet sauvignon. If a customer has ordered from the site before and enjoyed the wine that Granoff recommended, he or she will be receptive to that pitch. Besides, people in the market for exceptional and interesting wines are not all that price sensitive to begin with. What they are looking for is an opportunity to get an education on information-rich products while they shop. And Virtual Vineyards was among the first Web retailers to capitalize on that.

SELECTION, SELECTION, SELECTION

The ultimate in information-rich products may be books. You could even consider them pure information. Books are so information-rich that one connoisseur or reviewer, no matter how talented and dedicated, cannot possibly have an opinion on even a small fraction of what's available. In fact, with more than three million titles in print worldwide at any given time, books by far have more variety than any other product category.

Claiming itself as the world's largest bookstore, the Amazon.com site takes full advantage of this breadth. In 1994, Jeffrey Bezos, a Wall Street investment whiz in his early thirties, became intrigued with the idea of selling something, anything on the Web. After contemplating many different product categories and deciding on books, he relocated with his wife to Seattle and wrote a business plan. The premise for his Web-based bookstore was that there would be three main attractions that would bring book buyers to the Web: selection, selection, selection. Convenience, price, and reliable service were important, albeit secondary, factors, Bezos says.

Unlike Virtual Vineyards, where there are only a few hundred carefully chosen products to consider, Amazon offers up a huge inventory. Indeed, Bezos chose the name Amazon because that river is orders of magnitude larger than the next biggest one. By creating a database of more than 1.1 million book titles, Amazon.com is likewise many times bigger than even the biggest of book superstores, which typically stock up to 175,000 different titles at any given time. Instead of one person reviewing all the products, the Amazon site draws on snippets of reviews published elsewhere. Plus, it relies on its own customers to write their own short reviews for one another.

< W E B O N O M I C S >

Visitors to the site can search for books just as they do in a library's computerized card catalog: by author, by title, or by subject. But the key to selling lots of books isn't just to supply what readers are looking for but also to generate fresh demand for titles that readers might not know about. Readers are always looking to come across an intriguing book while browsing. In traditional bookstores, the serendipity factor is responsible for a large chunk of sales. Unplanned, impulse purchases account for 60 percent of all books sold, according to the Book Industry Study Group, a trade organization.

A small staff of book mavens at Amazon.com try to encourage serendipity by posting lists of the most interesting or obscure or funny new books in forty-five subject categories. And by stepping back and allowing readers to post their own reviews, Amazon.com has created a community of people who enjoy browsing through what their fellow members are saying.

"We want to make the experience every bit as fun and enjoyable as real bookstores," Bezos says. "Only instead of doing it with latté and sofas, we do it with customer-to-customer interaction and customer-to-author interaction." Amazon also simulates bookstore serendipity by presenting virtual "end-caps," which are the end-of-aisle displays that present hot titles. Amazon editors chose fifty interesting, strong-selling titles. Then anytime someone visits, it will display at random two of those titles and short reviews. If you reload the Web page, two different titles will show up.

In addition, the site makes use of its ability to collect data on customer preferences. "Amazon is creating a [customer] database that doesn't exist anywhere else," Albert Vitale, chairman of publishing giant Random House, told the *Wall Street Journal.*

Adhering to the third principle of Webonomics, Amazon provides members with something in return for their information. Armed with knowledge on the tastes of its individual members, the site can regularly E-mail them recommendations on new titles in categories that they select—say the Internet, ecology, and sex. Members can also choose to be notified when books from favorite authors are released and when certain books come out in paperback. Bezos says he does not provide reader-preference data to anyone outside the company.

Without any advertising in its first year, Amazon.com immediately attracted enormous attention—via the word-of-mouth powers of the Internet. "In our business plan, we projected a 10-times impact from word of mouth," he says, meaning one satisfied customer's experience would influence ten other people. Instead, he estimates that the site gets a 100-times impact.

Bezos doesn't disclose revenue and profit figures. But he says that sales grew an average of 34 percent month over month in its first year in business. In addition, he says, the company was poised to bring in more revenue in 1996 than the average book superstore, which generates about $5 million annually. *Business Week* pegged that annual sales figure at $17 million. Bezos has said that he has been investing profits back into the company. He expects to actually report profits by 1998, which is much faster than most equally ambitious start-ups.

While selection is the primary factor that drives people to Amazon.com, price cannot be overlooked. Books sold by Amazon are discounted by 10 to 30 percent. Besides the margins it makes on each book, Amazon charges a $1 per book and $3 per order service charge. But customers don't seem to mind the added fees. More than 40 percent of current orders come from repeat customers, and some buyers have ordered dozens of times. Customers hail from all fifty states and more than ninety-five countries, including Brazil, Finland, Japan, and Tanzania. And like Virtual Vineyards, the site has encountered little resistance to paying via credit card over the Web. About 90 percent of Amazon.com's customers transmit their card numbers online, while the others fax or phone it in.

Bezos doesn't expect sites like his to put traditional booksellers out of business. In fact, his site could be unwittingly helping them. Some customers use his database to search for books they want, then proceed to buy them at a traditional retail outlet. And he's under no illusion that a Web site, no matter how sophisticated, can ever replicate the sensory experience of being in a bookstore, especially the newer stores with cafes, lounges, entertainment, and well-designed displays.

But Bezos says he can do things that real bookstores can't. For instance, by ordering books from publishers in tiny allotments that mirror current orders, he not only maintains a small inventory but also offers publishers a new way to cut losses from returns, traditionally a huge cost problem for them.

In addition, under a marketing plan called the Amazon.com Associates Program, Bezos has deals with more than 5,000 other Web sites that put books in an editorial context and then refer prospective buyers his way—simply by building in a hyperlink. "There are Web sites and books on every subject," he says. And many of those single-subject sites are run by what he calls "passionate domain experts." For instance, a site called Pure-Bred Puppynet recommends a list of books about dogs and then sends visitors over to Amazon. Such partners get paid an 8 percent commission on sales. This is a way to set up what Bezos calls "micro-franchises" with zero overhead.

There's little doubt that Bezos has found a niche that will keep growing bigger and bigger. Len Vlahos, a spokesman for the American Booksellers Association, told the industry publication *WebWeek*, that he estimates the online market will account for 5 to 10 percent of total book sales by 2001. Currently, the U.S. book industry rings up about $25 billion annually and is growing at a healthy 8 percent clip year over year. Much of that online market share will be incremental, not replacement, business. No wonder Bezos is already attracting competing booksellers such as Borders and Barnes & Noble to the Web. We're talking about a multibillion-dollar opportunity here.

JOIN THE CLUB

Another highly successful way of retailing on the Web is not to be a retailer at all. NetMarket (formerly Shopper's Advantage), a shopping service run by Stamford, Connecticut-based CUC International, is essentially a giant wholesale club. The company maintains a database of some 400,000 different choices of name-brand consumer electronics, computers, appliances, and other big-ticket, information-intensive items. CUC has also branched out into other buyer's clubs offering cars, travel, dining, and financial services.

CUC claims to offer these products and services at or close to wholesale prices. "We don't make money on the transactions," says Rick Fernandes, executive vice president. So how did CUC quietly grow into a $1 billion company? The answer lies in the deal it offers consumers. The company makes nearly all its revenue selling memberships to consumers who want to bypass retail channels altogether and buy directly from manufacturers—at least for certain types of products. All told, CUC's shopping services have nearly fifty million members worldwide who pay a $50 per year subscription fee. (Trial subscriptions are available for $1 for the first three months.)

In 1974, founder Walter Forbes started the company as Comp-U-Card with the vision that some day consumers would shop from their homes using computers. Forbes, of course, was way ahead of the game. Back then, personal computers had not yet been invented, and it would be twenty years before a significant number of consumers would have PCs with modems in their homes. But the basic idea of bypassing traditional retail channels was dead-on. The company began by providing consumers with catalogs and taking orders over the phone. The service went up on CompuServe in the 1980s. And by the early 1990s, CUC was offering shopping services on Prodigy, America Online, and other online networks.

In September 1995, the Shopper's Advantage site went live on the Web. It quickly became the fastest-growing part of CUC's overall business. Visit the site and you might think you've entered some sort of postindustrial, virtual version of Sears. Only instead of *aisles* stocked with televisions, stereos, computers, refrigerators, microwave ovens, dishwashers, clothes dryers, and vacuum cleaners, the Shopper's Advantage site has *database categories* stocked with these items.

Consumers browse the product database by filling out multiple-choice forms with a few clicks of the mouse. For instance, you can tell the database that you're looking for a notebook computer with at least sixteen megabytes of memory, a one gigabyte hard drive, a 120 megahertz Pentium chip, a color, active-matrix screen, and a price tag of under $3,000. A database query could even be as simple as "refrigerator, under $800." The site will present all the models, if any, that qualify, and give you more information about each one. CUC doesn't accept advertising so as to keep its ratings objective and give all manufacturers a level playing field.

The Shopper's Advantage site can then take your order, charge the credit card number you gave when you enrolled, forward the order to the manufacturer, and make sure the product is delivered to your door. The company has no need for warehouse space, inventory systems, or retail stores. Additional costs are eliminated when consumers shop on the Web because CUC no longer has to pay as many sales clerks to field phone calls, answer questions, and search the database for customers. Now, consumers can do that themselves. And in general, customers are happy to get the chance. "It's a lower cost way of doing business," says Fernandes.

WHAT HAPPENS TO RETAIL STORES?

The best places to shop on the Web don't just rely on the fact that some people want the convenience of shopping at home. After all, there are other ways to do that besides going online. These sites distinguish themselves by building information-intensive services that offer something consumers would be hard-pressed to find anywhere else. Virtual Vineyards does it through product expertise. Amazon.com does it primarily with selection. CUC does it mainly by price. None of these companies had any brand awareness to speak of. Rather, they established themselves by virtue of the authority of the information they present.

Whether business models such as these present a real threat to the retail industry depends on what the industry does in response. So far, the response has been largely one of confusion. "The retail industry doesn't know what to do about this yet," Fernandes says.

When it comes to taking away market share from the retail business, Web-based shopping services would not have to win over a large percentage in order for retail chains to feel the pain. Profit margins in the industry are typically so slim that a small but permanent loss of customers could send a store into a tizzy. Fernandes's theory is that it only takes a 5 percent swing in revenue to bring a retail giant to its knees. "We don't have to take a huge percentage of business to have a huge impact," he says. As examples, he cites Caldor and Bradlees, two national chains selling housewares and apparel. While it didn't have anything to do with the Web, sales at those stores dipped only a few percent at the same time costs also increased a few percent. That was enough to throw each company into bankruptcy reorganization and cause them to begin closing down many of their stores.

But the retail industry has time to respond to this threat—and even capitalize on it. Online shopping has a long way to go before it captures 5 percent of the retail industrial complex. Forrester Research is expecting online sales to ring to the tune of about $1 billion in 1997, then grow to $6.6 billion by the year 2000. Even that latter figure is less than 1 percent of the gargantuan $1.7 trillion U.S. retail economy. (Although it does represent nearly 10 percent of the catalog shopping business.) Meanwhile, Jupiter Communications projects that the number of U.S. consumers regularly shopping on the Internet for certain items will approach 4.5 million by the year 2000. That's only about 3 percent of adults.

In a sense, retail establishments have been responding to the general shop-at-home threat for a long time. With the rapid rise of catalogs, mail order, and cable shopping networks over the past twenty years, retail businesses have recognized that they must create compelling reasons for people to drag their butts out of the house and into the store. What they lack in service, retail makes up for in entertainment. While shopping has always been a form of entertainment, in recent years it has been forced to become more so.

To this end, malls have become sophisticated entertainment zones, complete with arcades, stores from Disney and Warner Brothers, and theme restaurants such as the Hard Rock Cafe and Planet Hollywood. Furniture superstores such as Ikea have restaurants and play zones for kids. Record stores have installed listening stations. Bookstores have opened sit-down cafes and beefed up the scheduling of author appearances. Liquor stores now host wine-tasting parties. Once the entertainment draws the people in, they usually buy stuff.

The social experience of real live shopping is something that the Web can never match, no matter how good virtual reality and other technologies become. People will always want to get out of the house and experience the world firsthand. All bets are that retailers will continue to add entertainment to the shopping experience as one of the primary ways to distinguish themselves from all forms of home shopping.

But they must embrace online shopping as well. Physical stores and virtual stores can work in tandem and support each other as parts of the process of winning over customers, ringing up sales, and maintaining brand loyalty. Neither a Web site nor a real store is an isolated island. Rather, they can both pick up where each other leaves off and help compensate for the weaknesses of the other.

THE INTIMATE BOND

An example of how this can work can be found at the Web site of JCPenney. As the second-largest chain of department stores in the United States, behind Sears, JCPenney could very well view the Web as a threat to its enormous investment in brick and mortar. The company spends nearly $1 billion per year in advertising alone trying to get people into its 1,300 stores. In addition, JCPenney operates one of the world's largest catalog businesses, publishing and mailing ninety-one different editions annually and selling $3.7 billion in merchandise this way. Its catalog fulfillment centers handle seventy-five million inbound calls per year. All told, one out of every three families make at least one purchase from this retail giant each year, the company claims.

When JCPenney launched its Web site in November 1994, the most obvious idea would have been to put their catalog online so that shoppers could place orders for merchandise over the Web. But the company had already experimented with online catalogs and order taking via Prodigy and CompuServe since 1988—and those ventures were less successful than expected. So, it didn't rush to do that. The fundamental reason, says Marisha Konkowski, JCPenney's electronic retailing manager, is because the advantages to shopping in an online catalog versus a paper one are negligible.

"There *are* no advantages," Konkowski says. Customers enjoy getting glossy catalogs in the mail and flipping through them in search of something that catches their eye. On the Web, you have to wait for the pictures to appear on your screen, and the resolution is not as sharp.

But what about creating unique, information-rich services, such as an online bridal registry? Typically, if a bride and groom registers at a department store chain for dozens of gifts, friends and relatives have to visit one of those stores, go to the bridal registry department, ask a clerk to print out a list, and then proceed to select one of the items from that list. But what if some of the guests don't live near a JCPenneys—or don't have the time to get to one? Often, they would pick up a gift at a more convenient place, which means lost business for JCPenney.

At JCPenney's Web site, visitors can visit a virtual bridal registry department, enter the first two letters of the bride's or groom's last name, scroll through their list of chosen gifts or print it out. Then, the gift buyer can either try to find it in the online catalog that the company added to the site—or they could order and send it to the couple's home by calling Penney's 800 number. They don't necessarily have to see the gift because they already know that the couple likes it and wants it. "Customers perceive this as an added value because there is no other way to do it," short of visiting a store in person, Konkowski says.

The online bridal registry consistently attracts among the highest traffic on Penney's Web site, she adds. It's success underscores the department store's very raison d 'être. The protracted bankruptcy reorganization at Macy's in the early 1990s caused some retail analysts to write off department stores as a thing of the past. (Macy's was rescued from Chapter 11 by merging with Federated Department stores in 1994.) But in these days of superstores and specialty retail, a service such as a bridal registry shows off the splendor of the traditional department store.

Newly engaged couples don't register at Wal-Mart or Circuit City—and the reason is obvious. Only through a department store can you get all your friends and relatives to buy you towels, sheets, a bread maker, a blender, a coffeemaker, a microwave oven, flatware, china, a knife set, picture frames, lamps, pots and pans—not to mention furniture, clothing, and the quintessential wedding gift: candlesticks. "JCPenney is a department store," says Edward W. Sample, manager of communications research. "We're not a discount store. We're not a single-category store. We're not a specialty shop. That's not our competition. We're a department store."

The future of Penney's Web site lies in using information to strengthen the company's bond with individual consumers—and win over more of their business. That's what a department store in this era must do.

Penney's already has troves of information that it can leverage in its effort to strengthen that bond. Its customer account database contains records on 98 million consumers, including very rich data on its 17 million JCPenney credit-card customers. Konkowski says that the possibilities for using this data to create new information-based services are endless. For instance, if a certain customer tends to buy clothes in extra-tall sizes, he will be presented with specials in that category every time he logs on. This way, says Konkowski, Penney's can create a customized shopping presentation for each individual, based on that shopper's buying history.

Other options might seem frivolous, but could actually work. Suppose that frequent shoppers could look up pie charts, for instance, that show what percentage of casual clothing, dressy outfits, and business attire they have bought over the past five years. As the country's largest seller of women's business attire, Penney's can speak with authority on such matters. In fact, its Web site already has a pie chart showing that a working woman's wardrobe should consist of 60 percent business, 30 percent casual, and 10 percent dressy clothing. By looking up her own personal chart, a woman could order the right type of clothing to get her proportions more in line.

By using information to demonstrate knowledge of a customer's lifestyle, a Web site such as this could help forge an intimate relationship between a company and its most loyal customers. The ultimate goal is to use the latest technology to emulate the days of really personal customer service. At the turn of the century, James Cash Penney operated a single store in the town square of a small Wyoming city. He took pride in knowing exactly what his customers needed. Says Konkowski: "He knew what type of hose every woman in town wore."

THE BIG-TICKET PURCHASE

Some big-ticket items require buyers not only to see and touch but to feel the ambiance of the product before they buy it. Think of two of the purchases that represent the biggest investments a typical family will make—their car and their home. Consumers are unlikely to purchase these "products" over the Web. But since both are ultra-information-rich, the Web has already become an integral part of the decision-making process for each.

There are countless places to shop for a car online. Nearly every automaker has established a Web site. Many of these are huge productions with thousands of pages of information and entertainment. Auto companies were the first and most aggressive category of marketers to take their message to the Web. This was only natural. The auto industry spends more money on advertising than any other, laying out about $10 billion per year in the United States alone.

Smart automakers are using their Web sites to occupy the vast information gap that exists after a consumer sees an advertisement but before actually walking into a dealer for a test drive. "The Web offers the ability to close the communications loop that was opened by traditional advertising," says Rich Anderman, general manager of marketing communications at Mercedes-Benz of North America.

But once a consumer has done research on the cars that have caught his eye, once he has visited Web sites for specific information on certain models, it all comes down to agreeing on what the car should cost. Walking into a dealer showroom to negotiate the price is often about as pain-free as a trip to the dentist. Perhaps the high-pressure, sleazy auto salesman is an unfair stereotype. But now that there are more and more ways to bypass such salesmen, consumers are jumping at the chance to avoid the antagonism, aggravation, and self-doubt that often accompanies the car-buying process.

Used-car superlots have sprung up in the past few years, offering up huge selections at no-haggle prices. These lots are run by Circuit City,

Blockbuster Video, PriceCostco, and other companies that have already transformed other sectors of retail. Manufacturers are testing the waters, trying to grant new-car franchises to a few of these new super-lots without infuriating their traditional dealers.

The Web already eliminates haggling on new car purchases. By joining CUC's AutoVantage service, consumers fill out an online form specifying the exact car they want, complete with a list of options and their color preferences. Within a day or so, they receive a firm price quote via E-mail. It may not always be lower than the price they could negotiate themselves, but that extra discount is not worth the hassle for many buyers. Buyers also get the name of a contact person who works at a nearby dealer that has joined the AutoVantage network. More than 2,000 dealers now participate, and more than two million consumers pay $49 per year for membership in this shopper's club.

AutoByTel, another car buyer's Web site, works in a similar fashion, only it's free to the public. Dealers themselves cover the cost of the service by paying subscription fees of $250 to $1,500 in return for a stream of interested leads. More than 1,400 dealers have signed up. And the company had planned to turn a profit on $6.5 million in sales in 1996.

Here is where the Web once again shifts power into the hands of consumers. Since buyers need to test-drive the car before they buy it, they won't actually order the car via the Web. But by forming virtual buyers pools, buyers are forcing car sellers to standardize their prices and cut out the wheeling and dealing. More than 100,000 cars were expected to be purchased through online brokers such as these in 1996. That's only a small fraction of overall new car sales. But since these big-ticket shopping services are catching on so fast, they are beginning to transform the way cars are sold.

House hunting with a mouse is also starting to click. At first, real-estate agencies that had bothered to build Web sites were only referring house buyers to their agents in local areas, not providing actual listings of available homes. If you were planning a move across country and didn't have access to the Yellow Pages in the new area, these Web sites might be of some help—but not much. Some real-estate Web sites have gone a bit further, putting up elaborate menus of information that include local and national home-price indexes, mortgage-loan information, SAT scores for local high schools, and regional economic forecasts.

But the gauntlet was laid down in the spring of 1996, when Abele Information Systems Inc., a San Francisco start-up, launched the Owners' Network, a national home-listing and real-estate information service on the World Wide Web for people selling their homes themselves, rather than through an agent. Suddenly, more than $1 billion in property was available to anyone anywhere who pointed their browser at Owners.com. Users could define their search for homes by price, number of bedrooms, type of property, and metropolitan area. They could obtain a customized list of homes and choose to have free E-mail updates each week of new listings that meet their criteria.

In the real-estate industry, these for-sale-by-owner homes are derisively known as FSBO's, or "Fiz-bo's." But one out of every five homes is sold this way. For sellers, the motivation for selling their own homes is to avoid paying the typical 6 percent commission to a real-estate agent, thus saving themselves $10,000, $20,000, or more. The downside, of course, is that these homes are not entered into the multiple-listing service (MLS), the big kahuna database that all real-estate agencies use to find homes for buyers. Consumers typically cannot access the MLS directly. They must go through an agent or broker.

With the Owners' Network now on the Web, there was suddenly an alternative to the MLS. Individuals could list their homes in the database for free, then edit their listing, changing the price, open-house dates, and other details whenever they log onto the Web site. (For a $10-per-picture scanning charge, sellers could also offer a visual glimpse of their property.) The site makes most of its money by selling advertising to moving companies, furniture stores, mortgage companies, and other businesses that want to target the lucrative market of people on the move. The formula is working. In its first six months on-line, listings on the Owner's Network led to sales of at least 500 homes, and the site took in about $200,000 in advertising revenue, enough to break even on operating costs.

As Web sites like the Owner's Network catch on, Century 21, Cold-well Banker, RE/Max, Prudential, and the other giants of real-estate agency franchising are faced with a dilemma: Do they agree to put the MLS online for the public? If they do, buyers and sellers could use the information to cut the agents out of the process. The National Associ-ation of Realtors, the industry trade group that governs the MLS, had hoped to maintain control of the industry by developing an advanced, $16 million, private listings network for personal computers. But in August 1996, the group's board of directors voted to abandon the pro-ject and expand its Web site instead. The move does not bode well for agencies that want to keep things as they were.

But Hans Koch, a twenty-seven-year-old former property manager and CEO of the Abele Owners' Network, doesn't think that agents will be forced out of their jobs. The Web could even present a new growth business for real-estate firms. Agents who become expert at surfing the many different real-estate databases on the Web would become even more valuable. After all, searching for homes on the Web and knowing which information to look for and what to trust can be rather tricky. "There is a need for agents, but the value of their service isn't in pro-portion to what they charge," Koch says. He believes it will become more of a fee-for-service business, in which agents charge à la carte for preparing and filing documents, negotiating, marketing, holding open houses, and other items.

Agents who can navigate this new terrain could find additional work as buyers' brokers, rather than just sellers' agents. This way, they can leverage their know-how for the benefit of the buyer, surfing all kinds of databases in search of the perfect homes for their clients, then ar-ranging showings, negotiating the best deals, and smoothing out the complex paperwork. Getting paid explicitly for personalized service and specific expertise rather than proprietary access to a database is a purer way of making a living, he says. "We encourage this," he says. "Buyers brokers are canvassing our site for their clients."

"No longer do real-estate agents have a lock on information," says Becky Swann, founder and president of the International Real Estate Directory, a real-estate information service that lists and rates thousands of real estate-related Web sites. "Anyone can learn with the click of a mouse what he might expect to pay for a home that meets his needs. A seller can judge for himself whether he should sell and what he can expect to recover. From now on, agents will have to earn their fees, and those who only wait for 'pennies from heaven' will have to move on. If I sound cynical, I am, but for the consumer I am very optimistic."

The Web may never serve as a replacement for face-to-face buying and selling of homes. People in the market for a home will always want to visit personally a number of houses before laying down a deposit. Even if virtual reality technology improves to the point that consumers could get complete, three-dimensional walk-through tours of houses based on actual video footage, they'll still want to stroll through the house with their own bodies. Yet because shopping for a home is such an information-rich process, the Web is transforming the economics of yet another huge industry.

PITY THE INFORMATION-POOR

As more and more marketers of consumer products build Web sites, and as the novelty of the Web wears off, consumers will resort to paying attention only to Web sites that really matter to them. In this Darwinian battle for attention, promotional sites *for information-poor* products will fare the worst.

The prospects for attracting visitors to Web sites for detergents, shampoos, shaving cream, toothpaste, toilet paper, potato chips, candy bars, cereals, pet food, gasoline, and beer are shabby. On TV, ads for these products come at people. On the Web, the people have to go to the ads. People won't spend their time learning about these products on the Web; there's just not much to learn.

Information-poor products aren't very good at attracting attention. The theory that one-to-one marketing represents the future of all products and services is a powerful one. But it doesn't hold up in all cases. In their groundbreaking book *The One-to-One Future,* authors Don Peppers and Martha Rogers assert that people will take the time out to order customized breakfast cereals. "Kellogg's could customer-ize its products and begin offering . . . particular blends of cornflakes, fruit, bran flakes, and puffed wheat" to satisfy individual requests, they write. More likely, breakfast cereals will remain a low-involvement, mass-marketed product. Yes, consumers will take the time out to order a custom-configured automobile or a custom-designed mutual fund portfolio. But ordering custom-made cereals? One would worry deeply about people with that kind of time on their hands.

That's not to say that there isn't a role for selling information-poor products over the Web. Only instead of creating Web sites based on information about the *product itself,* the potential lies in services in which the information-richness has to do with the *delivery* of those products.

Online grocery ordering services offer compelling benefits. Food shopping is time consuming: The average shopper spends ninety minutes per week buying groceries, according to Raymond Burke, a consumer-behavior analyst at Harvard Business School. It's repetitive: 85 percent of purchases are the same stuff week after week. And groceries are heavy, especially items like laundry detergent, bottled water, and cat litter.

Even so, driving the car to the supermarket and shopping for food and household items is an age-old ritual that will be hard to replace. People may complain about having to shop for groceries, but most of us accept it as a part of the human experience.

Past efforts in this realm have flopped. In the early 1990s, Prodigy

canceled a grocery ordering service offered in several metro areas because of lack of interest. Consumers never became comfortable having
their food delivered without seeing the stuff first. Food is an intimate
thing. People didn't seem to want other people squeezing their melons
and picking their bananas. Plus, the prices on the Prodigy service
weren't very competitive. Prodigy chalked up the entire experience as
a bad idea. "When you're blazing new trails," a Prodigy executive told
me back then, "you're bound to take some wrong turns."

That was then, this is now. Plenty has changed over the past several
years. For starters, tens of millions more homes have personal computers. The number of dual-career households has grown. In general,
people are busier and more accepting of technology.

In an attempt to ride the high-tech wave, a company called Peapod
has made the most headway in setting up a workable online grocery
store. Headquartered in Evanston, Illinois, Peapod was founded by
Andrew Parkinson, a former Procter & Gamble brand manager, and
his brother, Thomas Parkinson, a software designer. The company
strikes deals with traditional grocery stores, linking their computerized ordering system with the stores' real-time pricing database. First
available in the Chicago and San Francisco areas, Peapod's service
has expanded to Boston and other regions filled with high-income,
high-tech, highly time-constrained people.

While customers can order via phone, fax, or computer, 80 percent
use their computers. At Peapod's Web site, members must enter their
passwords to get into the virtual store. Once inside, they can look at
photos of the products, see the nutritional information, and sort like
items by price, calories, fat content, and other factors. They can search
the store by entering a brand name, such as Del Monte, or by entering
product type, such as green beans. But the most popular feature is the
ability to bypass "shopping" altogether and simply create a list of staples.

When a customer is ready to send in her order, she must choose a
ninety-minute delivery time window later in the day or the following
day. A more precise thirty-minute window costs extra. Payment is ac-

cepted by cash, check, charge, or an electronic payment. The typical cost: a $4.95 membership fee, plus $6.95 per delivery.

Peapod has done well overcoming the online gender gap. About 75 percent of Peapod users are women. And it has been able to retain four out of five customers who sign up. But the number of people using it is still relatively small. By the summer of 1996, only 7,500 homes were using its services, and the privately held company was reporting steep losses on its $16 million in annual revenues.

The winning formula for services such as Peapod would be to offer the customer both convenience *and* lower prices. Peapod, after all, is simply a delivery service for existing grocery stores, where retail space typically costs $18 per square foot to stock, manage, and maintain. Other online grocery startups such as Streamline Inc. and Hannaford's Home Runs, both based in Massachusetts, bypass grocery stores altogether. They maintain huge food warehouses and fulfill orders from there. The cost of that space is typically about $6.50 per square foot. If these services can manage to deliver groceries for a lower overall price than people pay in stores, consumers would find it hard to resist.

<Chapter Summary>
• Information is what sells products on the Web. Marketers and online retailers must stock their site with facts, news, knowledge, wisdom, and advice about their products.
• Geography is irrelevant on the Web. Since cyberspace is boundless and can be traversed with the click of a mouse, so-called cybermalls of many stores "under one roof" will not dominate retail as they do in the physical world.
• Retailers on the Web must distinguish themselves by providing broader *selection*, superior product *expertise*, or below-retail *prices*.
• Buying online will *never* replace the in-person shopping experience; instead, it will force massive change upon it—such as the current movement to create sophisticated entertainment zones.
• People won't spend time comparison shopping online for *information-poor products*, such as grocery items, but they will go online to place *home-delivery orders*.

<CHAPTER FIVE>

Self-Service Provides for the Highest Level of Customer Comfort

SHIP IT YOURSELF

Just as automatic teller machines transformed the customer experience in the banking industry and self-service pumps have taken over gas stations everywhere, self-service applications on the Web are changing the rules in dozens of other industries. Customers are comfortable doing things themselves because it provides them with control and convenience. They don't have to rely on someone else to enter and read the correct information. And they can do all kinds of tasks whenever they want, without leaving their desktop—or their laptop.

For many industries, self-service isn't just a nice little novelty anymore. In a short period of time, it has become mandatory. The shipping industry, for instance, is engaged in an especially contentious race to export more and more of its work onto the desks and into the laps of its own customers. And as long as the work remains fairly easy, customers are gladly obliging.

The first company to exploit this was Federal Express. The Memphis company typically delivers more than two million overnight packages daily. Many of those are sent by customers who may want to check the delivery status of their urgent parcel at some point. Fielding calls on its 800 number, FedEx had been spending tens of millions of dollars on phone charges and customer-support personnel. But since the fall of 1994, when FedEx established its Web site, customers have been helping themselves to that package-tracking information.

Hundreds of thousands of customers per month began visiting FedEx.com for one simple reason: When they type in the tracking number of their package, they instantly get routing and delivery information. Customers are presented with a detailed list of checkpoints that the package has passed through, plus the time of final delivery and the name of the person who signed for it. The Web site not only saves FedEx millions of dollars. Surveys have shown that it actually enhances customer satisfaction.

How *much* money does it save? Nancy Raileanu, FedEx's Webmaster, says that an average of 500,000 packages per month were tracked on the site over the first six months. She figures that half of those were "curiosity" tracks by people just checking out the feature for the fun of it. But the other half would have called the company's 800 number. Such phone calls average two minutes each, she says. At an independently estimated cost to FedEx of about 50¢ per call, including personnel costs, that works out to about $125,000 in saving per month—due to just one simple feature. Raileanu says that the company spent only $50,000 developing the original site and $50,000 promoting it. The site "pays for itself many times over," she says.

Like far-flung ATM networks, the FedEx tracking system, called COSMOS, seems simple to consumers even though it's really a complex jumble of sophisticated technology. FedEx personnel scan the bar codes of every package at a number of checkpoints along the route. When the package reaches its final destination, the delivery person collects a time-stamped signature on one of those handheld wireless terminals. When the driver goes back to the truck and plugs the scanner into a data port, all delivery data are relayed over FedEx's private data network to its Memphis headquarters. Customers with a Web connection simply point their browsers at the FedEx server computers and access the database by typing in the number on their shipping receipt.

In 1996, United Parcel Service (UPS) leapfrogged FedEx by creating a Web site that not only offers package tracking but an entire slew

of self-service options: Customers can calculate the cost of their ship-
ment by entering the weight. They can prepare their own export documents. They can locate the nearest UPS drop-off points by typing in
their zip code. UPS has even moved into full-fledged electronic commerce applications, such as allowing business customers to manage
accounts receivable, reorder inventory, and preprogram customer orders.

Even ye olde post office has gotten into the act. The U.S. Postal Service delivers more than a half-billion pieces of mail every day. It may
have a monopoly on lick-'em and stick-'em mail. But as a self-
supporting, nontaxpayer financed arm of government, the Postal Service has much the same goals as any business—to increase revenue
while slashing costs. Waking up to the fact that FedEx and UPS are its
competitors, the Postal Service is also using the Web to provide customer service without actually having to service customers. Web
surfers can now order stamps, look up postal rates, obtain zip codes,
get tips on addressing envelopes, and register a change of address.
Philatelists can boot up at all hours of the night, enter the stamp col-
lector's gallery, and peer at whatever turns them on.

The Postal Service has truly joined the ranks of for-profit businesses. While its Web site can only claim a tiny bit of credit for its
turnaround, the nation's mail system posted $1.8 billion and $1.6 billion in earnings in fiscal 1995 and 1996, respectively. Postmaster
General Marvin Runyon called it "the best financial one-two punch in
our history."

As more and more people pile onto the Web, the basis of competition in the shipping business is shifting. As the Web becomes the point
of customer contact in this and other industries, more and more resources will be invested into making self-service on the Web efficient,
easy, even entertaining. Although this might seem like an impersonal
way to do business, a growing number of companies are coming to realize that self-service provides for the highest level of customer comfort.

WEB TRAVEL: WHERE TO?

The most likely business to find success on the Web is travel. That was a major finding in a 1996 study of more than 1,000 Web-based marketers, conducted by ActivMedia, a research firm in Peterborough, New Hampshire. Contrary to the popular perception that computer and software companies are the Web's most prosperous shopkeepers, travel sites are actually the most likely to be generating revenue and reporting substantial profits, the study showed.

"Travel sites are a natural match for the Web," says Jeanne Dietsch, an analyst with ActivMedia. Consumers who surf the Web are likely to be professionals who travel frequently, she says. In addition, travel is an information-rich business, a worldwide business, and a business that sells products—tickets, reservations, itineraries—that can be easily sold and relayed to customers living anywhere.

But the overarching reason for the success of so many travel sites is the ability for such sites to offer self-service. The Web may never surpass the experience of dealing with a good travel agent. Who wouldn't rather talk with a real, live, friendly human being who knows your personal preferences and has a vast array of knowledge about faraway places, including where to stay, what to eat, things to see, and how much it should all cost? Unfortunately, few people have a travel agent quite like that. While most agents are friendly and knowledgeable, they may not know anything about the particular place you want to go. Travel agents aren't necessarily well traveled. If you're going to Sydney or a secluded spot in the Caribbean, and the agent hasn't been there, you might walk away with little more than a few glossy brochures.

The Web can easily beat that. Every day, it seems, another local tourism board or chamber of commerce from somewhere builds a Web site. The Web is already stocked with more brochures, maps, travel tips, and other information than you could possibly want. Interested in taking a boat cruise around Manhattan—or the Greek Isles? Go to a search engine, type in a few key words, and you'll be presented with several sites that tell you where to go and what to do.

Likewise, the typical agent might not provide much in the way of added value when it comes to their most common task: booking airline seats. Travel agents search for the best prices and book seats by logging into massive computer reservation systems—or by contacting individual carriers. But consumers are more and more often doing this on their own. Direct booking was practically unheard of fifteen years ago. But in 1995, about 20 percent of U.S. airline seats were booked by consumers directly with carriers, while the rest was done through agents.

Most of that direct booking is done over the phone, by calling United, American, Delta, or another carrier's 800 number. But *online* bookings have been growing at a rapid clip. In the mid-1980s, American Airlines made its famous Sabre travel reservation system available directly to consumers for the first time. The so-called Easy Sabre system became one of the most popular features on Prodigy, America Online, and CompuServe. Consumers now had the chance to view all available flights for their chosen route and order tickets from the carrier that offered the best price. By 1995, the Easy Sabre system was handling more than one million bookings annually.

Self-service in the travel industry is a win-win-lose situation. Large numbers of the airlines' best customers are coming to realize that they now have essentially the same information and the same choice of fares that they would get through a travel agent. Meanwhile, by encouraging online booking, the airlines are drastically reducing the costs of servicing those customers directly. Indeed, the cost of fulfilling an online reservation is only about $2, as compared to $10 for fielding an 800 number call. Everyone seems to like this setup—that is, except for the travel agents. The airlines are using their direct bonds with consumers as leverage, literally slashing the commissions that they pay to agents.

"The airlines are squeezing the agents out of the middle," says

Dietsch. Initially, travel agents tried the lawsuit route for striking back at the airlines, eventually reaching a $72 million settlement just before a class-action, antitrust case was about to go to trial in September 1996. But while the agents got some cash, they weren't able to force the airlines to lift the caps on future commission payments.

Some travel agents are more cleverly wielding the Web as a weapon to fight back. The Internet Travel Network, based in Menlo Park, California, was founded in mid-1994 by two technologists and Bruce Yoximer, an owner of a travel agency for the past fifteen years. ITN's Web site provides user-friendly access to Apollo, a major online reservation system. But unlike Easy Sabre, which allows you to order your tickets directly from the airlines and have them delivered to your home or office, the ITN site doesn't actually fulfill orders. Instead, it instructs travelers to select a traditional travel agent from a list of 12,000 agencies in seventeen countries that have agreed to be part of the network. By typing in their zip codes, travelers can choose agents in their local areas. The agents handle the paperwork, perform follow-up customer service, and collect the usual commissions. ITN then charges the agents a flat fee of $3 per trip booked.

Yoximer claims that the benefits of doing it this way are numerous. Consumers, he says, get the best of both worlds—quick, easy self-service for airline tickets, plus a link to a real agent for help with more complicated parts of the trip, such as where to stay and what to do.

In addition, he says, corporate clients such as American Express can customize the ITN software for their internal "Intranets," the secure, Weblike, company-wide networks that allow employees to enter only relevant parts of the Internet. Silicon Valley clients such as Netscape Communications and Cisco Systems preprogram the software for their employees—routing their workers to preferred airlines and hotels, for instance, or imposing price restrictions, such as no first-class bookings or no rooms over $150.

But sites such as ITN may be fighting a losing battle against some powerful forces. Airline companies and hotel chains are hell-bent on cutting travel agents out of the self-service process for several reasons. Not only do they want to save money on commission payments; they also want to forge direct bonds with their best customers. Sites such as ITN encourage travelers to pick and choose among dozens of brand-name hotels, airlines, and tour packages. By contrast, most of the large travel-related companies that have launched their own Web sites naturally focus on increasing sales for just their own brand.

Travel companies can use their Web sites to offer powerful incentives to their most loyal customers. These incentives go a long way toward assuring that those consumers stop by their favorite travel-related Web site before going anywhere else. American Airlines, for instance, has been posting special "Internet fares" for customers who are interested in booking last-minute weekend getaways. Every Wednesday at midnight, American flashes the data on unsold seats. These seats are often sold at below market prices on an auction basis to the highest bidder. Consumers may pay by credit card or with frequent flyer points.

The Internet is the perfect place to sell tickets this way. Unlike a newspaper ad or a TV commercial, the Web enables up-to-the-minute data to be posted immediately. And it has an insider edge: Because such prices aren't advertised in a mass medium, the customers who already paid full price won't likely find out about this and become infuriated.

For the airlines, the economics of doing business this way are compelling. Airlines typically fill only two-thirds of their available seats. By auctioning off unsold inventory for imminent flights at low prices, the potential exists to fly at 100 percent capacity. Salomon Brothers airline analyst Julius Maldutis told the *Wall Street Journal* that average fare prices would drop 25 percent if this practice became widespread. However, profits would go way up. These planes are flying anyway; except for a few extra chicken dinners and a round of complimentary beverages, fixed costs would remain so. Almost all the commission-free revenue from those now-empty seats would go straight to the bottom line. Such a strategy has the potential to triple net income in the airline industry.

Hotels, cruise ships, tour operators, car-rental companies, concert and event promoters, and other travel-related companies have the same exact problem—and opportunity. By forming these special auction clubs, they can gain an underground channel for unloading unsold seats at the last minute without alienating those paying full freight. Unique values such as these will become more and more compelling as travel companies race to offer self-service in cyberspace.

Soon, every travel company will have to play by these new rules. Consumers who surf the Web for travel information have already raised their level of expectations. It's already becoming mandatory for travel sites to offer a full range of applications. Consumers are coming to expect real-time flight arrival and departure information, access to their frequent flier account data, and a help system for specific questions.

Moving way beyond just reservations, the most valuable travel sites are also offering to keep track of personal profile data. When a consumer cites preferences for aisle/window seating, special meals, rental-car size, and hotel-room requirements, it's up to the Web site to make use of that knowledge whenever that consumer requests a reservation. As these Web sites become more and more sophisticated, they can "get to know you" almost as well as a human agent. In fact, as the software learns more and more about your preferences, it can become your intelligent agent, searching the entire Web for the exact travel arrangements you want and returning a few seconds later with a list of choices and prices.

But perhaps the biggest potential for truly value-added services lies in simulating the word-of-mouth recommendations that travelers are always on the lookout for. According to a study in the *Journal of Travel Research*, 85 percent of tourist visits are to places that travelers had recommended to them by people they know. These "first-level" destination suggestions from friends, family, coworkers, and acquaintances are the lifeblood of the travel business. But most cyber-travelers would be hard-pressed to find recommendations that they trust on the Web.

Henri Poole, CEO of the Vivid Travel Network, a collection of Web sites based out of San Francisco, aims to capitalize on this opportunity. He notes that the travel and tourism is right up there with agriculture as one of the world's largest industries. But it is also "extremely fragmented," with information about each of more than 10,000 tourist destinations controlled by "culturally centered" and "biased" sources that most people have trouble finding and deciphering.

Poole's goal is to form a network of Web sites each designed in a standard format by thousands of local partners at each destination. The Vivid travel site in Rio, for instance, might be run in partnership with a magazine based there. Vivid makes its money by licensing its special software kit, brand name, and expertise to each partner. "Our role is to integrate all these information resources," Poole says. He expects content to be published in as many as twenty-five different languages, with information at each destination available in several of those languages.

Ultimately, he expects each local site to be a "community of interest" in which travelers could not only read brochures, view video clips, and obtain standard tourist information but also participate in interactive discussions. At a site to promote tourism in Italy, for instance, a visitor could search a bulletin board or a membership database for a person who not only has been to Rome but also to San Francisco. They could strike up an online conversation about San Francisco to see whether they have the same tastes and sensibilities. If so, Person A might come to trust the opinion of Person B when it comes to recommending out-of-the-way places to stay and fun things to do in Italy.

This idea of forming relationships with people all over the world based on common curiosities could represent the Web's ultimate destiny. Interactive travel services, to be sure, will be among the first to take advantage of this potential. Instead of just reading travel information, travelers from all over the globe could gather at a virtual version of the Spanish Steps, introducing themselves and exchanging points of view.

WEB BANKING: PUT YOUR MONEY WHERE YOUR MOUSE IS

In the banking world, the race is to the interface. A bank that builds a user-friendly, graphical user interface on the Web can invite millions of consumers and business clients to help themselves to a wide array of financial services. A bank that fails to design such an interface won't be in business for very long. Welcome to the age of the virtual bank. Like the Web itself, the bank of the future will know no borders in the global marketspace. Yet such an entity can forge intimate relationships with individuals, reaching into your home and taking your money with the nicest smile that software can simulate.

If you compare banking today with the way it used to be done, it's nothing short of a revolution. In the olden days, consumers chose their bank based on where it was. Location was the key criteria. People wanted to be able to deposit and withdraw money during "banker's hours," generally from 9:00 A.M. to 3:00 P.M. on weekdays, or before noon on Saturdays. This meant choosing a bank close to your office or home.

In the United States, strict interstate banking regulations assured that all banks remained local and catered to their local customers. As a result, banks generally had high fixed costs, often owning the most impressive piece of commercial real estate in town—and staffing these places with scores of well-trained employees who often knew their customers personally.

Behind the scenes, of course, there was always a different story going on. The real action has always been not with the tellers but among the bank's investment specialists. Banks have never made their profits providing services to consumers. To a bank, customer service is simply a cost. They have always made their money by seeking the highest rate of return on the consumer's deposits. For a kid visiting the bank on Saturday morning with his or her parent, finding out that banks don't really "keep" your money in the building is akin to being told that there is no Santa Claus. But just like Santa, banks have always existed on faith.

Automated teller machines got the public in the habit of servicing themselves. Not only did these cash-dispensing devices keep many of those pesky consumers from coming in the building, but they made banking more convenient, as consumers got more control over their money. Suddenly, in the 1980s, people started choosing their bank not based on where its branch offices were but by the positioning of its ATM machines around town.

For the banks themselves, ATMs seemed like a blessing. They could reduce the staff and resources it took to serve customers in person. And at the same time that banks were reducing their service costs, the government bestowed another blessing: a phasing out of the prohibition on interstate banking. Suddenly, local banks saw a whole new world of opportunities—and lots of new competitors.

The sheer logic behind the ensuing merger frenzy was straightforward and compelling. Starting around 1991, the banking industry came to resemble a food chain. Small banks were gobbled up by bigger and bigger and bigger ones. Hundreds of billions of dollars in assets changed hands, and the industry was left with an armful of regional powerhouses staring one another down. Driven by the rush to cut fixed costs even further, merged banks closed branches and laid off tens of thousands of redundant employees. Meanwhile, they expanded their investment portfolios, seeking a wider range of deals in the global economy.

For consumers, mergers and deregulation weren't necessarily all that good. A Gallup Poll found that 71 percent of customers of banks involved in a merger reported that their bank did nothing extra to try and retain them. A smaller number, 15 percent of customers, actually went through the hassle of closing their accounts and taking their business elsewhere after a merger deal was announced. With new competition and eroding customer loyalty, most banks now have no choice but to go far beyond ATMs, using technology to expand their franchise and win back the allegiance of consumers.

The first bank to wholeheartedly embrace banking on the Web was Wells Fargo. The San Francisco-based bank actually jumped into the online waters back in 1990, with an online banking service on Prodigy. Customers could check balances on their PC screens and transfer funds between accounts. In 1994, it introduced a software package that enabled PC users to dial in to the bank directly to perform such tasks. But by the beginning of 1995, only 20,000 customers were using those online products, and that number hadn't been growing much at all. "It was flat," says Gailyn Johnson, a senior vice president responsible for Wells Fargo's online banking efforts.

The company had launched a Web site at the end of 1994, but only for promotional purposes. "We didn't think the Internet was ready to do banking," says Johnson, citing security concerns at the time as the main roadblock. But an online customer survey turned up the fact that a large percentage of customers wanted to be able to check their balances on the Web. The bank figured that it was taking 60 million phone calls per year, and 80 percent of those were balance inquiries. If they could find a way to minimize the risks, there was an opportunity to dramatically reduce telephone servicing costs and increase customer satisfaction at the same time.

Wells Fargo claims it was the first to offer banking on the Web when, in May 1995, it offered the ability to view balances and the past forty-five days of transactions. The bank addresses security concerns by requiring a unique password, only transmitting partial account numbers during transactions and never displaying a customer name on a Web page. Johnson says that there were attempts at break-ins to online accounts, but that none were successful and that some perpetrators were traced back through the Internet and punished.

As the growth of the Web exploded, the bank suddenly became

keenly aware of the demand for such online services. Based in the most techno-saturated region in the world, with more than 50 percent of households owning PCs, bank officers became determined to stay out in front of the technology curve. In May 1996, it offered Web surfers the ability to transfer funds between accounts and open mutual funds. A month later, it started an electronic bill paying service to replace written checks. By the summer of 1996, the number of Wells Fargo customers doing banking online shot up tenfold, to 200,000.

In the meantime, Wells Fargo had completed its merger with First Interstate, a deal that propelled it into the ranks of the top ten biggest banks in the United States, with assets of $116 billion and more than 38,000 employees. By obtaining branches in thirteen Western states, the deal in a sense sent Wells Fargo back to the future. Founded in the wake of the San Francisco gold rush, the company started by Henry Wells and William Fargo was as much an express service as a bank. In those days, securely transporting gold, silver, and U.S. mail via horse-drawn stagecoaches was the mainstay of its business. It established offices in a dozen Western states, only to be forced to exit all of them and retreat to San Francisco in 1918, when the federal government took over the express business as a wartime measure.

Now that Wells Fargo has once again reentered those twelve states *physically*, it is also racing to enter the other thirty-eight *virtually*. And online technology is the only way it can serve customers all over the world without a huge jump in fixed costs. "Serve," of course, is not really even the right word. The Web is for people to serve themselves and only turn to bank personnel for help in rare situations. Banks are thus reaching out from their local roots and struggling to become global brand names. The game is now to use their new technology-driven economies of scale to offer higher rates and new services.

And that game will be won or lost at the user interface. Wells Fargo, for instance, believes that the winners will be the banks that can pull off "integration," says Johnson. She says that the bank may actually lose money on specific services. For instance, the $5 per month that customers pay for the bill payment plan may not cover the cost of delivering the service.

For proof of how difficult it is to make a profit paying people's bills, one only has to turn to CheckFree Corp., the Columbus, Ohio, company that has been offering an electronic bill-paying service to consumers since 1981. Consumers fill out the payee and amount fields in on-screen checks, then transmit the information via modem to Check-Free. Payment is usually made directly through the Federal Reserve's Automated Clearinghouse. If the merchant or person is not hooked up to accept electronic payments, CheckFree simply cuts a paper check and mails it the old-fashioned way.

Not long ago, CheckFree was charging $9.95 per month for twenty electronic payments. That was in the early 1990s, when stamps cost 29¢ each. If a consumer took full advantage of the service, and paid twenty bills online, she would be saving $5.80 off the cost of stamps. However, using the service would actually cost extra—$4.15 extra, to be precise. The entire value proposition was counterintuitive. Which is a big reason why the service was fairly slow to catch on. By 1992, after more than ten years in business, only 100,000 households were subscribing to the service.

But in 1996, CheckFree suddenly lowered the price. Faced with new competition from dozens of banks offering electronic bill-paying, CheckFree lowered the monthly charge to $5.95. With stamps now costing 32¢, consumers were now able to *save* 45¢ on their first twenty transactions. Finally, with savings now exceeding the cost of the service, electronic bill payment made sense for consumers. Not only did it save time, but it was cheaper—as it should be. CheckFree's membership jumped rather dramatically, to more than 500,000 households. But the company was now struggling to turn a profit. After going public in 1995, the company reported a long string of steep quarterly losses.

Banks, however, do not have to make a profit on electronic bill payment. The goal is to "manage the entire relationship with the customer," says Johnson. As long as the overall relationship is profitable, the bank will be, too. To this end, leading-edge banks such as Wells Fargo are bundling as many services as possible at the point of contact with the customer—be it on the Web, over the telephone, or at ATMs. "It's a convenience thing," she says. "People want all their accounts integrated and consolidated in one place."

This integration strategy is perhaps the best way for banks to stave off competition not only from other banks getting into their territories but also from nonbanks. Mutual fund companies and investment houses that offer their customers no-fee checking accounts have already captured billions of dollars of assets from banks. And technology companies such as Intuit and Microsoft are developing software and services that consolidate a wide range of financial services in one user interface.

But banks, even though they are traditionally thought of as slow-moving, low-tech, and regional, have a small window of opportunity. And that opportunity stems from the one advantage that banks still largely retain. It all goes back to the old joke: When Willie Sutton was asked why he robs banks, he gave the reply, "That's where the money is." But if banks fail to take advantage of Webonomics, the cash won't be there for very much longer.

WILL PEOPLE BE REPLACED BY SOFTWARE?

Jobs that can be automated will continue to disappear. But at the same time, people who can perform a valuable skill that cannot be automated will be in higher demand than ever.

Consider the fate of telephone support personnel. At banks and mutual fund companies, for instance, consumers used to obtain account balances and portfolio values and execute transactions by calling the customer service line and talking to a person. The phone clerk would punch the customer's account number into a computer and read numbers out of a database. Now, huge numbers of bank and mutual fund customers are performing these tasks themselves—using touch-tone keypad services or by logging onto a Web site.

Meanwhile, the people who man the phone lines are freed up to focus on higher-level tasks. They are performing the jobs that machines can't do, such as answering complicated questions that require advanced levels of training. Right now, you can call up any major mutual fund company's 800 number and ask the person who answers the phone to explain the bond market to you. Just try it. Ask that person the perplexing question: Why does an increase in the yield of a bond lower the value of the bond? Then try putting that question to someone working the register at The Gap. This is not something an ordinary human would know.

Likewise, look what is happening to 411 operators. Telephone companies have been laying them off by the tens of thousands and replacing them with voice-recognition software that does this low-level job automatically. "What city, please?" is now a refrain uttered by a computer in many parts of the country.

In fact, with national telephone directories coming online, this annoying question itself is becoming obsolete. On the Web, national directory sites such as Switchboard.com and Four11.com have become huge hits.

The Switchboard site is a giant national database that contains the names, telephone numbers, and addresses of more than 100 million households, plus millions of businesses. Visitors simply type in a name to get a White Pages listing of all people by that name in the country. Use of this site has grown beyond just being a self-service replacement for dialing 411 or 555–1212. Switchboard.com has also become a way of helping people get back in touch with long-lost friends. Because of its national reach, people use it to look up former boyfriends, girlfriends, college buddies, high school pals, long-lost relatives, and former coworkers.

PC Meter, the ratings service that tracks consumer usage of Web sites, has reported a surprising fact about the Switchboard site: People dawdle there longer than at any other site on the Web. Steve Coffey, chief technology officer at PC Meter, says that consumers view an average of two to three pages at the typical Web site. As a reference point, the Disney site is far above average, with an average of eight page views per visit. But at Switchboard, the average is *eighteen page views per visit,* by far the highest of all Web sites in a recent PC Meter survey.

Ironically, the Switchboard site was not developed by a telephone company, but rather by Banyan Systems, a computer networking company based in Marlboro, Massachusetts. The company invites consumers to update their own listing, if out of date, plus add their E-mail address. By enlisting consumers in its effort to keep its data up to date, the Switchboard database becomes even more valuable. The site has been so popular that Banyan has been able to sell advertising, thus putting it in the role of a telephone directory publisher. Caught flat-footed, telephone companies have been racing to develop something similar.

Other services provided by phone companies can also be moved to the Web. Imagine a phone company that lets users tap into its customer service database and access their own account. Customers could not only maintain an updated list of their most frequently called numbers but also tell the system what time of day and week they usually do most of their calling. They could order premium features such as call-waiting and call-forwarding. Such a Web site could make it easier and more convenient for customers to create their own customized calling plan—at a favorable price. "To present your needs and have AT&T come back with a plan for you—it doesn't get any more perfect than that," says Mary Lou Floyd, business manager of AT&T's promotional Web site.

Of course, this kind of service-based marketing is easier said than done. Not only does it involve a new mind-set, but it involves implementing new technology. The trickiest part of the procedure is often the linking of your new Web site with your customer account database, which might date back ten or twenty or more years. The marketing department can put in the request. But around corporate computing departments such requests are facetiously known as SMOPs, for a "simple matter of programming." Most corporate information systems departments are saddled with software backlogs that range anywhere from three months to three years. And software always takes longer than expected to develop, especially when it comes down to the final debugging and testing of the program. The old joke is that when 90 percent of the development is finished, it's then time to finish the next 90 percent.

But that kind of work must be done—and quickly—if traditional telephone networks are going to remain competitive with the Internet, which is handling more and more communications tasks (including voice and video conferencing). The Web itself has been built on a self-service model from the beginning. For instance, those wishing to register a new "domain name"—the Web site address that ends in .com, .org, .net, .edu, or .gov—must visit the Web site run by the Internet Network Information Center, also known as the InterNIC. Once there, visitors fill out a simple electronic form stating who they are, how they can be contacted, what domain name they'd like, and for what purpose they would operate their Web site.

Based in Herndon, Virginia, the InterNIC automatically searches its database to determine that every tom.com, dick.org, and harry.edu is indeed an original name. The software evaluates all of these applications, registers them, and bills the applicants. Developers of Web sites must pay a $50 annual maintenance fee for exclusive use of a new domain name.

The miracle of the InterNIC is that it is managed by only a handful of people. This self-service system is run by a small government contractor called SAIC Network Solutions, which in 1993 was awarded a five-year contract by the National Science Foundation. Yet this small company managed to register, bill, and maintain records on more than a half-million Web sites in its first three years. In the first quarter of 1996 alone, the InterNIC approved new domain names at the rate of one for every minute during business hours.

This is the kind of business model that, if applied elsewhere, could transform the economics of what could be called "the lagging industries." Lagging industries are ones that are underinvested in information technology. As a result, productivity tends to be low. Traditionally, industries such as government services, highly regulated utilities, and bureaucratic health-care organizations have fallen into this camp.

Some government agencies are already taking advantage of Webonomics. In 1995, the Internal Revenue Service, for instance, created one of the most popular government Web sites. With all tax forms and filing instructions in one easy-to-access place, calls to the IRS information line have been reduced, enabling the agency to cut its overhead dramatically. In 1996, the IRS said it would lay off 4,800 customer service workers, representing about 15 percent of its overall staff. This plan, which includes reducing its regional service centers from seventy to twenty-three, is expected to save $500 to $750 million over five years. Under pressure to slash costs even further, the IRS will continue to provide more and more self-service applications on the Web.

The U.S. Patent & Trademark Office is also moving in this direction, providing the forms and information to businesses and individual inventors on its Web site. Although this is a step in the right direction, it still can take about a year for the government to evaluate a new trademark application, as opposed to just a few days for the InterNIC to approve a new domain name. Ultimately, the massive, across-the-board budget cuts in government will force a choice: Use self-service technology to deliver the same range of government services more efficiently, or deliver fewer services in the same old way.

For example, in the state of Massachusetts, employees at the famously grumpy Registry of Motor Vehicles have created what they believe is the first online motor vehicles department. Consumers can now log on to the registry's Web site to renew their vehicle registration, order vanity plates, and pay their speeding tickets with a credit card. "We believe the public would rather be online than in line," a registry spokesman told the *Boston Globe*. Another registry spokesman put it more bluntly: "Our goal," he said, "is never to have to see a customer again."

Speaking of people you don't want to see ever again, consider the fabled insurance salesman. Since its launch in April 1996, a site called LifeQuote has been providing consumers with free price quotes on life insurance policies. Visitors to the site choose the benefit level and other terms of their own policy, in a sense selling themselves on the product. As soon as a visitor submits his or her request, they can see their annual premium figure instantaneously.

Ross Burger, the Webmaster at Miami-based LifeQuote of America Inc., says that the company invested less than $50,000 to develop the site. Yet it quickly started bringing in 60 percent of the eleven-year-old company's overall business. Out of the 200 people per month who use the site to request quotes, 17 percent get converted into paying customers, he says. That compares to a 1 to 2 percent conversion ratio for direct mail, and a 5 percent ratio for cold calling. LifeQuote acts as the insurance agent, representing more than 250 insurance companies. It makes its money from fees paid by those companies, collecting 50 percent of the first year's premium for each policy it sells.

Burger says that there is incredible pent-up demand for these kinds of self-service applications, built up over decades of bad experiences with overzealous salespeople. "We handle people who don't want to see a salesman in a bad suit sitting across from them, pointing a pen in their face."

<Chapter Summary>
• Self-service is becoming mandatory in many industries—as consumers demand increased comfort, control, and convenience.
• Open twenty-four-hours per day, seven days per week, the Web is well suited to be the point of customer contact for a wide range of self-service applications, from overnight shipping to technical support to travel reservations to at-home banking.
• Industries such as the airline business are aggressively promoting direct customer booking as a way to reduce costs, increase efficiency, and boost customer loyalty.
• Banks and other financial services companies are rushing to integrate as many services as possible within one, easy-to-use user interface—thus becoming one-stop financial shops.
• Human service personnel won't be obsolete, but rather freed up to focus on higher-level tasks. They are performing the jobs that computers can't, such as answering complicated questions that require advanced levels of training.

<CHAPTER SIX>

"Value-Based Currencies" Enable You to Create Your Own Monetary System

WHAT ARE VALUE-BASED CURRENCIES?

One of the biggest questions concerning electronic commerce has to do with how people will pay for whatever they purchase online. Several different electronic currency systems, known as digital cash, are being marketed as answers to this question. Most of those payment systems are doomed to failure. Meanwhile, a form of online money that people *are* accepting happens to be right under our noses.

Consumers are already amassing fortunes in new forms of "value-based currencies" that aren't directly tied to dollars, yen, pounds, deutsche marks, or any other national currency. These new forms of currency are not backed by the U.S. Treasury, or any other country's treasury department for that matter. These currencies are not legal tender for all debts public and private. Unlike credit card transactions, these currencies are not even backed by banks.

Instead of asking you to put your faith in the government, which in turn asks you to put your trust in God, these new forms of digital currency ask you for something more modest: to put your faith in a company that you do business with regularly. We're talking about airlines, hotels, car rental companies, Internet and online service providers, software companies, computer makers, auto manufacturers, retail chains, entertainment conglomerates, and telecommunications giants.

Using the Web, such companies have new opportunities to issue and control currencies that are backed by and redeemable for valuable goods and services. Then, they can use these entirely new monetary systems to engender loyalty among their customers. Ultimately, such currencies enable companies to preside over a new type of monetary system that can be used for strengthening their relationship with consumers and broadening the appeal of their products.

The implications are enormous. The online money of the future won't "consist of interchangeable, uniform markers that provide a universal standard of value," says David Reed, a former senior scientist at Interval Research Corp., a technology lab in Palo Alto, California. "Instead, it will become like frequent flier miles, or the national currencies of small countries. It can expire, get revalued at will, and it will be designed to manage the microeconomies of corporations, industries, and institutions."

The perfect example of this, of course, comes from the airline industry. In 1981, American Airlines revolutionized its industry when it invented its Advantage program. The idea was to issue points to frequent flyers based on the number of miles flown. Those points could later be redeemed for free trips. The program became wildly successful, forcing every other airline to follow suit. Consumers began choosing their carrier based on which airline offered the best route to a future free ticket.

As frequent flier miles took off, these incentive systems began to take on a life of their own. Airlines signed up dozens of partners, such as hotels and car rental companies, that also offered ways of earning mileage points. Credit card companies issued mileage points based on the number of dollars you charged. Soon, families were amassing these points in the same way that they fed their traditional savings accounts. Consumers began coveting frequent flier points precisely because they have real value.

Another breakthrough came in 1994. American began selling miles—at 2¢ apiece—to any company that wanted to offer them as a sales incentive. Everyone from restaurants to furniture stores to charities began offering miles to consumers as an added bonus for doing business with that organization. Eat an expensive meal, earn 100 points. Within two years, more than 1,000 companies began offering incentive miles. American was now issuing hundreds of millions of dollars' worth of mileage points to other companies. Consequently, industry analysts estimate that nearly half of frequent flier miles are now earned on the ground.

Suddenly, the airlines are finding themselves doing much of the same thing that the Federal Reserve does, namely tightening and loosening the supply of currency in the marketplace. With consumers holding literally trillions of mileage points, frequent flier miles have indeed become "a second national currency," declared the *Wall Street Journal.*

This phenomenon all happened without much help from the Web, of course. But airlines now need the information-management functions of the Web to help people keep track of this new money supply. As people pay more and more attention to the value of their frequent flier accounts and as the options for earning and spending these points widen, the Web becomes the natural way for people to control their accounts. Consumers want to know how many points they have. They are no longer satisfied to receive quarterly updates in the mail. They want to be able to check their balance and view a list of all recent earnings twenty-four hours a day.

To satisfy these needs, nearly every airline has built a Web site that enables consumers to access their frequent flier account information. Not only do the self-service applications at these sites enhance customer satisfaction, but they also reduce costs compared to providing this information in other ways, such as telephone 800 numbers. Most important, once these points go online, they take the final step in becoming a totally informationalized form of currency—true digital money.

NOT FOR AIRLINES ONLY

Companies of all kinds would do well to create their own monetary systems, offering loyal customers points that can later be redeemed for goods and services. The Web will be the place where such points can be earned, bought, sold, traded, and redeemed.

Online surfing time is a perfect example of a new form of digital cash in the Web economy. America Online, for instance, offers a no-annual-fee Visa card to its members. For every dollar you spend on anything using the card, you earn one "reward point." This is a form of currency that America Online just invented out of thin air. But the Vienna, Virginia company has something of value to back it up. It even invented its own valuation system: Every 200 reward points that a consumer earns is redeemable for one free hour online.

But here's the clever part. For the money you spend specifically on America Online services, you earn *two* reward points. In this monetary system that AOL created, not all spending is created equal. If you have the option of shopping online, as opposed to a brick-and-mortar store, AOL provides an incentive to go online. This is a positive cause-and-effect loop that has the potential to greatly increase the loyalty of AOL members. The more money you spend in AOL's digital economy, the more free time you earn. The more time you earn, the more incentive you have to spend *even more time and money* online. This loyalty effect is no small matter. Lack of loyalty has been AOL's biggest problem, with its "churn rate," or the number of customers who quit the service every year, estimated at around 50 percent.

Telephone companies have also jumped into this game. AT&T, with its True Rewards program, offers one point for every dollar spent on calls. Customers can already use the points to buy stuff ranging from CDs to magazines to baseball cards to U.S. Savings Bonds. Such offers usually come in the mail every so often. But AT&T could turn its Web site into a nonstop electronic bazaar where TrueValue points could be used to fund a digital shopping spree.

The possibilities for entirely new monetary systems are fascinating. The Walt Disney Company, for instance, has been reportedly studying ways of offering frequent flier miles to people who watch the Disney Channel on cable. But why play the airline industry's game when the company can create its own form of digital cash? Consumers who order Disney videos from its Web site could get 100 Magic Kingdom points credited to their online account. Purchases of Disney's endless array of branded products could also come with point incentives.

The points could be redeemable for free admission tickets to Disney's theme parks. The company could even make the award level for Disneyland Paris a lot lower to finally get people interested in going there. People would constantly return to Disney's Web site again and again to check on their Magic Kingdom accounts and find out about new ways to earn and spend these points.

There are even ways to integrate activity at a Web site with purchasing that must be done in person. Imagine, for instance, if the Starbucks coffee chain issued smart cards instead of those "buy ten cups, get one free" stamp cards that are offered at so many coffee shops these days. Here's how it could work: Every time you bought a cup of coffee at Starbucks you would hand the clerk your card. She would swipe it through a special card reader that would be programmed to add ten points to your account. The information would be instantly uploaded from each store location to the company's central computers in Seattle.

These points could even be called Star-bucks. As usual, the card would tell the counter people in the store when a customer was entitled to a free cup. Further benefits would await consumers in cyberspace. You could visit the Starbucks Web site whenever you wanted to check your account balance. At the site, you could learn about new ways of redeeming your points while learning more about new types of coffees. An accumulation of 500 Star-bucks could buy you a groovy T-shirt or a pound of Kona delivered to your house. Maybe you could compete in a coffee trivia contest to win yet more Star-bucks. Instead

of being addicted to just caffeine, you could also be addicted to amassing more and more coffee points and redeeming them for real beans.

Even sellers of information-poor products could mint their own digital money. Oil companies such as Exxon, Mobil, Shell, Texaco, and
Gulf have for years been trying to differentiate their products by tout-
ing "high-octane" or "clean-system" gasoline in their TV commercials. To consumers, however, gas is gas is gas. They don't really want
to know much about it. So they certainly aren't going to visit the newest
Exxon Web site to find out about the latest Ultra Ultra formula.

Oil companies engender customer loyalty not by coming up with
better names for their gasoline formulas but by coming up with better
payment systems. A holder of a Mobil credit card is very likely to seek
out Mobil stations only. The convenience and control of consolidating
your gasoline purchases in one monthly payment is often incentive
enough. But gasoline companies could go further. Imagine trading in
your gas card for a smart card that could keep track of special incentives. Imagine earning 1,000 "shells" for buying $1,000 in Shell gaso-
line. Consumers could visit their gasoline brand's Web site to access
their account information, check their award status, and use their
shells to buy various products and services—including a certificate for
a free fill-up.

In nearly every industry, value-based currency systems will determine customer fidelity. The incentive to keep earning valuable points
will keep people coming back for more. The loyalty effect will not only
manifest itself at airports, theme parks, coffee shops, and service stations all over the world; it will also show up in cyberspace. People will
return again and again to the sites where their digital cash is kept—to
check on their personal accounts and find out what they can buy with
their points.

Marketers can spend millions creating the world's greatest interactive commercials for the Web. But ultimately, people don't want to
know more about products; they want to know about themselves.
Value-based currencies exploit this natural inclination.

WHY "DIGITAL CASH" WILL FAIL

The question of how people will pay for items they purchase on the Web has led to an impressive array of purely information-based currencies. While credit cards have become the dominant way to buy products from mail-order catalogs, the argument goes, many people are nervous about entering their card numbers into a computer network. They fear their transactions will be tracked, that their data will be traded among intrusive marketers, that their privacy will be obliterated, and that having their card numbers (and expiration dates) floating around in cyberspace leaves their credit card open to fraud and abuse at the hands of hackers.

"Digital cash" is the proposed solution to this. Such payment systems work like this: First, you visit the Web site of the company or bank issuing digital cash. You register at the site, providing your name, address, and password, then download the necessary software to your hard drive. The software usually contains special security codes and other encrypted identifiers so that hackers can't intercept your account information as it travels over the Internet.

This so called "digital wallet" software can work one of two ways: When you register for your new digital cash account, you must provide either your existing credit card number or your existing checking account information. If you choose to operate your digital cash account on a *credit* basis, your software will transfer electronically a specified lump sum from your credit card to your hard drive. (Usually, you won't get charged the usual cash-advance fee.) Then, when you purchase something from an online merchant, you will send a payment from your hard drive to that merchant by filling in the amount in an online form. As long as the balance on your hard drive can cover your purchases, you can keep on buying.

If you choose to operate your digital cash account on a *debit* basis, you will shop and pay the merchant the same way, except that your software will retrieve electronically the funds from your checking account every time you buy something. Your bank account will get charged as if you were simply writing out a check.

When you want to shop online, you can enter your password to activate the software on your hard drive. This software can actually store value, credited from your regular bank account, enabling you to exchange digital currency with any merchant—or a friend—who conducts commerce this way. Supposedly, the advantage here is having the convenience and anonymity of real cash. When you buy something, the merchant doesn't have to know who you are.

These electronic greenbacks and cybercoins are issued by companies with names such as First Virtual, Mondex, NetCheque, NetBill, DigiCash, and CyberCash. Since these currencies are indigenous to the Web economy, such cash can be spent only at Web sites that have agreed in advance to honor a specific brand of digital cash; they can't be spent elsewhere. Think of them as a bit-based version of the beads you buy at a Club Med—to exchange for fruity beverages.

"Ecash is a software-only form of electronic money that provides all advantages of cash and then some. It is *the* money for the Internet . . . and cannot be exchanged for real money," announces the Web site from DigiCash, an Amsterdam company founded by data encryption expert David Chaum. It all sounds so seductive and alluring—as if these companies were inviting you to be part of a secret club where members wear digital decoder rings.

The problem with these new forms of payment is that they are not needed. Several of these digital cash start-ups will likely go out of business in the next few years due to lack of consumer acceptance. People don't want to be confused by what are essentially new forms of credit or debit cards. For buying products on the Web, the current choices are just fine. Credit card companies and banks have woken up to the fact that consumers worried about online security are a huge market opportunity. Thus, they are already deploying advanced solutions to the security problem on the Internet. And consumers in turn are growing more comfortable using their card numbers online.

At bottom, these new digital cash start-ups on the Web aren't actually offering a new form of money, just new payment systems that add another layer of costs to the way we pay for things now. Many of these companies are likely to get acquired or go by the wayside as soon as the traditional credit card companies perfect new security technologies and consumers become more comfortable with them.

SECURITY MATTERS

Whatever form payment on the Net takes, security is an overriding issue. It's a tricky one at that, mainly because it is governed more by perception than by reality. Many of us misperceive security threats in everyday life. For instance, people fearful of flying typically hop in their cars without a care, even though the chance of getting killed in a car accident is about 100 times greater than perishing in a plane. Similarly, many of those who say they'll never pass their credit card number over the Internet will gladly order merchandise from a cable TV shopping network—in the process giving out their card number over the phone to some twenty-two-year-old stranger in Phoenix.

When it comes to credit cards, most of the hundreds of millions of dollars' worth of fraud that happens every year is the result of terribly low-tech scams. Security is most often breached at the point of sale. Thieves will pick up carelessly discarded receipts. They'll stand by and listen to you read out your card number over a public phone. They'll buy numbers from unscrupulous employees who wait tables or work in a store.

The Internet, of course, has higher-tech security dangers. But the danger is also focused at the point of sale. Although it's rare, wily programmers have ways of intercepting messages—including credit card numbers—that travel over the wide-open Internet. The security features built into the Netscape Navigator, Microsoft Explorer, and other Web browser programs go a long way to thwart this possibility. Included in these programs is a so-called Secure Sockets Layer that encrypts credit card numbers and other data deemed sensitive by online merchants. When such data is being transmitted via Netscape's browser, users can see that the SSL has been activated because a key at the bottom of the screen lights up.

By virtue of this feature, purchasing things over the Web is probably at least as secure as doing it over the phone or in person. Still, credit card companies have gone even further. The secure electronic transaction (SET) standard backed by MasterCard, Visa, IBM, Netscape, and Microsoft allows purchases to occur while hiding the consumer's full credit card number from the merchant, thus protecting consumers from the sleazy ones.

This is how SET works: The consumer clicks a button that transmits a message containing the type of goods being purchased and the price. The message also includes a "digital certificate"—supplied by the consumer's credit card company—that specifies the consumer's name, a few digits of the card number, and the name of the bank that issued the card. The merchant uses a special key to unscramble the message and verify the consumer's identity. That information is used to check the buyer's credit with the bank. Only the bank has the full credit card data. The entire transaction happens without the merchant seeing the whole number.

Even if all these precautions somehow failed, many consumers know that federal law caps an individual's liability in credit card fraud at $50. It's the card companies that have to pick up the rest of the tab, which is why they are working so hard to minimize the dangers.

After years of media reports that have focused on security flaws on the Internet, the public has indeed been cautious. But the message that the Internet is actually less risky than using your credit card in a restaurant is finally getting through. Merchants on the Web are reporting that between 75 and 95 percent of their customers are comfortable using their credit cards online, with most of the remainder calling in their order over the phone. Digital cash from companies such as CyberCash, DigiCash, and First Virtual also offers top-flight security. But only a tiny fraction—less than 1 percent—of Web transactions are done with such payment schemes.

Some online merchants, such as JCPenney, offer credit card payments as the *only* way to buy things. And customers are by and large comfortable doing so. Out of the more than 1,000 E-mail messages that JCPenney gets from customers every month, the vast majority are typical customer service questions as well as queries about when they can use their credit cards to buy new types of merchandise online, says Marisha Konkowski, the chain's electronic retailing manager. Virtually no one has written to express security fears or concerns about shopping online via credit card, she says.

WHO HERE WANTS ANONYMITY?

Besides security, some of the new Web payment systems also offer the added benefit of anonymity. When you use paper dollars or coins to buy, say, a magazine off a real newsstand, the seller can see you, but he has no idea who you are. On the Web, when a consumer uses electronic money from DigiCash and other providers, the merchant can neither see nor identify that consumer. No name or user-ID number or even an E-mail address is passed along. Such transactions cannot be tracked and filed in a database for future reference. The money is simply debited from the consumer's account and credited to the seller's account—anonymously.

This benefit, however, is not winning acceptance, despite the layer of privacy that it promises. The reason that anonymous cash won't fly on the Web is because it's not in the best interest of the merchant—or, ultimately, the consumer. Merchants want to maintain *relationships* with consumers. If they don't know who you are, they can't work to get your repeat business and engender loyalty. They can't offer you membership in a buyer's club—or in a community of people with common interests. They can't offer you volume discounts. They can't tailor products and services to your specific needs. They can't contact you with special offers.

Anonymity breaks down some of the primary driving forces that make doing business in the Web economy so compelling in the first place. This is one of the main reasons that value-based currencies are catching on as a form of online money, while digital cash schemes are not.

For the very same reasons, anonymous transactions aren't in the best interests of the consumer, either. Consumers prove every day that they prefer doing business with companies they trust. As the third principle of Webonomics implies, consumers don't mind telling those companies who they are if they get some sort of reward, incentive, or discount in return.

There may be a few exceptions to this. If you are paying to peep at porno pictures, for example, anonymous cash may be the way to go (especially if you're a U.S. senator). But aside from potentially embarrassing transactions, anonymous E-cash will be used only in limited circumstances by a limited number of people. (As an aside, DigiCash takes great pains to point out that while consumers remain anonymous under its system, the merchants do not. To receive real money in return for the Ecash they have collected from consumers, merchants must reveal their identities to a bank affiliated with the Ecash system. This is designed to eliminate the type of illegal money laundering and tax evasion that currently happens in many "cash-only" businesses.)

If merchants decide to stick with familiar credit and debit instruments, anonymous Ecash will have a tough time reaching a critical mass—something that charge cards have already achieved. More than 12 million merchants all over the world accept Visa and MasterCard, and millions of others accept American Express. Visa alone has more than 400 million active credit card holders, issued through more than 20,000 banks that pay to be associated with this powerful and trusted brand. This is a level of acceptance that would be almost impossible for any new digital cash scheme to match.

MICROPAYMENTS

The third and final reason that these new digital payment schemes give for being is a concept known as micropayments. Unlike security (which is increasingly available via traditional payment methods) and anonymity (which is something that the market is rejecting), the prospect of using new forms of digital cash to buy lots of little cheap things online may sound compelling at first. If you've ever tried to use your American Express card to buy a pack of Chicklets, you know firsthand that credit card companies discourage small transactions. Because of the significant fees they must pay to the card companies, stores generally do not accept credit cards for purchases under $5.

On the Web, however, one can envision lots of things costing less than $5, even things costing less than $1. Possibilities include online newspapers, research reports, pay-per-play video games, even Japanese phone directory listings. There are even entrepreneurs planning businesses that sell tidbits of information—cookie recipes, for example—for a fraction of a penny. These so-called nanobucks take the concept of micropayments to the extreme. But for all of these pocket-change transactions, there exists a central hurdle: The cost of the item sold has to be greater than the cost it takes to process the transaction.

Based in San Diego, digital cash start-up First Virtual Holdings believes that micropayments on the Web can enable a new multihundred-million-dollar business opportunity. The company's Web site hosts the InfoHaus, a place where people can come to buy everything from batches of inspirational quotes to horoscopes for pets to a list of pres-elected personal ads—all for as little as 50¢ a pop.

Here's how First Virtual's system works: Consumers register their name and credit card information at First Virtual's Web site. (The company says it stores the information off-line, to increase security.) In return, consumers receive special ID numbers, which could be compared to the serial numbers on dollar bills. When the consumer wants to buy something, he sends one of his serial numbers to the merchant via E-mail or by typing it into a form at that merchant's Web site. The accumulated transactions are charged to the consumer's credit card.

One boutique business, called the Mind's Eye, uses the First Virtual system to sell stories and poems written mainly by unknown writers. Readers choose from stories by reading short synopses and reviews. Each story is priced between 50¢ and $1. To buy one, readers simply enter a First Virtual serial number into one of Mind's Eye's purchase forms. The transaction is confirmed via E-mail.

These tiny transactions are not without overhead, of course. First Virtual takes 29¢ per transaction, plus 2 percent of the price of the goods sold. That works out to 30¢ out of every 50¢ transaction, and 31¢ from each $1 transaction. By the time the fees from First Virtual, plus the fee from Mind's Eye, plus the normal government taxes are taken out, an author would net 12¢ for a 50¢ transaction and 46¢ for a $1 transaction.

That could earn a writer a fine living, if there are at least tens of thousands of people buying his stories this way. But that, as they say, is a big "if." When it comes down to adding up the dollars and cents, it's hard to come up with the numbers to make micropayments a viable way of doing business.

Brock Meeks, a contributor to *Wired* magazine, claims that 800,000 people read his Cyberwire Dispatch column, which gets sent out for free on many different Internet mailing lists. Meeks says he'd like to harness a micropayment system in which people who want to read each dispatch would just hit their F1 key to debit 3¢ from their digital cash account. He believes that there would be no resistance to that price, as many people don't even bother to pick up three pennies when they drop them in the street. If just his current readership agreed to the payments, he would make $24,000 per article. "When that happens," he says, "I'll be a millionaire."

But Meeks is unlikely to inherit the earth anytime soon. Here is why his scheme probably won't work. First, Meeks wouldn't be the only person who would like to write a column every week or so and make

$24,000 each time. Wouldn't you? If it were so easy to collect so many micropayments, it would be likely that lots of writers even more well-known than Meeks would be syndicated this way. Let's say Steven King, Michael Crichton, David Broder, Ann Landers, Maureen Dowd, David Barry, and hundreds of others all decided to have regular columns or features or book excerpts distributed directly to readers for a few pence. Let's say you as an Internet user started getting fifty or so solicitations per day to buy articles for 3¢. Wouldn't it quickly become a chore to sift through all of that to decide which two or three you should buy in a given day?

With so much competition for people's time, attention, and pennies, it would be highly unlikely that all 800,000 readers on Meeks's Internet lists would buy each column. Let's be optimistic and say 1 percent of them, or 8,000 people, actually accepted Meeks's offer each week. At 3¢ apiece, that's only $240 per article. Instead of becoming a millionaire, he'd have trouble paying his health insurance.

Such bleak predictions have not deterred start-ups that see megabucks in micropayments. For instance, Clickshare Corp. of Williamstown, Massachusetts, has developed a transaction system that keeps track of the whereabouts of Web surfers and settles charges for digital information. Under Clickshare's model, users would jump from page to page across many different Web sites that license the company's technology. Consumers would pay as little as a few cents for each page they view. Presumably, these micropayments would take the place of and possibly exceed the much higher monthly subscription fees that some content sites have been trying to charge.

But the reason micropayments is an idea that will meet only with limited success has less to do with price resistance than it does with the limited supply of attention. Asking consumers to pay 3¢ or 5¢ or 10¢ or 50¢ every time they want to do something on the Web means asking consumers to make too many decisions. The prospect of getting nickeled and dimed to death can't be very appealing to most people. In the end, micropayments will fail mainly because they are really, really annoying.

THE TRUST BUSINESS

 When all is said and done, consumers need to have the utmost confidence in any monetary system in which they participate. They aren't going to invest their time, money, and energy in a digital cash system that might be extinct in a few years.

"We're in the business of creating peace of mind and trust," says John Donegan, a vice president at First Virtual Holdings. CyberCash Inc. founder William Melton says that contrary to popular belief, banks and credit card companies are not in the business of money or credit. "A bank's primary function is credibility," he says.

Any online currency system must establish trust. Not only between banks and merchants, as today's credit card companies do, but also between individuals, just as today's coins and bills do. This fact means that anyone in the business of winning the trust of consumers could get into the digital cash business.

That actually puts companies such as CyberCash and First Virtual at a distinct disadvantage. Although they are by all accounts fine companies, why would anyone put their trust in a company with virtually no name recognition, no widespread brand identity, very little personal contact with consumers, and no long-standing reputation for living up to its promises. If consumers are given the choice of putting their trust in CyberCash or AT&T, whom do you think they'd choose? If it's between First Virtual or Disney, which one would inspire more confidence?

It's the companies with strong brand-name recognition and a long track record that have the best chance of creating successful new monetary systems. In the end, consumers will not need nor will they accept an entirely new payment system. Traditional credit cards will do just fine. The real opportunity in online money lies in issuing currency backed by valuable products and services. In every industry, the companies that want to keep their customers faithful will realize that value-based currencies are the money of the future.

<Chapter Summary>
• "Value-based currencies" are monetary systems in which corporations reward loyal customers with points that can be redeemed later for real goods and services.
• These new currency systems will reach way beyond airline frequent flier miles, spreading to nearly every industry.
• The Web is the ultimate tool for enabling consumers to manage their many different value-based currency accounts in new ways. As consumers go online to check balances and spend their points, marketers win over their attention and form closer relationships with them.
• The other form of online money, known as digital cash, promises security and flexibility when purchasing products in cyberspace. However, these payment systems are either failing to catch on or are being integrated into traditional credit card purchasing.
• Micropayments, too, are failing to catch on, mainly because consumers find that being asked to pay pocket change for digital information is both annoying and unnecessary when so much online information is free.
• Trust is the most valuable commodity in cyberspace. In the end, the companies that are most successful issuing and backing value-based currencies will be the ones that establish a strong sense of trust among consumers.

<CHAPTER SEVEN>

Trusted Brand Names Matter Even More on the Web

CUTTING THROUGH THE CLUTTER

Just try to avoid brand names. They're on the tube, in what we read, on the awnings of the stores as we walk by, with more brand names waiting inside for us. They're on our shirts, our pants, our shoes, on our cars, on our watches and clocks, on big signs at the side of the road, on our refrigerators and microwaves, and they're on the toys and all the things that kids want. If space on the moon, the sun, and the stars were for sale, eager marketers would rush their logos there. So, of course, these names are also on our computers and in our software, and they're everywhere in cyberspace. Of course.

But brand names aren't just here to bombard us. They have a benefit. When you as a consumer have many choices and limited time, it pays to be loyal to brands you trust. A brand can serve as a mark of quality, of something familiar. As such, they can actually save you time and aggravation. Reach for that comfortable brand name, and you don't have to bother sorting through all the other choices, all the noise and clutter in the marketplace. Here's the question, though: Do brand names cut through the clutter—or are they the clutter itself?

The basic process of building brand equity is the same everywhere. Not only do you have to get the word out that the brand exists and that the product has benefits, but the product must live up to these claims. Whenever a consumer drives a car, wears jeans, reads a name-brand newspaper, or embarks on a Web search using a branded search engine, the response to that experience increases or decreases brand equity. If the experience meets or beats expectations, brand equity is strengthened. If not, the brand equity is diluted.

For something that's so intangible, brand equity is surprisingly real. If you look at a company such as Coca-Cola and take away all its physical assets—including its real estate, offices, plants, equipment—you would be left with more than just a recipe for colored fizzy sugar water. Its brand equity is worth more than all of that stuff combined. The company's balance sheet, in fact, lists its brand name as an $86 billion asset. (A stock market valuation of $101 billion minus physical assets of $15 billion, as of year-end 1995.) This is the real "real thing," as valued by shareholders.

Before you can build brand equity, you have to start building brand awareness. Strong brand images are becoming more difficult and expensive to establish in the first place. TV audiences are fragmenting into smaller and smaller camps, with prices going through the roof for the rare mass audiences that do gather during the Super Bowl, the Olympics, or the very top rated TV shows. The Web takes the fragmentation of TV to the extreme. It's getting harder and harder to launch a new brand name product by marketing solely on the Web. The audience is simply too spread out, in too many places at once. There are too many sites to see, too many voices calling out to us.

"The noise level on the Web is getting higher and higher," says Mark Kvamme, chairman and CEO of the CKS Group, a multimedia marketing firm in Cupertino, California. "Every day it gets tougher to establish a new brand name. A couple years ago, if you had a Web site, it was written up in every newspaper. Now, you're lucky to get a single mention somewhere."

Since they are becoming harder to come by, well-known brands are thus becoming more and more valuable to have. This corollary of the law of supply and demand is the seventh principle of Webonomics: Because they are becoming more and more difficult to establish, trusted brand names matter even more on the Web.

WEB-BASED BRANDS

Economic life moves much faster on the Web. With new sites cropping up at the rate of one per minute and current sites changing at an
even faster pace, the Web is in a state of perpetual motion, constantly
struggling to satisfy the public's obsession with "what's new." This
stepped-up pace of change goes a long way toward explaining what
companies must do to establish a new brand name on the Web.

In the traditional media, the brands that were first to stake out a
novel piece of turf became the undisputed market leaders. In the world
of cable TV, viewers think of CNN when they think twenty-four-hour
news. HBO comes to mind first for movies. ESPN for sports. MTV for
music videos. And more recently, Comedy Central, for funny stuff. In
all of these markets, whoever was first got the prize.

But even though they were first, those brands took years to establish. On the Web, it seems like the early bird can get the worm in a
matter of months, even weeks. Consider the case of Yahoo!, the Mountain View, California company known for its directory listing of virtually everything on the Web. The company was launched in March 1995
by Jerry Yang and David Filo, a pair of Stanford University grad students (just a couple of self-proclaimed Yahoos). By the fall of that year,
the Yahoo! brand name was universally known among Web surfers
everywhere. Just thirteen months later, the company's rocket ride of a
public offering stunned Wall Street, fertilizing the market for still more
Web-related offerings.

"They spent maybe a couple million dollars establishing the brand
name," says Kvamme, who has counted Yahoo! as one of his firm's
clients. "That's nothing!" When the company went public, sharehold-
ers put a value on the brand in the neighborhood of $500 million. By
any measure, that's a lightning-fast rise in brand equity.

The Yahoo! name is now right up there with Netscape in awareness
for a Web-based brand. Even people who have never been on the Web,
indeed people who have never seen a Web page in their life, will typically be aware of the name. "I want to get on the Web," they'll say.

"What should I use, Netscape or Yahoo!?" When you try to tell them that Netscape is a browser and that Yahoo! is a directory, they'll ask, "What's the difference?"

Consider all the search engines and directory services that came out after Yahoo! There's InfoSeek, Magellan, Web Crawler, Lycos, Alta Vista, Excite, HotBot. With the possible exception of InfoSeek, which was launched around the same time as Yahoo!, none of the others have been able to match Yahoo!'s brand awareness, even though many sport excellent technology. Much of that awareness came from free mass-media hype. And some came from Yahoo!'s own subsequent mass-media advertising campaigns. But most of that awareness came from the fact that Yahoo! was first out of the gate. Web surfers spread the word among themselves remarkably fast.

This keen brand image has enabled Yahoo! to extend its brand into a whole family of Yahoo! branded media properties. There's the magazine *Yahoo! Internet Life*, as well as Yahooligans!, a Web guide for kids, and geographic adaptations of the directory such as Yahoo! Japan and Yahoo! Canada. Not to mention a personalized news service called My Yahoo!

Other Web-based brands that were first to enter a particular market have also taken off. As the Web's first book superstore, Amazon.com in a matter of months gained the reputation as the place to go for books online. By the time Borders and Barnes & Noble were able to respond, millions of Web surfers were shopping at Amazon and recommending it to their friends.

Some categories, however, are so rich with well-known brand names that it becomes prohibitive to invent your own. When Starwave launched the SportsZone site, it knew that there were just too many well-known places for sports information on the Web. After all, *Sports Illustrated, USA Today,* and other brands were already coming online. So, it contracted with the ESPN cable sports channel to not only share content but to brand the Web site with a famous name. As a result, ESPN SportsZone got instant credibility and awareness in a very competitive and crowded field. Hotwired was able to benefit from a similar strategy. An offspring of *Wired* magazine—already established and revered by the Net crowd—Hotwired instantly benefited from the irreverent, high-tech, insider sensibility for which its parent is known.

Establishing a new brand name very quickly on the Web has become so important that it has led to a general rule: Give your product away for free, then use the brand to make money on related products and services. Netscape, of course, pioneered this concept. By giving away its browser software for free to consumers, the ubiquitous N symbol instantly became nearly synonymous with the Web itself. The company then proceeded to leverage its brand by selling sophisticated server software to corporations. Digital Equipment Corp. did the same with its Alta Vista search engine. Anyone can use it for free. But Digital charges companies that want a customized search engine for their internal corporate Intranet.

Of course, the most popular way to make money from a newly minted brand is to sell advertising. That strategy alone is self-limiting, however. If all of your products are free and all your revenue is from advertising, you often must become an advertiser yourself in order to keep awareness high.

Indeed, among the top twenty-five recipients of advertising revenue on the Web, many of them must spend a considerable portion of that revenue on—you guessed it—Web advertising. The InfoSeek search engine, for example, has garnered more advertising dollars than any other site, according to data from Jupiter Communications. But it typically spends 10 percent of that revenue on its own Web advertising campaigns, placing banner ads at other sites to generate traffic. Netscape, meanwhile, spends nearly 50 percent of its ad revenue on ads that bolster its brand on the Web. So does C/Net, the popular digital magazine and Internet news site.

The practice seems to have a circular reasoning to it: If you want to maintain a high traffic site so that you can sell ads, you must advertise your site by placing hyperlinks at other high-traffic sites. It's not uncommon for C/Net to place an ad on InfoSeek's site, which places ads at Netscape's site, which in turn places ads at C/Net's site. What you end up with is an infinite traffic loop of sorts.

Some Web-based brands hit the mark just right and can be parlayed into huge new business opportunities. The Java programming language and Web software distribution methodology from Sun Microsystems is the perfect example. Java caught on not only because it's a great technology but also because the name is so cool—spawning endless bad coffee puns in trade magazine headlines, such as SUN PERKS NEW JAVA BREW.

Java took off instantaneously upon its introduction in early 1995. Thanks to lots of free publicity, distribution deals with Netscape and Microsoft to integrate Java into their browser programs, plus strong word of mouth among programmers, the Java brand became the basis for countless books and trade shows, spawning a entire subindustry onto itself. As a maker of high-end desktop workstations, Sun Microsystems had become a pretty powerful brand name, rocketing onto the Fortune 500 list after only about nine years in business. But that was nothing compared to this. "The Java brand," says Sun CEO Scott McNealy, "has become bigger than Sun itself."

GLOBAL BRAND ICONS

A well-known brand name can serve as a beacon on the Web, in a sense casting its glow in all directions and compelling loyal customers to come toward the light. The opposite can be true as well. A brand name that stands as an icon in one-way media can fail to understand the principles of the Web economy and get crushed to dust by the new interactive media.

When the Home Shopping Network launched its Internet Shopping Network site way back in 1993, it certainly seemed to be way ahead of most other retailers that may have had visions of doing business on-

line. As a brand icon, HSN is known as the cable channel that pioneered the shop-at-home, order-by-phone experience. Yet when it extended its brand onto the Web, it clearly failed to realize its aims as a
broad-based cybermall that sold everything from clothing to jewelry to
consumer electronics.

"They didn't put the right resources into it," says Mark Kvamme, of
the CKS Group, which performed contract work for ISN. He agrees
that when ISN retreated to the niche of only selling computer gear, the
move served to dilute the powerful brand equity that the Home Shopping Network had built up. In hindsight, HSN might have been better
off not entering Web space until it better figured out the dynamics of
online shopping. In general, it's better for a well-known brand not to
go on the Web at all, rather than be there with a halfhearted, inferior,
or totally useless Web site.

The tobacco industry seems to be taking this very nonapproach to
the Web. Cigarettes are perhaps the only category of consumer products that has all but completely stayed away from the Web. Why don't
brands such as Marlboro, Camel, and Kool have Web sites? Perhaps
it's because this is an industry that doesn't need a new way to boost
customer loyalty. The industry's physically addictive products already
compensate many of its best customers with the ultimate reward: a
slow, painful, early death.

There also might be a regulatory reason why well-known cigarette
brands don't have Web sites. It's not entirely clear whether the Web
falls into the category of a print medium, a broadcast medium—or
something else entirely. The Federal Communications Commission,
which regulates U.S. broadcasters, banned cigarette ads from the airwaves some twenty-five years ago. The jury is still out as to whether
the FCC has any jurisdiction over computer-based communications
media. The cigarette companies seem to be waiting for this issue to
sort itself out.

Other global brand icons would be conspicuous if they opted out,
however. This is why Coca-Cola had a lot riding on its effort to rein-

vent its brand image for the Web generation. As a pop icon, the Coca-Cola brand has for decades been inseparable from mass culture.

When Coca-Cola introduced its first crack at a Web site in 1996, the focus was on information about the company and the brand. One on-line feature, "The World of Coca-Cola Museum," was a series of Web pages stocked with brand imagery and advertising artifacts going back to the early part of the twentieth century, when the beverage was first introduced.

The original Coca-Cola site also included a message from the company's chairman, a company stock quote button, and the ability to send E-mail about product satisfaction to unnamed "executives." The Atlanta-based company wisely warned consumers not to send in ideas for new products. "Unsolicited product ideas are a real quagmire," the message said. "Please resist the urge to send them." Well-known companies like Coca-Cola are cautious about unsolicited ideas received via E-mail because if they do happen to introduce something similar to what someone suggests, they are often subject to lawsuits charging them with ripping off that concept.

One gets the sense that this initial Web presence is simply a place holder for Coca-Cola, that the company will and should introduce something more spectacular, something more worthy depicting the company's high production values. But since Coke, Diet Coke, and the company's other brands are the quintessence of information-poor products, what can the company do? The natural direction for a brand like Coke is to use its Web site to showcase its products using state-of-the-art digital technology, such as video streaming and 3-D animation.

Coca-Cola should, in fact, be in the business of selling or giving away eye-popping screen savers that consumers could download to their hard drives. The "Always Coca-Cola" TV ad campaign, with the rapid-fire imagery based around the big red Coke bottle cap, would make for the perfect screen saver. This would put Coca-Cola in the software business, which would make for an unexpected but logical extension of its brand image.

"On the Web, brands must become technologies," says Less Ottolenghi, director of emerging technologies for Holiday Inn.

McDonald's is in the same boat as Coca-Cola. It, too, is a global
brand icon for information-poor products. Consumers will not go on
the Web to seek out information about what's available at McDonald's restaurants; there's nothing essential to learn that isn't already
known.

No doubt, McDonald's will continue to use mass-media advertising
as its primary vehicle for brand awareness. McDonald's is the fourth
most advertised brand in the United States, accounting for nearly $500
million in spending in 1995. Worldwide, the Oak Brook, Illinois company spends more than $1.5 billion on advertising. Total revenue in
1995 was $9.8 billion. So, the king of burgers spends about 15 percent
of its revenue just on advertising. To promote the new Arch Deluxe
burger alone, McDonald's was planning to spend about $200 million in
1996. First year sales for this adult burger are projected to be from
$750 million to $1 billion. So roughly 20 to 25 percent of revenue from
Arch Deluxe will go to advertising. And the burger only sells for about
$2.39. How do you make money on selling such a low-cost product
with such high overhead? Volume!

Judging from McDonald's recent mass advertising slogan, "Have
you had your break today?", the goal of the company has clearly
shifted to something more than just brand awareness. After all, if you
aren't fully aware of McDonald's, chances are that your body has been
cryogenically frozen for the past fifty years. Since everyone already
knows McDonald's, the goal now is to quite literally get every single
person on earth to eat there every day.

There are 11,500 McDonald's in the continental United States. You
can work out the numbers, dividing the land area (3.5 million miles)
by number of restaurants (11,500), coming up with a 304-square-mile
area, which is a 17.4 mile by 17.4 mile box. That means the average
time someone would have to drive to come upon a McDonald's is about
twenty minutes or so. Of course, that includes vast stretches of rural

land and national parks where there aren't any golden arches. In most populated areas, there's usually a McDonald's every couple of miles.

In recent years, McDonald's has been proceeding to saturate the rest of the world. A new franchise opens every four hours, according to the McDonald's Web site, which offers pictures from restaurants in Beijing, Paris, and Moscow (touted as the world's busiest restaurant). Meanwhile, despite this aggressive expansion of new stores, McDonald's same-store sales in the United States have actually been going down slightly, in recent years.

Clearly, McDonald's is maxing out on its mass-media saturation strategy. To boost same-store sales, McDonald's needs to come up with a strategy that tries to boost loyalty among existing customers as well as make non-McDonald's families frequent customers. The company could E-mail everyone on the Internet every day, asking them, "Have you had you break today?" But that would probably meet up with fierce resistance and unleash a wicked backlash.

Another strategy would be to form a frequent eaters club. Consumers would get a Smart Card that gets swiped through a reader at the counter or at the drive-through window. Points could be credited to each consumer's account, according to how much food is purchased. As a form of value-based currency, the points could be redeemable for toys for the kids and free bonus meals for the adults. (Of course, this service should also come with a health insurance plan.)

But instead of designing its first-generation Web site to execute some sort of loyalty strategy, McDonald's simply took the opportunity to offer "information" about its products and brand image. One feature on the site is a Q&A with "the Nutritionist." The feature is not interactive, as consumers don't even get to ask the questions. One of the canned questions in this feature is: "How does McDonald's fit into a healthful eating plan?" That's a fair question. But get a load of the reply: "All foods fit into a healthful eating plan because it's the total diet that counts. There are not good foods and bad foods." How's that for being gastronomically correct?

THE GREAT BRAND MIX-UP

Brand names often stand for something much broader than it would otherwise appear. Instead of just being the name and logo for a specific category of products, many well-known brands are actually symbolic of a certain sensibility, attitude, or lifestyle. Nike, for instance, spends more money on building its image than it does on making sneakers. And it is parlaying its "just do it," in-your-face attitude into a host of new businesses, including retail megastores like the giant Nike Town in Chicago.

The king of forging a multifaceted brand identity is Richard Branson, the brash, British billionaire. For more than twenty-five years, Branson has been launching business after business; the only thing they have in common is the Virgin brand name. He initially chose the name because of his inexperience in business. But he believes the brand has grown to stand for a bold, fun, playful sensibility.

In 1970, Branson launched his Virgin Group of companies by starting up Virgin Records, a mail-order record business. Twelve years later, he started Virgin Atlantic Airways, challenging British Airways in lucrative U.S. to London routes. In 1992, to raise cash for the airline, he sold Virgin Records—by then one of the world's largest independent music labels—for $1 billion to Britain's Thorn EMI. (Branson, however, retains the title of honorary president for life.)

In the 1990s, the Virgin name has spread to dozens of businesses. In 1994, Branson began marketing the new Virgin Cola in the United Kingdom. He also started operating blimps, hot-air balloons, resorts, a tour company, hotels, a radio station, a video postproduction studio, and a chain of huge media megastores. He is the publisher of books, video games, and interactive CD-ROMs. All of these new companies leverage the Virgin brand name. Branson has even launched a bridal consultant business in the United Kingdom called—what else?—Virgin Brides.

Naturally, his privately held, $2.5 billion empire has spilled onto the Web as well. Virgin Atlantic was one of the first airlines to launch a Web site and sell tickets online. Branson also uses the site to stage playful promotions. An early one was in conjunction with the Joe Boxer underwear company. Buy five pairs and get a free companion ticket to London. Visitors to the Virgin Interactive Entertainment site can meet fellow players of hit games such as 7th Guest, trading playing tips and finding out about sequel releases.

This idea of extending a brand name—and the attitude and attributes associated with it—can be a powerful formula for growth in the Web economy. Consumers want to do business with names they know and trust. As a result, we are witnessing the beginning of what can be called the great brand mix-up: Well-known companies are starting Web services that have nothing to do with their core product areas. The Web is the perfect place for such businesses to take root, as the newness of the Web can ensure a level playing field for start-up ventures.

High-tech companies have been among the first to employ this strategy. Consider these moves:

Microsoft is now jointly operating an online travel agency—with American Express.

IBM has opened up a cybermall, called World Avenue.

Intuit, the maker of the popular Quicken brand of personal finance software, is now selling life insurance on its Web site.

America Online, leveraging its experience creating digital content, is now serving as an advertising agency, selling Web space for clients such as Netscape.

All of these companies seem to be going far afield. But consumers already associate these brand-name companies with high-tech product development, ease-of-use, and aggressive promotion.

At the same time, Web-based brands are encroaching on the turf of some of the world's most venerable companies. InfoSeek and Yahoo! have moved into personalized news services, offering visitors to their sites a complete rundown of customized lists of stocks, news categories, industry happenings, and sports updates. Traditional journalistic organizations, long stuck in a one-paper-fits-all mentality, have suddenly realized that these personalized news services should be their bread and butter on the Web.

It almost seems ridiculous. But we have a situation in which the most respected names in journalism, such as the *Wall Street Journal,* the *New York Times,* and *Time* magazine, are all aggressively trying to beat back services such as "My Yahoo!" These well-established brands will hold sway not just by matching Yahoo! and listing news stories that contain certain key words, but by somehow putting news into context in a highly personal way. Says Walter Isaacson, managing editor of *Time* and former editor of *New Media* for Time Warner: "When we're swamped with information, and you have a thousand different sources for each piece of data, you look to certain brand names and certain types of journalism you trust, to make sense of it, to be your intelligent agent, to sort it out."

The most prestigious news and information brands, however, shouldn't just be playing defense in the great brand name mix-up. Instead of simply providing want-ad listings online, for instance, perhaps the *Times* could become a full-fledged employment agency for the New York region, taking commissions on the salaries of workers that are placed by the service. In other worlds, holders of valuable brand names should be playing offense as well.

BRAND AS IDENTITY BADGE

Some people have such an affinity for certain brands that they go so far as to integrate those brands with their own identity.

Saturn cars is one such brand. When the new Spring Hill, Tennessee division of General Motors began marketing the first line of Saturns in 1990, the ad campaign trumpeted "a different kind of company, a different kind of car." The message took hold. When the car received rave reviews in the auto trade press, Americans were intrigued. They were eager to buy a sporty new American-made car that promised the feel and quality of a Japanese-made compact.

The first owners of Saturn cars naturally felt as if they were getting in on the ground floor of a truly different phenomenon in American automobile manufacturing. The fact that Saturn dealers took a decidedly different no-hassle, no-haggling price policy solidified the image that Saturn was more like a club than a company. Instead of doing heavy negotiating, Saturn salespeople focused on singing the praises of the car and, more importantly, how all Saturn workers felt they were part of something special. This approach was widely recognized as an enormous success. And the basic reason for that success goes to the heart of human nature: Everyone wants to belong to something. And Saturn was something that people deemed worth belonging to.

The Saturn Web site not only took advantage of this brand affinity; it reinforced it. Instead of simply providing electronic versions of Saturn brochures, the site invited Saturn owners to register in an online Saturn club called the Extended Family Database. And instead of simply asking people to send in their names, addresses, and car models— information the company already had anyway—this Web site asked people for much more detailed information: Why do you like your Saturn? Have you driven it anywhere interesting? What color is it? What are your interests and hobbies? What do you do for a living? Within two years, nearly 10,000 people entered their answers.

Here's the ingenious part: Instead of just storing all that information in an internal corporate database, Saturn made the information available to anyone who visited the Web site. Visitors could punch in the name of their town and look up all the registered Saturn owners in their neighborhood, viewing all kinds of fun facts about these people and their cars. The result is to further boost word-of-mouth support for the car. Fellow Saturn owners who lived nearby could be prompted to get to know one another. In addition, this approach makes prospective owners want to join the club. The subliminal message is this: You are a superior human being for being intelligent and cool enough to own a Saturn.

Not all brand names can serve as an identity badge, of course. Many people are indeed proud of the car they drive and believe their choice says something about their personality. But not all products produce this kind of close identification. There's a reason, for instance, that people don't go around wearing T-shirts advertising Preparation H. People generally don't go around boasting about the relief they feel from the itching, burning, and swelling.

One category of products that serves as an identity badge is alcoholic beverages. In today's brand-conscious economy, the brand of beer you drink says a lot about you. But even a well-conceived identity site can flop if it promotes a product that fails to connect with consumers.

Consider the sad case of Zima. Beginning in the fall of 1994, this new clear, malt alcohol beverage from the Adolph Coors Co. became one of the inaugural sponsors of Hotwired and a handful of other content sites. To introduce the drink, Zima not only advertised on TV and in print but had turned to a new media agency called Modem Media for a high-profile Web campaign. The Zima.com address mysteriously appeared on the bottles, at a time when such a thing was unheard of in consumer marketing.

The site invited Web surfers to follow the adventures of a techno-savvy, twentysomething character named Duncan. In addition to getting consumers to identify with this character, the site also encouraged visitors to join Tribe Z, registering their name, address, and other data in exchange for goodies sent via regular mail, such as those hologram illusion cards that you're supposed to stare at until an image pops up.

Back when the Web was young and marketing sites were few, the Zima site was an instant hit. Since it was one of the first marketing sites specifically designed for this new medium, it drew an immense amount of coverage. The Zima site was written up in countless newspapers and business periodicals. It was also featured on the NBC Nightly News and in a PBS special on the Internet. All told, the site received 100 million impressions in free media, according to the company.

Hundreds of thousands of people joined Tribe Z. People were curious as to what Zima was. And the Web site seemed cool. Then, toward the end of 1995, the site experienced a precipitous drop-off in traffic. People who had visited once were not coming back. They had learned what Zima was, looked around once, and that was it.

The problem here was not with the Web site but with the fact that the product itself was not catching on. Zima was targeted at the nebulous Generation X crowd as an identity badge. But what was the product supposed to say about you? Some of the women who used to drink wine coolers in the '80s started buying it. But there's a reason that Bartles and James took early retirement; that market is pretty small. Then, the beverage was marketed to men as an alternative to beer (The slogan: "zomething different."). But beer drinkers did not want to be seen drinking sissy wine coolers. Hence, a marketing failure. Sales fizzled and investment in the Web campaign was slashed. The site didn't disappear entirely, but it became stagnant. And on the Web, stagnation is death.

One problem with Zima is that Gen Xers had no natural affinity for the Zima product; nor did the Web site or any of the marketing efforts succeed in cultivating one. Zima was simply a good Web site for a lackluster product. By 1996, the Coors company shifted the marketing message once again: Zima was now being marketed, in part, as something you mix with something else, such as Schnapps, Grand Marnier, Chambord, or another liqueur. The unspoken admission: People aren't thrilled with the taste of Zima itself. And the lesson: Even the best Web site can't rescue a dog.

WHEN DAVID FIGHTS GOLIATH

While trusted brand names do take on a heightened importance on the Web, it's also true that not being on the Web with a quality site can leave that brand open to attack and erosion.

One example of a little-known brand that has forged a connection with consumers online is Annie's Homegrown Inc., a Hampton, Connecticut company that makes macaroni and cheese. This is an unusual example of an information-poor product that has attracted attention on the Web by placing itself at the center of an information-rich experience. This experience is designed to form a bond with people who aim to live an antimainstream, "green" lifestyle. But such lifestyle connections must be carefully considered and done well.

In this case, Annie's is up against one of the world's best-known food brands: Kraft. And if you look closely, the entire company is built on a subtle anti-Kraft message. Started in 1989 by a young entrepreneur named Ann Withey (she is also the cofounder of Smart Food popcorn), the Annie's brand achieved national distribution and $5 million in annual sales by 1995. It did all this without any advertising whatsoever. Word about the product spread quickly among friends who may have grown up on Kraft macaroni and cheese but now prefer natural foods. Withey simply relies on attracting customers who are clued in enough to realize that the color of Kraft's orange cheese does not occur in nature. In fact, the only other place you might see it is in Strom Thurmond's hair.

In the fall of 1995, Annie's started putting its Web address on its boxes. Within a few months, an average of 2,000 people were visiting the site every week. Web surfers are greeted by Bernie the rabbit, the company's mascot. People use the site to send questions and comments to the company and receive speedy replies via E-mail. They also can order cases of twenty-four boxes of the product shipped to their home or sent to a friend. The company now does 10 percent of its direct sales to consumers through the Web, says Heather Keenan, a marketing manager. (The other 90 percent happens over the phone.) The site is also stocked with information on how to get involved with the proenvironment volunteer efforts that the company supports and integrates into its overall image.

Annie's Web site also allows consumers who may have heard about the product to punch in their zip code and find the nearest store where the product can be purchased. Some of those stores are creating their own Web sites, and consumers can hyperlink over to them. Keenan sees this as a new form of low-cost cooperative advertising. "We didn't anticipate that," she says, "but we'd rather provide links than spend $5,000 on a co-op advertisement that we can't afford."

Let's contrast this form of word-of-mouth marketing with Kraft's mass-media efforts. In 1922, the Phoenix Cheese Company signed up with the ad agency J. Walter Thompson, which advised the company to change its name. The newly christened Kraft Foods began an unprecedented mass-market push to implant that brand name into the minds of every consumer in the country. When TV came along, the company in 1947 created Kraft Television Theater, thus launching the concept of the regularly sponsored commercial TV show.

Due in part to its many highly successful mass-marketing campaigns, Kraft's products now account for 10 percent of all branded food sales in the United States. Maintaining that market share has a high price tag. Kraft's parent company Philip Morris spends $3 billion per year on advertising alone, making it the second biggest American advertiser (after Procter & Gamble).

But when the Web came along, where was Kraft? The reason Kraft has been a latecomer to the Web (it finally launched a site in late 1996) may be because this medium could never provide the mass exposure the food maker has been used to all these years. What's more, the company in all likelihood just isn't comfortable being in direct contact with its customers. Kraft simply makes its products and hires an ad agency to tell the world that they exist and that they are good. That's not good enough anymore.

Annie's success selling a rival product via word of mouth and a Web site does not mean that Kraft should immediately halt its TV and print ads and start hawking its individually wrapped cheese food slices and other products exclusively over the Web. Kraft is addicted to the mass-market way of thinking and probably always will be. But small success stories like these do portend a future in which hundreds or thousands of niche and regional brands of all kinds will be using interactive media to form individual relationships with customers. The net result may be a slow erosion of dominant brand fortresses that fail to change their basic thinking.

<Chapter Summary>
• Major brand names are up for *reevaluation* in the Web economy. Those that build Web ventures that live up to and exceed their reputations will become even more valuable. Those that do not stand in danger of losing their eminence.
• Consumers recognize that brand names are more than just marketing slogans. It often pays to be loyal to trusted brands because these names *save the time and aggravation* of sorting through the increasingly cluttered marketplace.
• Establishing a new brand image is difficult on the Web, but can best be done *by being the first* to do something, such as creating a new type of product or service.
• The Web is the perfect place to catapult a trusted brand name beyond the original products for which it is already known. Brand names that evoke a certain sensibility, core competency, or comfort factor can be used to sell almost anything on the Web.
• Ultimately, companies that establish a strong affinity with customers can establish an online community of interest around their brands.

<CHAPTER EIGHT>

Even the Smallest Business Can Compete in the Web's Global "Marketspace"

FROM MARKETPLACE TO MARKETSPACE

In the Web economy, consumers and businesses don't so much meet in a marketplace; they interact in a "market*space*." As defined by Harvard Business School professors Jeffrey F. Rayport and John J. Sviokla, the marketspace is the domain of computer networks. "Every business today competes in two worlds: a physical world of resources that managers can see and touch," the professors wrote in the *Harvard Business Review*, "and a virtual world made from information."

When a business moves from the marketplace into the marketspace, it must recognize three key changes in the terrain: First, the computer network serves as the infrastructure, not buildings and other brick-and-mortar real estate. Second, the computer screen simulates face-to-face contact. Third, people trade information instead of physical goods.

The computer-mediated marketspace doesn't go so far as to *replace* the traditional marketplace. It would be wrong to say that place is place, and space is space, and never the twain shall meet. There certainly is plenty of interplay between the two economies. For instance, online contact often *leads to* face-to-face contact. And sometimes, online digital information *represents* the physical goods that are to be shipped directly to consumers.

But the Harvard professors note that the process of doing business and creating value in each of these worlds is different. Instead of taking raw materials, fashioning those materials into a product, then physically shipping that product, businesses in the marketspace must engage in a newly learned sequence of gathering, organizing, selecting, synthesizing, and distributing information.

Perhaps the most dramatic advantage of doing business in the marketspace is that even the smallest of businesses can go global with unprecedented low costs. This global marketspace, unfortunately, is often an afterthought among companies setting up shop on the Web.

Many Web-based businesses ignore the international opportunities because of an all too common nationalistic mind-set. Nowhere is this more true than in the United States, where the mass media hammers home the message that we are citizens of a particular country, often without regard to how national interests are intertwined. News reports are completely dominated by issues and events that happen within the country's borders. Politicians focus their message on the national economy, the Federal budget, and so forth. Advertisements are almost always geared for the "American" market.

The global marketspace effectively erases national borders and gives even the smallest of companies a worldwide reach. The first two W's in WWW actually stand for something quite radical. This technology enables consumers to buy what they want, when they want it, with little regard for the location of the company selling that product or service.

An overseas shopping excursion no longer requires consumers to show their passports or even leave their homes. In most cases, government permission is no longer needed to make the marketspace journey to another country. In cases where paperwork is required to import certain goods, shipping companies such as Federal Express, UPS, and DHL are making it easier and easier to prepare export and import documents. In fact, much of that work can now be performed on the Web.

The main requirements for participating in the worldwide digital emporium are a personal computer, a Web browser, and an Internet connection. Someone in Kansas City can order fresh coffee beans from

Costa Rica just as easily as someone in Tokyo can order a basket of almonds from California. Often, online prices will be cheaper than buying locally. But perhaps the most common type of product that will be bought and sold across borders will be purely digital information: news reports, pictures, music, business information, and the like.

Companies do not have to achieve a critical mass to sell and service these bits. Nicholas Negroponte of the MIT Media Lab notes that a company needs a certain number of buyers in a certain city in order to make money selling products made from atoms such as hydrogen and oxygen—Evian water, for instance. "With atoms, you need a market where the consumption of those atoms is big enough to justify moving them there," Negroponte says. "But with bits you don't care. You can have just one person from a city buy your bits."

In addition, companies can provide customer service for all bits from one location. Negroponte cites another example: If a car company stops selling its cars in a certain country, as Peugeot did in the United States in 1991, it becomes more and more difficult to get parts and service. However, a company providing entertainment and information over the Web can easily service its digital assets all from one place. "This is a wonderful difference between bits and atoms," he says.

THE WEB'S BALANCE OF TRADE

Not surprisingly, companies with Web-based businesses are finding success doing business globally. According to ActivMedia, a Peterborough, New Hampshire research firm, one in three U.S. companies selling products and services over the Web are reporting export sales, as compared with one in ten of *all* U.S. companies doing business via traditional distribution methods.

Overall, about 18 percent of total sales from U.S.-based Web sites were exports to other countries, the firm found in a recent survey. That is a very healthy percentage. Indeed, it is slightly higher than the percentage of revenue due to exports reported by global giants such as General Electric, Chrysler, and Kodak.

U.S. companies have had an advantage in that they generally discovered the Web first and developed an online presence much sooner than their counterparts around the world. In the early days of the Web, the vast majority of revenue-producing sites were based in the United States. That lead, however, is rapidly eroding. As of mid-1996, only about 10 percent of revenue-producing sites were based in Europe. But such companies are more likely to be selling their products and services around the world. The ActivMedia survey found that one in *two* European companies reporting sales on the Web sites are engaged in exporting.

And while only 5 percent of sites reporting revenue were from the Asia-Pacific region, the survey found that companies in this region are developing Web sites at a much faster pace than any other region in the world. Overall, the survey found that one in three Asian-Pacific companies are engaged in exports—roughly the same proportion as the United States.

With all these companies getting online and setting themselves up for selling their goods and services everywhere, there will be an even bigger battle for the mind of the global consumer. American consumers are an especially fertile market. "The predominance of American consumers online will make them a juicy target for direct marketing by overseas firms," concludes ActivMedia's Jeanne Dietsch.

But most likely, the balance of trade on the World Wide Web will be in, well, a balance. In the traditional economy, large imbalances of trade are often a source of political tension. The massive annual trade deficit that the United States has been running with Japan, for instance, has produced endless rounds of high-level negotiations. Envoys from America try to get Japanese government officials to lower what they perceive as deliberate or culturally based trade barriers. The Japanese government, meanwhile, tends to resist such efforts.

Often left out of these negotiations over rules and regulations are the consumers themselves. On the Web, such trade deficits aren't likely. Tariffs, quotas, and restrictions are not in the vernacular of electronic commerce. In the Web economy, consumers are pretty much given complete freedom to choose which products to buy, no matter who is selling them.

And consumers from all over the world are exercising that free choice every day. A study by Internet Profiles (I/PRO) revealed that traffic from non-U.S. users at U.S.-based Web sites jumped to 30 percent of total traffic by June 1996. That was up from just 15 percent of total traffic just six months prior. In other words, nearly one-third of the people visiting some of the most popular American sites are not Americans. As that kind of global Web browsing grows, it matters less and less where you are and where the Web site you're visiting is hosted. Location as a barrier to trade goes away. What matters is human creativity, intelligence, and skills. The sites that are most worthy of attention can succeed everywhere at once.

SMALL COMPANIES ACTING BIG AND BIG COMPANIES ACTING SMALL

Some of the first companies to take advantage of the global reach of the Web were, in fact, start-ups specializing in Web site development.

A U.K. company called Web Media began in 1994 as a one-stop shop for all aspects of getting companies up and running with eye-catching Web sites. Within two years, the London-based company was reporting about 90 percent of sales from clients in the United Kingdom, according to new business director Tarnya Norse. But most of its sales *leads* were coming from companies in Israel, France, Germany, Japan, and six other countries.

Web Media was able to establish a global presence, despite the fact that the company had only about fifty employees. Most of those leads came from companies that learned about its capabilities from its Web site. With a worldwide base of clients such as The Body Shop, *Reader's Digest*, Netcom, Lufthansa, and Lloyd's Bank, the company attracted the attention of British advertising kingpin Maurice Saatchi, whose Megalomedia venture fund purchased a 20 percent stake in Web Media.

In addition to small companies acting as if they are big, the Web enables big companies to act as if they are as agile, flexible, and responsive as a small company.

Digital Equipment Corp., for instance, is a $15 billion giant of the computer industry. However, when a small team of programmers in its Palo Alto, California research center created the Alta Vista search engine in 1994, the fast-paced business environment of the Web enabled this team to introduce, promote, and improve upon this new product as if Digital were a nimble start-up. Within a few months of introducing the new search engine, Alta Vista became a global brand name. And Digital started collecting millions of dollars in license fees from corporations all over the world that wanted to use Alta Vista as the search engine on their internal Intranets.

Sometimes, the Web enables global giants to communicate with people it never would be able to reach otherwise. One example of this comes from Korea. To draw expatriate Koreans back to Seoul, the electronics giant Samsung advertised extensively in Korean-language newspapers in the United States but achieved almost nothing in the way of results. But when the company put up an English-language Web site called the Samsung Human Resources Development Center, it received instant attention and dozens of applicants for job openings at its headquarters. Fully 80 percent who applied for those jobs did so by filling out applications on the Web. And all of those who eventually were hired were Internet applicants.

The list of other examples of companies ramping up global businesses at low cost is virtually endless. The Amazon bookseller site and the Virtual Vineyards wine-seller site, for instance, each have been shipping their products to consumers in nearly 100 countries. Neither

Amazon nor Virtual Vineyards has a physical presence in any of those countries. They hardly even do any advertising outside of the United States.

Direct marketers of personal computers such as Dell Computer and Gateway 2000 allow Web surfers around the world to learn about the features of their systems, then build and configure their own custom machines by choosing options such as RAM, hard-drive size, and processor speed from online menus. Customers can receive a total price, enter their credit card number and shipping address, then transmit their order to the company. At any time, customers can log back on to check to estimated delivery date of their system.

Dell reported that 34 percent of its overall $5.2 billion business came from overseas in fiscal 1996, as compared to 31 percent of its $3.5 billion in sales in 1995, the year it introduced its Web site. Of course, the Web site itself cannot take very much of the credit for boosting international sales so heartily. But it does have the potential to cut down significantly on the costs associated with setting up expensive telephone sales centers around the world.

PENETRATION OF THE INTERNET

Of course, just because the Internet *can* go anywhere doesn't mean it does. In reality, there has been a huge imbalance in Internet infrastructure, with some countries all wired for access and some with barely any computing capacity at all.

The best way to measure which countries are the most wired is to count the number of Internet "host" computers stationed in each. A host computer can be anything from a souped-up PC to a large mainframe. Such systems have a direct, high-speed link to the Internet backbone, which is the main fiber-optic network that carries data traffic among hosts. Individual users either dial into host systems from their homes using modems, or connect over a local-area network installed at a company, university, or other institution. A single host system can support as few as two or three people and as many as several dozen active users. But the general rule of thumb from the Internet Society and other trade groups is that the average host computer supports ten users.

Simply put, once a country has one host computer for every ten people, then we'll know that the country is saturated with Internet infrastructure. But in all practicality, that kind of ratio would probably amount to an overcapacity. No need to worry about that. No country has that kind of capacity as of yet.

In an extensive study, Killen & Associates, a Palo Alto, California research firm, collected data about host systems from around the world. The study amounts to perhaps the best apples-to-apples comparison of Internet infrastructure in dozens of countries.

In the survey, the United States weighs in with 3.7 million Internet host computers as of the beginning of 1996. With a population of 263 million, that works out to about seventy citizens per host system. Surprisingly, even though the United States has more than one-third of the world's nearly 10 million host systems, it doesn't have the highest capacity of Internet infrastructure as measured against the size of the population. That honor belongs to Finland, with twenty-four citizens per Internet host. Others with a higher ratio than the United States are Sweden and Australia, each at fifty-nine, and New Zealand at sixty-three.

As one might expect, the most industrialized nations of western Europe follow pretty closely behind the United States in terms of Internet capacity. In this study, the Netherlands has a ratio of 88, while the United Kingdom is at 129, and Germany is at 179. France lags in this group, at 390. Meanwhile, Israel, with a small population but with highly concentrated high-tech enclaves, also falls into this range, at 183 people per Internet host.

Japan and some of its neighbors in the Asia-Pacific region are among the fastest-growing countries in terms of Internet infrastructure. But in this study, these countries lag. Japan has a people-to-host ratio of 466, while Hong Kong is at 311, Taiwan at 851, and Korea at 1,553.

ActivMedia estimates that Japan was about eighteen months behind the United States in online commerce as of the end of 1995, but only a year behind by the middle of 1996. Japan had approximately 1.6 million Internet users as of the beginning of that year, according to the country's Ministry of Posts and Telecommunications. ActivMedia was projecting that Japan would fully catch up with the United States in terms of sophistication in online commerce and in the proportional number of surfers and commercial sites by 1997.

South and Latin American countries generally have poor Internet capacity relative to the population. Chile is among the best in the group, with a people-to-host ratio of 1,562, followed by Argentina at 6,438, Brazil at 7,990, Venezuela at 18,026, Colombia at 16,004, and Nicaragua, with a ratio of 29,787 people for every Internet host.

As one might expect, most African and many Middle Eastern countries also fare poorly in Internet infrastructure measures. South Africa leads the region with 932 people per host. Way behind are Tunisia with 108,171, Zimbabwe with 119,355, Morocco at 124,359, Iran at 238,376, and Uganda at 337,414.

But the poorest countries in this respect are the ones with the largest populations. Ranking way at the bottom of the survey is China, which has more than a half-million people per Internet host. India, although it has a few pockets of high-tech development, ranks dead last in the survey, with more than one million people for every Internet host. Those two countries, however, are generally regarded as the ones with the most explosive growth potential in the world Internet scene. If just 2 percent of the population of those countries go online, it would quickly double the worldwide total number of Internet users.

Overall, Killen & Associates expects the number of host systems worldwide to increase tenfold by the year 2000, to a total of nearly 100 million machines. Meanwhile, the company projects the worldwide total number of people surfing the net to grow almost as fast in that time frame—from 30 million people in 1996 to a mind-boggling 250 million people in the year 2000. If that projection holds, it would mean that the number of people online by then would nearly match the current population of the United States.

LANGUAGE IS A VIRUS

Just because people can *access* the Web from all over the world doesn't mean that the Web is *accessible.* The majority of content on the Web is in English, and most of the world doesn't understand much of it.

"The American view of the world is that English is the center of the universe, and that it will continue to be in the future," says Bill Washburn, general manager of international business development for Killen & Associates. "But then there is reality."

It's true that English is becoming the most popular language for business people worldwide. And the United States is the largest exporter of "culture"—movies, videos, and television programs. As a result, English is becoming a standard second language taught around the world. However, it's also true that billions of people simply aren't very comfortable with it. "Especially if it's technical or business issues that they want to be clear on," Washburn says. "If it's not your primary language, reading English is very taxing on your brain and eyes. Those people can do it, but it's a struggle. It's sort of like doing math all the time."

Catering to many different language groups is an imperative, Washburn says. "Why would we as business people ever think of limiting ourselves in the linguistic sense?"

Over time, the Web is likely to alter the language patterns of the world—just as information technology that came before it already has. Prior to Gutenberg's invention of the printing press in the fifteenth century, Latin was the official language of scholars and the sacred language of the church. Vernacular languages were considered "vulgar" by the powers that be. But the printing press created the pressure to start publishing in Greek, Italian, and other nonsacred languages. This helped spark the Renaissance and revive dormant dialects all over the known world.

Washburn sees a half-dozen ultraimportant languages besides English dominating the Web: German, French, Spanish, Japanese, Russian, and Chinese. He also believes Dutch may be significant, as many publishing, electronics, and high-tech firms are located in the Netherlands. Korean may also prove important, he says.

And just like the printing press, the Web is likely to spark an analogous revival of withering tongues. Until the Web, the economics of publishing books and magazines in languages with small bases of readers were prohibitive. The costs of printing and distribution were simply too high for the size of the market. Smaller groups who speak Armenian, Swahili, Kurdish, Yiddish, or other more obscure languages are beginning to get into the business of distributing products, services, and information over the Web. The Web's low costs may finally make those markets profitable. "Language," as Laurie Anderson writes, "is a virus." And it can be a computer virus, too. The efforts of just a few people could cause certain languages to take on a new prominence.

In some cases, those who want to do business internationally may not have to go to the trouble of translating their Web sites into different languages. More and more Web surfers around the world are plugging automatic language translation software into their Web browsers. A company called Globalink, for instance, sells a program called Web Translator that works with the Netscape Navigator. The software automatically translates Web pages designed in French, German, and Spanish into English—and vice versa. All of the page's hyperlinks, graphics, and formatting are preserved. The best part of the program is that it enables you to surf in real time, as if everything were originally written in your native tongue.

Such programs, however, are known to produce highly imperfect translations, with choppy grammar, an occasional mistranslation of an idiom or ambiguous word, and no provision for accounting for cultural differences. For the foreseeable future, the only way to avoid such glitches is to actually have your Web site translated by hand by people who know both the native and target languages intimately. That, in fact, is what Killen and many other consultancies around the world specialize in. If you really want to impress citizens of the world that your Web site is targeted to them personally, you must realize that language is inseparable from culture. Any mess-ups in language could reveal an ignorance of local culture.

Indeed, many products sold on the Web must be customized for the different cultures. Just think of a simple product like pizza. It might not be the best product to sell over the Web (ordering one by phone is just fine). But it serves to illustrate that there are profound cultural differences in what different people expect from a pizza. According to a survey by Domino's that was published in *Food & Wine* magazine, the most popular pizza topping in the United States is, not surprisingly, pepperoni.

But the survey found that the most popular topping in Japan is squid. In Australia, it's eggs. In Brazil, green peas. Pickled ginger is the favorite in India. Guatemalans prefer black bean sauce, while pizza eaters in Chile like mussels and clams. Barbecue chicken is the big topping in the Bahamas, and fresh cream the favorite in France. Leave it to the world's culinary mavens in England to crave tuna and corn. If you don't live in these countries, not only might you not know about these popular toppings, but you probably wouldn't even know what to call these things. Pizza—and language—is culture.

THE WORLDWIDE WEBPHONE

The wild card in the Web's transformation of international communications is something known as the Webphone. Simply put, the Webphone bypasses the conventional phone system, allowing calls to originate from a personal computer rather than a traditional telephone.

The telephone has indeed made the world seem like a smaller place. But even though it bridges distance, the telephone system puts up the barrier of money. Making calls, especially international ones, is damn expensive. A midday call from Los Angeles to New York costs about $15 per hour, while New York to Paris could run between $60 and $120 per hour. By contrast, the cost of talking to people on the Webphone—no matter where they are—is usually no more than what people pay for Internet access, about $3 to $4 per hour. The location of whom you are calling no longer is a factor in the cost.

While the Internet was not intended to carry voice traffic, especially not voices traveling in real time, special Webphone software aims to take care of that limitation. It works sort of like the online chat feature on America Online. Only, instead of just typing, people can really talk. First, two people must arrange to be online at the same time. The coordination can be accomplished via E-mail, for instance. The Webphone software connects a caller to a special server, or host computer, where the names of all the people who want to engage in conversation are listed in an on-screen window. The caller simply clicks on the person he or she wants to talk to.

The caller speaks into a microphone on his or her PC. The Webphone software digitizes and compresses the sounds, then turns those sounds into thousands of packets of data that can be transmitted to the host computer of his or her Internet access provider. From there, the host system relays the packets over the Internet backbone network to the host system of the recipient. The recipient's PC at the other end gathers those packets, converts the digital data back into analog sounds, and pipes them through his or her speakers or headphones. When the recipient speaks, the process is simply reversed.

In other words, the "data" from Webphone conversations are pretty much treated by the Internet just like any other data. That makes the Internet a more efficient—and thus cheaper—way of handling voice traffic; all conversations use the same shared resources. By contrast, conventional telephone networks establish a special dedicated circuit that runs the entire distance and duration of each phone call. That's why at certain heavy traffic times—such as during an earthquake or on Mother's Day—telephone callers sometimes get an "all circuits are busy, try again later" message when placing a call.

This need for dedicated, totally real-time circuits has forced long-distance companies to undertake the great expense of laying fiber-optic cable along the ocean floors of the world. This eliminates the millisecond delays of the alternative: bouncing international voice signals off satellites. It also adds to the costs of international dialing, but the quality is usually excellent. As you might expect, the packet approach of the Internet is less reliable; it often produces choppy speech, and results in conversations with delays as long as a few seconds. That can be very distracting. This low quality gives the Webphone a certain CB radio quality. It may be fine for hobbyists, but it's not quite ready for mainstream users.

Among the first companies to tap into the Webphone phenomenon was VocalTech Inc. Based in Israel but with operations in New Jersey, VocalTech has said that 150,000 people downloaded its Internet Phone software in the first three months after its release in early 1995. At first, calls were half-duplex, meaning that one person had to completely finish speaking before the other replied. But a new version enabled normal, full-duplex conversations—although delays and choppy speech is still hard to avoid.

There may be many applications in which people will tolerate this lower quality in exchange for dramatically lower costs. For instance, there is something known as a "call-back" service. AT&T, for instance, has introduced technology called Instant Answers that lets visitors to a commercial Web site click on a button that says "call me now." A sales or service agent at a bank, retailer, computer, or any other company would get the message, then telephone the customers in the usual way to answer questions about their products and services.

Another application is the "shared whiteboard." This is a way of tying together voice with data. Engineers using a shared whiteboard could trade technical information such as digital drawings and blue-prints at the same time that they talked to one another about the material via their PC microphones. This application fulfills one of Tim Berners-Lee's original visions for the Web. As he invented the basic Web technology in the late 1980s, Berners-Lee predicted that it would enable people to work across great distances to solve complicated problems.

Other applications for the Webphone involve playing real-time games against people around the world, as well as the proliferation of Internet ham radio and Internet talk radio. But perhaps the most pervasive application would be an extension of what happens during on-line chat sessions: meeting and talking to complete strangers about total nonsense.

One thing is for sure: The technology is moving at a blinding pace. And some of the glitches may be fixed one day. At least one company, International Discount Telecommunications (IDT), in Hackensack, New Jersey, has introduced a call-back service called Net2Phone, which enables users to dial any telephone number from their computer. Instead of talking to someone who is using a computer, the recipient of the call simply answers his or her ringing telephone. With costs as low as $6 per hour, Net2Phone enables people to dial anywhere in the world at a dramatically lower rate.

Some of these Webphone software packages are already being bundled for free into new versions of browser programs from Netscape, Microsoft, and others. Since this makes it more likely that the Webphone will catch on, traditional phone companies are up in arms over the issue.

In the spring of 1996, a political action group known as America's Carriers Telecommunication Association petitioned the U.S. Federal Communications Commission, demanding that the government place a ban on Internet telephone services. The group is made up mostly of local phone companies. (Sprint, MCI, and AT&T distanced themselves from the coalition.) The amazing thing about this effort is that telephone companies began moving to quash this technology even before most people knew it existed.

Governments may be sympathetic to such lobbying, but for an entirely different reason. The data-packet technology of Webphones can make calls all but impossible to tap—especially if the packets are filtered through an encryption program before they are transmitted. Law enforcement agencies would have to engage in a technological arms race to keep up with criminals who use such calling systems for illegal purposes.

Still, it seems inevitable that the Webphone will catch on in some form. And when it does, it no doubt will make doing business globally that much more compelling. By erasing cost as well as distance barriers, the Web in more ways than one is proving that it's an even smaller world, after all.

<Chapter Summary>
• In the borderless "marketspace" of the Web economy, any business can go global with unprecedented ease and low costs.
• As location as a barrier to trade goes away, human creativity, intelligence, and skills matter more and more. The Web sites and services most worthy of attention can succeed everywhere at once.
• Well-designed Web storefronts enable small companies to act as if they are big and enable big companies to act as if they are as flexible and responsive as start-ups.
• At present, there remains a huge gap in Internet penetration between industrialized nations such as the United States and the developing economies of the world. The strongest growth is happening in Japan, while China remains the country with the biggest growth potential.
• Although a disproportionate amount of content on the Web is in English, at least a half-dozen other languages are ultra-important for reaching international consumers.
• The ability to place phone calls over the Web threatens to bypass traditional telecommunications networks and dramatically lower the cost of talking to friends, family, and business partners around the world.

<CHAPTER NINE>

Agility Rules—Web Sites Must Continually Adapt to the Market

Agility is the ability to move with quick, easy grace. An agile basketball player senses in a split second when the situation on the court changes. Instead of attempting to score, he'll fake the shot, then pass to a suddenly open teammate who has a better chance. There's no time for the coach to call the play. It has to happen in the now.

Running a business venture on the Web must work much the same way. Often, there's no time for information about changes in the marketspace to get reported up through the usual chain of command. Waiting for a decision on how to proceed could cause a company to fall hopelessly behind as competitors race ahead. The Web economy is a world in which a competitive advantage may last only a few months, if not weeks. Yes, the CEO must be actively involved in setting electronic commerce strategy. But he or she also must empower those lower down on the command chain to act quickly and independently.

Might those "empowered" employees who run the company's Web venture make mistakes? Absolutely. As *Technology Review* magazine comments, "A computer lets you make more mistakes faster than any invention in human history—with the possible exceptions of handguns and tequila."

But smart Webmasters should be able to sense what's not working, then quickly correct it. Indeed, netrepreneurs should count on misjudgments, errors, and glitches as a normal part of doing business. Advertising pioneer David Ogilvy liked to say that the most important work in advertising is "testing." He noted that twenty-four of twenty-five products fail in test marketing. You must keep testing, he said, and your products and your advertisements will always improve. While those who market and sell products on the Web should aim to achieve a better success ratio than that, the basic point holds true. Learning from failure is part of what it takes to gear up your business to the fast-changing Web economy.

Not only must successful business ventures on the Web continually adapt to market changes, they also must actually *drive* business change. Taking a proactive rather than reactive stance is imperative in a technology-driven society. For managers, the old approach to information technology was asking the question: "I have this business problem—can technology help?" But managers looking to succeed in the twenty-first century must seek new applications for emerging technologies *before anyone else does*—before it's even clear just how the technology will be of use. When you look at it this way, the question becomes: "Here are the latest developments in technology—how can we apply them to our advantage?"

THE WORLD (WIDE WEB) ON TIME

Federal Express has been proactive about the Web right from the start. The Memphis shipping company splashed onto the Web way back in November 1994. Whereas most first cracks at corporate Web sites amount to pages and pages of graphics and promotional material that's of little practical value to customers, the FedEx site consisted of little more than the corporate logo and a place for entering a package tracking number.

Although this may be considered ho-hum now, the feature enabling customers to obtain delivery information on their packages was revolutionary at the time. "Some people kidded us about having no bells and whistles," says Nancy Raileanu, Webmaster for FedEx. "But we got written up in the press big time because we were one of the first sites where you could perform a task."

This competitive advantage lasted nearly a year. About twelve months later, UPS unveiled package tracking and a bevy of other features on its Web site. Since then, the two shipping giants have been locked in a battle with each other, with the U.S. Postal Service, and with other smaller competitors. No longer do leads last a year. As each of these companies add new self-service features to their Web sites, they are often quickly matched by the others. "This is an ultra-competitive industry," says Raileanu. "I have to spend time looking at their [UPS's] site."

The best way to move quickly and effectively is to keep close tabs on what customers want. In the beginning, Raileanu personally would read and respond to all the E-mail that customers sent to webmaster@fedex.com. This gave her clout at meetings of the Internet Steering Committee, a small group of top managers assembled from divisions across the 125,000-employee company. "I got to be the voice of the customer because I was the one answering the mail," she says.

At those meetings, steering committee members have to decide how to proceed with the site. Technology makes many things possible. And different constituencies are always clamoring for their own pet projects. The freight operators want this. The billing department wants that. "The hardest part is deciding what to do next," she says. "It has to be a matter of what you *should* do, not what you *can* do."

And as far as customers were concerned, the number one priority was applications that made shipping packages easier. Early in 1996, the company introduced the ability to prepare and print out shipping slips, dispatch a courier, find drop-off locations, and even send E-mail to the recipients of packages to let them know they were coming.

Before long, Raileanu was getting about 2,000 E-mail messages per month from customers. She had to recruit a staff of four people to answer it and compile it into summary reports. Not only would FedEx correspond with these customers, but it also would recruit them to try out new online applications. Before the shipping features were introduced, for instance, loyal customers were asked to beta test them. They were given a secret Web address that the general public didn't know. And these customers gave their honest input via E-mail. In this respect, FedEx was acting more like a software start-up than a shipping company.

Continuous feedback from customers enables FedEx to stay on the edge. The fifteen employees who run what FedEx now calls the Virtual World Service Center are constantly honing a "priority list" of important applications and a "wish list" made up of more blue-sky items. Every month, the staff adds a select feature from the top of the priority list to the site. Visitors can now do things such as open an account online, download software, and adjust mistakes in their billing invoices.

Managing all these online applications takes a tremendous amount of agility. When it was first launched, the FedEx site contained just 5 pages. Now it's up to more than 500 pages of information and applications. Everything must constantly be revamped and reevaluated to make sure it's as easy-to-use, accurate, and responsive as can be. "We make a lot of little decisions every day," Raileanu says.

DEALING WITH DISRUPTION

The biggest test of agility comes whenever a new technology bursts on the scene and threatens to shake and rattle the very ground of an industry's competitive landscape.

There are many examples of these so-called disruptive technologies in almost every major high- and low-tech industry. An article in the *Harvard Business Review* cites some of the major disruptions in the computer industry: "IBM dominated the mainframe market but missed by years the emergence of minicomputers," the article notes. "Digital Equipment dominated minicomputers but missed personal computers almost completely. Apple led the personal computer market but lagged five years behind the leaders in bringing portable computers to market."

Often, customers as well as companies are caught off guard by disruptive technologies. "As a rule," the article says, "mainstream customers are unwilling to use a disruptive product in applications they know and understand. At first, then, disruptive technologies tend to be used and valued only in new markets and new applications. In fact, they generally make possible the emergence of new markets."

The World Wide Web itself is an example of a disruptive technology. It wasn't as if business executives were crying out for a multimedia information forum where they could post information, perform customer service, and sell products. Before its arrival, the concept of the Web wouldn't even have crossed the mind of the average consumer or business person. They didn't know they needed it. Now, they can't do without it. For the entire media industry and computer industry, the arrival of the Web has been something of a shock.

Even Microsoft was caught by surprise. In 1994, the software giant put much of its resources into developing the Microsoft Network (MSN), an online service that would compete with America Online and be bundled with every copy of its Windows 95 operating system for PCs. But when the Web took off the following year while membership in MSN didn't meet expectations, Microsoft promptly switched gears, devoting the lion's share of its interactive resources to Web-related ventures. The company moved much of the content from MSN to the Web and poured more and more resources into developing and marketing new versions of the Internet Explorer browser and creating new standards such as the ActiveX programming language for the Web.

Overall, at the outset of 1996, Microsoft was committed to spending an estimated $800 million to $1.5 billion on various interactive media efforts over the next five years, including its investment in the MSNBC cable network and Web site. The all-out response by Bill Gates to Netscape, Sun Microsystems, and other leading Web technology companies is a testament to his competitiveness and his clout, as well as his agility.

FROM PULL TO PUSH

The Web itself is not immune to such disruptions. The first significant disruptive force has come from a Silicon Valley start-up called PointCast Inc. Whereas most Web sites must entice you to seek out and visit it, then sift through and "pull" information onto your PC screen, the PointCast Network works more like television: It pushes the information at you.

The basic idea is simple: Better for the news to come at you, rather than your having to go get the news. You only have to visit PointCast's Web site once—to register your age, gender, zip code, and other demographic information in return for a free download of the company's software. After it's installed on your hard drive, the program takes the place of your screen saver, automatically dialing up and retrieving news, information, and marketing material from the Internet—then flashing it on your screen whenever you get up to take a break.

Upon your return, you see on-screen menus of news stories all neatly organized in categories, such as national news, politics, international, business, sports, and weather. There's also the ability to view bulletins on certain companies and industries of interest. A customized stock ticker running across the bottom of your screen shows the latest price of the companies you want to track.

Plus, of course, in one corner of the screen, there are advertisements. These aren't the static banner ads found at most Web sites but animated color graphics—complete with racing cars, flying planes, flashing logos, and streaming slogans. Since the company already has all that demographic information, the ads could be targeted to groups of individuals. Men could get ads for Armani suits and women could get ads for Ann Taylor business attire, for instance. Hence the name PointCast: This service can point broadcast material at individual consumers.

The ads, of course, pay for PointCast to deliver all this software and information to you. Christopher R. Hassett, cofounder and chief executive officer, explains that PointCast works somewhat like television.

All of the news, information, and ads are assembled on server computers in Cupertino, California, at what Hassett calls a giant "broadcast" facility, not unlike those built by NBC, CBS, or ABC. At preselected intervals during the day, the computers of PointCast users automatically dial up the Internet to retrieve the information. This way, says Hassett, getting all this content has the "effortless" quality of TV.

PointCast itself is the very model of the modern agile company. It's software was made available on a test basis in February 1996. After enlisting potential customers to help iron out the bugs, the program was officially released in May. By the end of the year, the company had attracted more than two million users and nearly $50 million in venture capital funding. Chris Hassett, who started the company with fellow software engineer and brother Gregory Hassett, has also struck alliances with dozens of content suppliers, including CNN, Reuters, Time Warner's Pathfinder site, the *New York Times*, many local newspapers, and wire services from all over the world.

The company was firmly established in the market for only a few months before competition began to strike. Berkeley Systems Inc., makers of the popular "flying toaster" screen saver programs, released a new screen saver that offers news "channels" from *USA Today, Sports Illustrated, ZDNet,* and the *Wall Street Journal.* Even Microsoft got into the act, announcing that it plans to build a set of programs, called Active Desktop, into the next version of Windows.

PointCast moved to hold onto its lead by striking a deal with Microsoft to become part of Active Desktop and by developing new products for the corporate Intranet market. A special version of its software, called OneCast, is able to feed to PCs not only mass media news but also the kind of stuff that is found in internal company memos. So, an employee of XYZ Corp. can sit at his desk and read the news of the world along with XYZ Corp. information such as earnings announcements, new product releases, benefit program changes, personnel news, and even details of how the corporate softball team fared.

All the agile maneuvering of PointCast has been highly disruptive to all the other news suppliers and content creators on the Web. The PointCast notion of pushing the information at the consumer, in a sense, does away with *browsing* altogether. At least for the time that PointCast is on your screen, you don't need to visit the Web to find stuff.

As such, this push model forces a *separation* between the content and the *delivery* of content. If this model comes to dominate the Web, those in the business of creating content—CNN and the *New York Times*, for instance—no longer have to build their own Web sites; they simply have to license their material to PointCast, Microsoft, Berkeley Systems, and others in the business of finding an audience for their push-news delivery networks.

This is especially disruptive if you consider the business implications. On the one hand, when the *Times* licenses its content to Point-Cast, it brings in a new revenue stream. On the other hand, if people look to PointCast and not the *Times* Web site for their news, it will be PointCast, not the *Times*, that collects the lucrative advertising revenue. Equally important, the *Times* may lose its direct, interactive relationship with its Web audience members.

AGILITY IN THE FUTURE

Navigating these tricky waters will require extreme nimbleness. And the straits will get even more precarious if new software from start-up Marimba Inc. becomes as popular as the hype surrounding it suggests. Founded by Kim Polese and other former members of the Java team at Sun Microsystems, Marimba promises to take information-push to a whole new level.

Marimba's software, named Castanet, works like a television channel tuner. You subscribe to channels that appear as icons on your screen. Let's say you want the *Wall Street Journal* channel, the Microsoft channel, the Dilbert channel, the Yahoo! channel, the Sega channel, the Gap channel, the ESPN channel, the MTV channel, and the Sony Pictures channel. Castanet is in charge of maintaining a twenty-four-hour-per-day connection to the Internet and receiving a steady stream of updated content for all such channels.

Under this kind of a setup, consumers will *subscribe* to software from Microsoft and others, receiving regular upgrades to their hard drives, rather than having to go buy a box in a store. In addition, when something new comes in, Castanet will alert you and ask you if you want to see what's new. When you click OK, you might see a live news report from a *Wall Street Journal* editor, a commercial for the Gap's new fall lineup, a preview of the new Jim Carrey movie, or Mariah Carey video, and so on.

"Take your favorite Web site and envision it as a TV show," writes Jesse Freund in *Wired.* "What will it look like? How will it feel? How often will it be updated? What would you see? If Castanet is to fly, someone had better figure it out in a hurry."

Now, *that* requires agility. Imagine that higher-speed Internet connections make it possible to deliver streams of high-quality, real-time video and audio, not the grainy snippets that most Webophiles have become accustomed to downloading. Imagine if Web sites gave way to Web channels. This could force every media company and every marketer to overhaul their plans for the digital landscape.

These information-push technologies are, in fact, so radical that they bring us back to the original motivations for surfing the Web in the first place. Remember the Saatchi & Saatchi study from this book's introduction? People often surf the Web for the same reason they take up any hobby: It's a somewhat challenging activity in which the journey, rather than any specific destination, is the reward. People like the thrill of the hunt, the mystery of seeing what's out there, the reward of stumbling across something of interest. They like to control what they see, not sit back, fold their arms, and stare. It's an interactive medium, not a passive one.

Tim Berners-Lee, the inventor of the Web, has something to say about this conflict between pull and push, about this battle to make the

Web into more of a TV-like experience. In the future, he says, we will not only have a combination of both, but that push and pull will become part of one cohesive process. He believes that people will continue to browse the Web and hone hotlists of favorite sites. In addition, certain content and personalized information will be pushed at them via PointCast, Marimba, and similar software. "Push and pull at the *moment* are visible Web concepts," Berners-Lee says. "But they'll disappear. What's important is that some information changes rapidly and some information is more static. Some information you let in, and some you don't."

In other words, it will make sense to get some things pushed at you. But by no means will the Web morph into a fully information-push, passive medium. The Web is too successful in its current state to transform into something that goes against the grain of its basic reason for being. The psychology of someone sitting close up to a computer screen is completely different than someone reclining and watching TV at a distance. People might resent marketers who broadcast full-screen commercials to their computers while they are trying to get their work done.

But that doesn't mean that the technologies now represented by PointCast and Marimba won't find new applications that no one has thought of yet. Perhaps such software could deliver finally on the promise of truly intelligent agents, alerting you to a great sale on a washing machine, tennis racket, or other item you are in the market for right now.

In the future, disruptive technologies will be introduced with regularity. Rapid change is the only sure thing about the future of technology. The people who first figure out how to best take advantage of these changes will generate enormous value for themselves and for their customers. Those that don't spot these opportunities will be left under water. In the end, only the agile will survive.

<Chapter Summary>
• The Web economy is a world in which a competitive advantage may only last a few months, if not weeks. Those running Web ventures must act quickly and take a proactive stance toward deploying new technologies before competitors do.
• Your customers are your best judges. Let your most loyal customers test, troubleshoot, debug, and try out new Web services before you formally introduce them.
• The best way to move fast is to keep close tabs on what customers want. Take E-mail feedback and suggestions from customers seriously—and respond to their questions and complaints.
• Develop a priority list of new features, improvements, and services for your Web site, adding new ones at regular intervals.
• Recognize when "disruptive technologies" burst on the scene and alter the way the Web economy works; develop a strategy on how best to capitalize on these technologies.

<EPILOGUE>

The Web Effect—How It's Changing Life As We Know It

NEW GROWTH THEORY

The Web is having a ripple effect that reaches well beyond its own waters. As individuals and companies adhere to the principles of Webonomics, it is already pushing wavelets of change into many aspects of our lives. We're not just talking about a shake up of the media business and new quirks in the way we communicate with each other, but a basic shift in the structure of the economy itself and how people and institutions fit into it. Depending on your point of view, some of these changes are for the better and some for the worse.

A microcosm of the information age economy in pure form, the Web represents a triumph of mind over matter. More than a new medium, it's an infrastructure for commerce, a universal conduit of ideas, a parallel universe where people are exchanging information on an unprecedented scale. Stock market valuations are so high for so many companies involved in the Web precisely because the Web is a world composed of the most valuable type of property: the intellectual kind. Much of the focus has been on these specialty companies, the software firms that sell products and services for setting up Web sites. But the biggest impact will come among mainstream businesses in every industry. And these changes are being driven by the customers who interact with those companies.

The biggest enemy and friend of companies trying to grow their business on the Web is free-market capitalism itself. True capitalists believe in efficient markets: business environments in which companies are free to connect with customers unencumbered by high transaction costs, poor communication, and middlemen that fail to add any value. The Web doesn't suffer from any of this. Indeed, the Web is often *too efficient* a marketspace, sometimes even too efficient to make a profit. The complaint of many companies that have set up shop here is that it's hard to sustain a competitive advantage. Customers are so empowered that they expect not only abundant choice and instantaneous service but also don't expect to pay much for it.

As more and more companies pile onto the Web, pricing pressure can only increase. "We will see price cutting and price pressure that we haven't seen since Sam Walton entered the retail business," says John Sviokla, associate professor at the Harvard Business School. Just look at the market for books. Jeffrey Bezos, founder of the Amazon book site notes that "net margins in traditional book stores are usually from 3 to 5 percent," meaning a bookstore will pocket a slim 60¢ to $1 on each $20 sale. On the Web, Bezos sees a lower cost of doing business, higher volume, and an even more hypercompetitive environment taking shape. "We won't have the luxury" of having even those kind of margins, he says. "In the long run, net margins should be lower in the online world because it enables frictionless comparison shopping."

Barely making a few pennies on each transaction sounds like pretty grim business. Unless you look at it from a different perspective. Amazon should not be compared to actual stores selling books. Rather, it's in the business of selling *information about* books. The authors and publishers make most of the money from the book itself. The value that Amazon adds is in the reviews, the recommendations, the advice, the information about new and upcoming releases, the user interface, the community of interest around certain subjects. Since it's in the business of selling information about books, it gets paid every time that information leads to a sale. Yes, Amazon will arrange to deliver the book to your door, but you as a customer are really paying them for the information that led to your purchase.

If sales volume gets high enough, this business of selling information about products can become a fabulously lucrative business. The cost of providing information on the Web is low, especially when compared to the high fixed costs of building, renting, and maintaining brick-and-mortar stores—and stocking and restocking inventory. On the Web, once you sell a piece of information, you still have the same bits to sell again and again. That's the beauty of intellectual property. And this model applies across countless industries. Virtual Vineyards doesn't sell wine but information about wine, and automobile sites don't sell cars but information about cars. And so on.

If one applies traditional economic thinking to such a world, the outlook, again, would look pretty dim. In the early nineteenth century, economist David Ricardo argued that competition in a capitalist society will drive down wages to subsistence levels, that competition between entrepreneurs will prevent consumers from paying more, while competition between workers will prevent raises. This is "the law of diminishing returns" and "the iron law of wages," which later prompted historian Thomas Carlyle to call economics "the dismal science." Malthus, Ricardo's contemporary, might have been the most famous pessimist in economic history, but it was Ricardo himself who most precisely defined this deep pessimism.

Webonomics splits with the dismal economics of the past. The Web economy is not necessarily a world in which competing companies fight over market share and the limited fruits of the marketplace, with diminishing returns for all. Instead, we are moving into a new era in which value-creation is the bottom line. Total consumption of books, software, knowledge, and indeed all intellectual property may be far greater than we ever imagined. Instead of fighting over a limited pie, companies that create something valuable could keep expanding these markets. As long as the information captures the attention of the right people, it will do well.

Look at all the high-tech companies with low or no profits but high stock valuations. Employees of these companies are creating value and taking paychecks home to their families, even though the companies they work for are for the time being spending more money than they are taking in. Such companies have succeeded in inventing new markets and capturing the attention of the public. Yahoo! and InfoSeek, for example, may not be profitable, but they are creating value and being rewarded for such.

Some of these developments can be explained by what's being called "New Growth Theory," best defined by Paul Romer, a young economics professor at Stanford University, and the son of Colorado Governor Roy Romer. Paul Romer adheres to the basic free-market principles of Adam Smith, but with some key twists. Traditional economic thinking only considers two main factors of production: capital and labor. Romer elevates a third component: technology.

Whereas traditional economists tend to view technological developments such as cars and computers as random discoveries, a sort of "manna from heaven," New Growth Theory holds that such development increases in proportion to the amount of investment people apply to it. Yes, any one individual's efforts to advance technology might be a random shot in the dark, but when many individuals are working on similar problems, someone is almost certain to create something valuable. Instead of being *exogenous* to, or outside, economics, he says, technology is *endogenous,* or central, to it. Thus, as we devote more and more resources to technology, we achieve permanently higher economic growth.

Ideas cause economic growth, Romer postulates. The U.S. economy used to be driven by the manufacturing of things. The people who worked on the assembly lines were paid to do a repetitive routine, not discover a better way to do that routine. The number of those repetitive manufacturing jobs has been on the decline in the United States for more than twenty years. Meanwhile, the number of jobs in which people are paid to invent new ideas, find new markets, and improve the process of making things are increasing. "Cognitive skills are going to be permanently more valuable and unskilled labor permanently less valuable," Romer told *Forbes* magazine.

All this is why the Web is a world of boundless opportunity. The Web is all about the discovery of ideas. There's no manufacturing going on. A person who is in charge of Web strategy for a corporation must be constantly on the lookout for better ways to market products, better ways to connect with customers, new graphic designs, new ways to bring in revenue. The discovery of such ideas brings growth. And it might not even be growth at a competitor's expense, but fresh growth that expands, not redivides, the economic pie. There are an infinite number of ideas in the universe waiting to be discovered. And knowledge can be organized in literally countless ways—some that have tremendous value to people. The job of those running Web start-ups or Web sites must be to seek and implement valuable ideas.

Another departure from classic economics is Romer's views on monopolies. Ricardo believed that monopolies are bad and for the most part won't happen because fierce competition enables smaller players to undercut the market leader's prices, thus gaining market share. The monopolies that do happen, therefore, are aberrations that should be busted by the government.

We now know that this thinking cannot easily be applied to high-technology industries, where monopolies happen all the time and governments can't keep up with the changes fast enough to exercise trust-busting. Microsoft, for instance, holds sway in the PC operating system market, and Intel controls the PC microprocessor market. The cost barriers to creating and establishing a new PC operating system or chip design is enormous. Even if a rival design is better and undercuts Microsoft or Intel on price, the company that controls the technical standards will be able to maintain the monopoly. Even the well-funded IBM, with OS/2, couldn't break Microsoft's hold.

Romer not only believes that monopolies are inevitable in high-tech; he believes they're beneficial. When the founders of Netscape, for instance, saw an opportunity to gain a monopoly in an entirely new area, they had great incentive to discover new ideas and create a valuable new market. This doesn't mean that monopolies are permanent.

Romer simply believes they should be allowed to run their course in the marketplace with minimal government intervention—until the technology landscape shifts. On the Web, software start-ups and media companies are constantly striving to invent and dominate new markets, in the process achieving economic growth that ultimately is to the benefit of everyone.

THE JOBS SHIFT

By now, everyone from left-wing academics to right-wing populists have blamed computer technology for killing jobs. No doubt, technology has played a key role in corporate downsizing and "reengineering" efforts at banks, insurance companies, manufacturing enterprises, and just about every other type of company. And the trend toward self-service applications on the Web may indeed have the potential to send additional categories of jobs the way of the milkman.

But on the whole, there's no evidence that computerization causes mass unemployment. "The question isn't about whether technology is killing jobs," says Arthur Andreassen, a senior economist with the U.S. Bureau of Labor Statistics in Washington, D.C., "but about the revolutionary change technology is having on the economic structure." Andreassen acknowledges that computer technology is indeed making certain jobs obsolete. But it's also creating new ones at the same time—with the net effect being positive.

Cars and software tell it all. About 800,000 people in the United States are now employed in automobile manufacturing—about the same number as the mid-1950s, despite a leap of 100 million in the overall population. Meanwhile, the high-tech sector has been booming. In the United States, for example, employment in computer software and related services has doubled, from about 500,000 jobs in 1984 to more than 1 million by 1994, according to the bureau. It projects that there will be a total of 1.8 million full-time positions in that field by the year 2005. If New Growth Theory is correct, that estimate might be terribly low.

In almost every industry, the rush to apply the principles of Webonomics will accelerate this massive shift in the workforce—not just in the United States but worldwide. This is not to say that those in fear of being among the next crop of downsized managers, laid-off manufacturing workers, and obsolete service personnel should all become HTML programmers. But they should understand the way technology in general and the Web in particular is transforming their jobs and their industry. And they should be looking for ways to ride the wave, not fight it.

A widely quoted study from Alan Krueger, a Princeton economist, found that people who use computers in their work earn an average 15 percent more money than those who don't. Meanwhile, a much more targeted study of real-estate agents found that those who use a personal computer in their job make $74,000 more—over double the salary—than those who don't. The fact is that these studies are all over the map. And it's difficult to measure precisely how much more money computer users earn. But the bottom line is clear: those who do have an edge.

That edge has something to do with using the computer to discover new ideas and to learn new skills. Staying ahead of the technology curve can be a do-or-die situation. "Technical change by its nature is a cruel process," says Joel Mokyr, an economic historian at Northwestern University. "It has a tendency to make your skills redundant when you're most vulnerable." Citing "the fallout from rapidly changing technology," Federal Reserve Chairman Alan Greenspan says that "human skills are subject to obsolescence at a rate perhaps unprecedented in history."

The pervasive fear in the 1980s was that manufacturing was declining and giving way to a lower-wage service economy, in which flipping burgers would become the new economy's signature job, if not the predominant one. That prediction was not quite accurate. While traditional manufacturing jobs have indeed continued to dwindle, what is rising to take its place is much better than most people imagined. The signature job of the current U.S. economy is not burger flipper, but bit flipper.

Many of the people who do stay ahead of the technology curve are among the growing numbers of people who make their living either partially or entirely due to the Web. How many jobs is the Web responsible for? It's hard to tell. But there is evidence of Web-fueled job growth at nearly every level of the workforce. Web-savvy kids now coming out of school—even kids *in* school—are making $20, $40, $50, $80 per hour developing Web pages. And just like every mom and pop started a video store in the 1980s, every geek and dweeb is starting an Internet service provider or Web site development shop in the 1990s. High-tech areas such as San Francisco and New York are each served by more than 100 companies that provide local consumers and businesses with access to the Internet, usually for a monthly fee.

Virtually all of these jobs have been created since 1994. And the largest category of these Web-related jobs are at mainstream companies in every industry. A study by *WebWeek* magazine found that most Fortune 500 companies now have Web departments. They tend to be relatively small, with half of those surveyed employing between two and five people. But about 12 percent of these departments employ twenty or more. And salaries are very good, especially for the top Webmaster in charge of the corporate site or strategy. About 68 percent of Webmasters surveyed reported making more than $45,000 per year.

The development of corporate Web sites has spawned a wide range of jobs based on a wide range of skills, some that don't even require much technical proficiency. The *WebWeek* study turned up dozens of corporate job titles that hardly existed a few years ago, among them digital communications specialist, electronic marketing manager, Internet developer, security administrator, new media manager, director of Internet services, network content manager, Web applications developer, multimedia technician, and online content developer. In addition, respondents to the survey reported some fairly creative new job titles, among them cyber commander, Webmeister, Web mistress, Web wizard and, supremely, Web goddess.

WHO NEEDS GOVERNMENTS, ANYWAY?

The most influential economist of the twentieth century, John Maynard Keynes, is most famous for his theory that high unemployment could only be fought with high government spending. The government, in his view, has the power to create jobs, stimulate growth, and manage the economy. Ever since Franklin D. Roosevelt based his New Deal programs on Keynesian principles—using government as a lever to catapult the country out of the Great Depression—this theory became the conventional wisdom of the land. Generations of postwar college students learned the basic principles of economics from the textbook by Paul Samuelson, an avid Keynesian. Even Richard Nixon once quipped: "We're all Keynesians now."

Keynesian economic policies have certainly served industrialized economies well—up to a point. But we seem to have already entered the post-Keynesian age, with President Bill Clinton declaring that "the era of big government is over" in his 1996 State of the Union address. Pure Keynesian economics is out of favor among both major political parties in the United States. With near universal pressure to cut spending, permanently downsize government, and put power back in the hands of entrepreneurs and families, the ability to use government spending to stimulate short-term growth has been dramatically diminished.

If Keynesian theories have faded, what's to take their place? In our high-tech, free-market society, who needs government to manage the economy, anyway? Romer, for one, argues that government has a role to play when it comes to investing in new technologies. While some libertarians argue that the invention of the Internet by a Pentagon research agency in the late 1960s was a fluke, Romer argues that it was the result of broad-based investment. And he believes that government should step up such investment in the future, supplementing private funding of technological research. Instead of trying to micromanage short-term economic cycles, the Federal government should be in the business of planting seeds for long-term growth.

That doesn't mean that governments should have the power to decide how people use technology, however. The intense public backlash against the Communications Decency Act should serve as proof of that. Supported by the Christian Coalition and other religious groups, the CDA was passed by Congress as a small part of a sweeping telecommunications reform act in 1995. An attempt to bar "indecent" material from appearing on the Internet, the law was deemed an unconstitutional restraint on free speech when it was struck down by a Philadelphia court in June 1996.

Governments without such constitutional protections are faring better at such clampdowns. The corporate nation-state of Singapore, for instance, became the first country in Asia to pass regulations to stop what it calls "Internet abuse." Singapore's definition of illegal and subversive material is vague but haunting: "That which tends to bring the government into hatred or contempt, or which excites disaffection against the government." With a population of three million and one of the world's highest densities of Internet subscribers, Singapore's attempt at censorship should be watched closely by governments and Internet users all over the world.

ACCELERATING TECHNOLOGICAL CHANGE

The nine principles of Webonomics are designed to withstand the test of time and any technological change. Since the principles are based on supply and demand, human behavior, and common sense, they will remain true, regardless of all the many unresolved technological issues. The quality of your Web site will *always* be more important than the quantity of visitors. Marketers on the Web should *always* be looking for results, not just exposure. Consumers will *always* want compensation for their data, and they will *always* seek self-service. And so on.

But that doesn't mean technological changes are of little importance. The mechanics and details of building a presence on the Web are very much affected by the accelerating technological changes that we see and read about every day.

Perhaps the hottest technological debate in the industry has to do with whether most people will continue surfing the Web using current personal computer designs, or whether a whole new class of "network computer" devices will reach a mass market looking for cheaper, easier-to-use information appliances.

Microsoft CEO Bill Gates has something to say about this issue. He maintains that the PC of the future will be smaller, cheaper, and more powerful—a safe bet, for sure. But he also says that one major change will be that the PC of the future will always be turned on and connected to the Internet, as opposed to cumbersome dial-up procedures that people have to go through now.

This prediction presupposes that the Internet will take on some of the qualities of cable TV networks. Currently, data on the Internet is now primarily delivered in small packets, or chunks, of bytes over ordinary phone lines and dial-up modems. By clicking on hyperlinks or typing in the address of a Web site, users are requesting to receive the packets. When too many requests flood the network during peak usage, network response time bogs down.

Cablelike networks would largely do away with such "packet-switching." With cable, programming is always flowing through the wires in a continuous stream. Instead of requesting data, the consumer simply tunes in what he or she wants. Quicker response time would encourage computer users to turn to the Web more often and integrate it more fully into their daily routines. Gates has predicted that cable modems and faster, digital phone lines will make such a scenario possible fairly soon—by 1998 or so. But full-fledged "video streaming," in which uninterrupted, full-motion pictures are delivered over the Web would still be a problem. Due to constraints on the main Internet "backbone," Tim Berners-Lee has said that he doesn't expect that technology to be feasible until early next century.

When it comes to basic computer designs, Microsoft's competitors see things differently. Scott McNealy of Sun Microsystems and Larry Ellison of database software giant Oracle Corp. believe that Web surfers don't need huge expensive hard drives that store more and more complex software. The Web, not the personal computer itself, is the "new center of gravity" for the computer industry, Ellison said, as he introduced the NC, or network computer.

Such machines, due to ship in volume in 1997, are priced under $500. Instead of buying expensive software in stores, users of NC's would rent cheap programs downloaded over the Web, for use as needed. That's the beauty of Java, McNealy argues. Once a program is written in the Java language, "it runs on anything, anywhere, quickly and safely." Such appliances are supposedly as easy to use as a coffeemaker with no complex hardware or software to tinker with.

Gates counters these arguments, saying that consumers like their full-blown personal computers, and they do not yearn for stripped-down terminals. Yes, computers are still pretty expensive, costing $2,000 and up for the typical new model. But that's what people want. "The market to date has opted for more power at the same price," Gates said. But that could change. New price competition has already prompted Gates to use his clout to convince Compaq, Dell, and other top makers to introduce full-functional PCs for well under $1,000, thus cutting the price difference between an NC and a PC. As usual, Gates seems to have the edge in this battle.

Another raging debate concerns whether so-called "Web TVs" will catch on. These are set-top-box-size devices that sell for under $300 and plug into your television set or VCR. Like a computer, it connects to the Internet via a standard phone line. Eventually, it should work through cable lines or satellite transceivers, too. To use it, consumers are supposed to sit on their sofas and click their remote controls, basically treating the Web as if it were another set of TV channels. These machines are sold by Sony, Philips, and other consumer electronics companies. Gateway 2000 also sells this kind of gizmo.

Similar devices have failed in the past. Remember CD-I, aka "The Imagination Machine," from Philips? You probably don't, despite Philips's all-out efforts to market it in the early 1990s as the ultimate Christmas present from Dad to the kids. This was a multimedia CD-ROM-type player that attached to television sets, letting people play games, consult encyclopedias, take tours of art museums, and other fun stuff. Even after Philips cut the initial $1,000 list price several times, it found virtually no takers.

Then came the promise of "interactive television," as envisioned by all the big cable and telephone companies. Remember 500 channels? Remember interactive shopping and banking on TV and play-along game shows and tens of thousands of movies on demand? Technical glitches and low consumer interest doomed most of the experiments. The fact remains that people have never expressed much of a desire to interact with their TVs in any meaningful way. They just want to plop down on the sofas, turn on the entertainment, tune out their higher brain functions, and exercise their constitutional right to stare vacantly at the tube, resting assured that interactive television is little more than an oxymoron.

This is essentially why the WebTV idea, as currently conceived, is doomed. TV is for entertainment. Surfing the Web can be entertaining, but that's not the primary purpose. When online, people are in an entirely different, information-seeking mode. Once Web surfing is transferred to a remote-control-from-the-couch experience rather than a mouse-and-keyboard-at-the-desk one, the Web simply ceases to be the participatory, interactive medium that it is.

It remains doubtful that people will ever enjoy sitting in their living rooms reading text or even looking at graphics. When they are watching TV, people expect not only full-motion, expensively produced video but also narrative stories that have a beginning, middle, and end. The Web has no beginning, end, top, or bottom. It's a hyperlinked world of interrelated information. PCs of the future will indeed become better and better at displaying video, and TVs of the future will have more and more computing power. But people will continue to want to have both machines, using them for different purposes.

THE NEW MEDIA LANDSCAPE

The sudden arrival of the World Wide Web over the past few years can be compared to "the first ten seconds of the big bang," says Jeffrey Bezos. "So much has happened in a very short time frame." Extending this cosmic metaphor, he says that we are entering a more gradual growth phase in which the new media landscape is forming right before our eyes. "Now," he adds, "we go into the process of planetary accretion."

How is this new media landscape shaping up? "Time has ceased, space has vanished. We now live in a global village . . . a simultaneous happening. . . . Electronic circuitry profoundly involves men with one another. Information pours upon us, instantaneously and continuously. As soon as information is acquired, it is very quickly replaced by still newer information."

It's been thirty years since Marshall McLuhan wrote those words. And it's a remarkably apt description of the World Wide Web. McLuhan's idea of a global village in which people could witness happenings in far-off cultures was widely believed to have come true in the TV age. With the advent of CNN in the 1980s, all the world had the same instantaneous news. People all over the planet were now watching events as they unfolded.

But in a way, mass-media culture didn't bring about greater understanding among the people of the world. The triumph of mass media over everything didn't forge a cohesive village of the world's population, as much as it simply enabled the world's population to tune into the antics of a relatively few elite entertainers. In the words of Paul Simon, "staccato signals of constant information" has produced a "loose affiliation of millionaires and billionaires." If we are living in a global village, then the village is run by Mayor Madonna and policed by Sheriff Schwarzeneggar. Wolf Blitzer is the town crier, with Jim Carrey as the village idiot. And the whole place is owned by Disney and Time Warner, which have joint marketing deals with McDonald's and Coca-Cola.

Only with the Web is McLuhan's prophesy fully realized. In his 1967 book, *The Medium Is the Massage,* he illustrated the concept of "electronic interdependence" with a picture of African villagers gathered round a tribal storyteller, the audience not only watching but reacting to the story in real time. In a true global village, ordinary villagers should be able to participate in the storytelling. In some of his writings, McLuhan seemed to fear his own vision, with all the world in reach of the same sounds suddenly panicking at the beating of tribal drums. At other times he was optimistic about it, foreseeing the day when instant communications would bridge ancient boundaries. Actually, it's difficult to find two readers of McLuhan who interpret the meaning of the global village in the same way. And that's probably the way McLuhan wanted it.

The future is anyone's guess. But it's conceivable to narrow down the possibilities. And some people are doing just that. In an attempt to prepare for the uncertain media landscape of the next century, advertising giant McCann-Erickson Worldwide developed what it calls its "visioning" process, breaking down the future into three potential scenarios:

The first scenario is called "TechnoUtopia." Everything works out as big corporations want. Everyone has their own personal media device, and that device tells them to buy, buy, buy. Marketers inhabit a heaven on earth, in which they are able to target their messages to the appropriate consumers—and always receive the desired response. Advertising and the media it sponsors become one and the same.

The second scenario is called "Pay to Play," and it's hell for marketers but sheer bliss for wealthy consumers. All the best media content—TV specials, live sports, valuable databases, well-edited magazines, and news reports—are only available via pricey subscriptions and pay-per-view. All the best Web sites are like cable premium channels. Those who can afford it pay for control, convenience, and the avoidance of advertising altogether. Intelligent agent software finds exactly what people want, charges their credit cards, and filters out the ads. An expanding underclass that cannot pay for any of this is left to watch only the leftover mind-pollution on free, ad-sponsored TV.

Finally, the third scenario is called "Revolution du Jour." Waves of media hype tout the latest and greatest innovations, with little regard for what's really good. Groups of consumers lurch to adopt what's new, only to find much of it obsolete within a short time. Business markets are chaotic. Polarized debate rages between Luddites and techno-savvy users, with the vast middle not knowing what's going on. There's a few hugely successful technology ventures and lots of failures. Big business alliances are struck—only to collapse as the market shifts.

This last scenario should sound somewhat familiar. It's largely what we've been experiencing in the digital future of the 1990s. In some ways, this big ball of confusion is fun, epitomizing the excitement of free-market capitalism. Whereas the first two scenarios are implausible, according to McCann forecasting, Revolution du Jour represents not only the present but the foreseeable future as well. But at the end of the day, all the hype in this scenario is besides the point. That's why it's so important for those navigating the new media landscape not to get swept up in the day-to-day confusion, but rather to stick to basic, guiding principles of doing business in such an environment.

If there's a central message in all this, it's that the future of all the communications technology being deployed all over the globe is in the hands of the individual sitting at his or her computer. The idea that the ordinary citizen would have immense control over far-flung computer networks is the opposite of what many people predicted. In the classic book *Nineteen Eighty-Four*, for instance, George Orwell wrote of a future filled with sheer horror, a society in which a central authority uses communications technology to enforce absolute power over everyone's lives and achieve the objectives of the state. The specter of a Big Brother has haunted us ever since.

Although he lived at the same time as Orwell, Vannevar Bush held a completely opposite vision for the future. He predicted that the natural outgrowth of information technology would not be totalitarianism but a world in which more and more power would shift to the ordinary individual. He hoped that people would one day be able to do great things with what he called "the great record" of all human knowledge. "The applications of science have built man a well-supplied house, and are teaching him to live healthily therein," Bush wrote. "They have enabled him to throw masses of people against one another with cruel weapons. They may yet allow him truly to encompass the great record and . . . to wield that record for his true good." Instead of technologies of enslavement, we have technologies of freedom.

<ACKNOWLEDGMENTS>

In March 1995, I sat down with John Battelle, then my editor at *Wired,* to discuss story ideas. It was a foggy Saturday morning, and the converted San Francisco warehouse that *Wired* inhabits was unusually quiet. But the idea John proposed to me sent my head buzzing. He wanted a story about business models of World Wide Web sites. How does one make money on the Web? Where does the revenue come from? Subscriptions? Advertising? Transactions?

The assignment was an especially tricky one. Every newspaper, magazine, publishing, and media company on the planet needed to know the answers to these questions. Not to mention marketers of almost every conceivable kind of product and service. Indeed, anyone in any kind of business—from retail to financial services to travel and tourism—had to figure out how the emerging digital marketplace would change the nature of their businesses. But it was simply too early to write this story. Back then, there were only a few dozen serious media and marketing sites on the Web. And not enough time had passed to see which business models worked and which didn't. I told John I would think about this idea and get back to him.

Then, that summer, Netscape went public, and the whole thing went into frenzy mode. I had been reporting on information technology for nearly ten years, but I had not seen anything like the cyclone of activity marking these early days of the Web. I zapped some E-mail to John telling him that I'd like to start working on the Web story.

As I delved into it, one question led to another. If the most successful Web sites weren't willing to charge subscription fees, would there be enough advertising to support these ventures? If advertising was the key revenue source, what then do the advertisers want out of the medium? If they themselves don't know, then what *should* they want? That begs another question: Why would a consumer spend time interacting with an advertisement? Could you even call it an advertisement?

I interviewed dozens of people, including marketers at companies such as AT&T and Chrysler, editors at media companies such as *USA Today* and Time Warner. I spoke to executives at advertising agencies and people running start-up businesses on the Web, with names such as I/Pro, Individual Inc., Organic Online, and Starwave.

While out for a walk one day, it hit me that what was emerging on the Web was nothing less than an indigenous, information-based economy. It wouldn't be long before every company, every media outlet, every social institution, every part of government, as well as millions of individuals would have a presence on the Web. The Web was looking more and more like a place where people would be spending a significant part of their day exchanging their money, their time, and their attention for information, goods, and services. There needed to be principles to explain why things happen as they do here. If the Web was an economy, then there had to be a field of study called Webonomics.

This epiphany finally gave shape and structure to all the reporting I had done. I was finally able to write the story, which was published in the February 1996 issue of *Wired*. The article, entitled "Advertising Webonomics 101," clearly tapped into a deep vein of interest, receiving more attention than anything I had ever written before. Some of the principles made some people uncomfortable. Advertising industry executives complained that I was going too far—that the entire field of advertising really didn't have to be reinvented. Most of the more than 100 electronic mail messages that came swooshing over the wires to me had a common theme: People simply wanted to know more about Webonomics.

I'm happy to say that I answered every one of those messages and have been keeping in touch with many of these readers. Some have invited me to speak at conferences, at corporations, and at universities. It was this feedback that convinced me to expand on the ideas presented in the *Wired* article and develop a full-blown exploration of the principles of Webonomics.

Thanks, of course, to John Battelle, and to *Wired* managing editor and my former *Business Week* colleague Russ Mitchell, who edited the story and forced me to produce something original; to my agent Elyse Cheney, who helped get the book project off the ground and to the right publisher; to my editor Lauren Marino, as well as to Kati Steele and the entire team at Broadway Books, who had the energy to publish on a tight schedule; to Lisa Braun, Eric Marcus, Annette Tonti, Chunka Mui, and Rich Schroth of the CSC Vanguard team; to Anthony Schneider of Webzeit; to Mark Katz at the Sound Bite Institute; to Russ Neuman at Harvard's Kennedy School; and to Edith Bjornson and Cathy Clark at the Markle Foundation. Special thanks to the scores of people who gave their time, ideas, and insights during interviews. Too numerous to mention here, they are listed in the Notes section. Finally, heaps of gratitude to my parents, my friends, and my family for their love and support.

<NOTES>

<INTRODUCTION>

Page 1: The July 1996 issue of *Wired,* page 36, reports that the InterNIC had approximately 205,000 registered domain names as of the beginning of 1996. The number jumped to more than 340,000 by the beginning of April. That's 135,000 new sites in three months, or 45,000 per month, or 1,500 per day, or 62.5 per hour, for an average of 1.041666 per minute.

Page 5: Neil Rudenstine speech at Harvard Conference on the Internet & Society; May 28, 1996.

Page 6: "As We May Think," by Vannevar Bush, the *Atlantic Monthly,* July 1945. Story downloaded from the *Atlantic*'s area on America Online.

Pages 7–8: "The Curse of Xanadu," by Gary Wolf, *Wired,* June 1995, page 137.

Page 7: "The World Wide Web: Origins & Beyond," paper by Lenny Zeltser, of the University of Pennsylvania. Published 1995. Available at homepage.seas.upenn.edu/~lzeltser/WWW/#History_Hypertext.

Page 8: "WorldWideWeb: Proposal for a HyperText Project," by Tim Berners-Lee et al, published November 12, 1990. Available at /www.w3.org/pub/WWW/Proposal.

Pages 9–10: Speech by and interview with Tim Berners-Lee at the MIT Media Laboratory's News in the Future symposium, May 24, 1996. Excerpt from his 1995 MIT speech was taken from Berners-Lee's home on the Web. An extensive biography and catalog of his speeches, papers, and presentations is published on the Web site of the World Wide Web Consortium at MIT; www.w3.org/hypertext/WWW/People/Berners-Lee-Bio.html.

Pages 11–12: "The Second Phase of the Revolution Has Begun," by Gary Wolf, *Wired,* October 1994, page 116.

Page 13: "Netscape Seeks Closer Probe of Microsoft: Letter to Justice Dept. Raises Allegations of Antitrust Violations," by Elizabeth Corcoran, the *Washington Post,* August 21, 1996, page F3; "U.S. Requests Microsoft Documents: Move in wake of Netscape demand for antitrust probe," by Hiawatha Bray, the *Boston Globe,* September 20, 1996, page C1.

Pages 15, 16: Results of the Georgia Institute of Technology's semiannual surveys of Web users can be found at www.cc.gatech.edu/gvu/user_surveys. The survey summaries present data on gender, income, frequency of usage, what people use the Web for, occupational categories of Web users, regional breakdown by continent, political affiliations, technical expertise, and suggestions for improving the Web. The site also points to other studies of Web demographics and usage.

Page 16: A. C. Nielsen figures from *Net Marketing,* by Bruce Judson, (Wolf New Media, 1996).

Pages 16–17: Coopers & Lybrand study, published in June 1996.

Page 17: "The Interactive Consumer," a Saatchi & Saatchi study, as reported in the February 1996 edition of BackChannel, the interactivity newsletter of the American Association of Advertising Agencies (AAAA).

Page 18: "Backlogs of History," by Cullen Murphy, the *Atlantic Monthly,* May 1996, page 20.

Page 19: "Web Sites: What Customers Want and Do Not Want," Gartner Group Research Note, November 9, 1995.

<CHAPTER ONE>

Pages 21–22, 26–27: Top-ten search terms provided in interview with Louis Monier, technical leader of Alta Vista at Digital Equipment Corp., April 1996.

Pages 22–23: Interviews with Eileen Kent of Playboy Enterprises, September 1995 and April 1996.

Page 24: Jupiter Communications data on the top twenty-five Web advertisers and top twenty-five Web publishers from "The Web Ads Up," *Information Week,* August 5, 1996, page 44.

Pages 24–26: Interviews with David Thau, cofounder of Bianca's Smut Shack, April and July 1996.

Page 28: Interview with Andrew Nibley, editor of Reuters NewMedia, May 1996.

Page 29: "Intellectual Popcorn for the Net," by Max Frankel, the *New York Times Magazine*, Word & Image column, April 21, 1996, page 26.

Pages 29–31: Interview with Lorraine Cichowski, vice president, USA Today Information Network, October 1995.

Page 30, *Presstime* magazine survey published April 1996. Results summarized in Associated Press story, April, 26, 1996.

Pages 31–33: Interview with Barry Parr, *San Jose Mercury News*, September 1995.

Page 34: Interview with Mark Kvamme, CEO of CKS Group, July 1996.

Page 35: Figures on the *Wall Street Journal* Interactive Edition from "Testing Whether Internet Readers Will Pay," by Mike Allen, the *New York Times*, September 16, 1996.

Pages 36–38: Interview with Mike Slade, CEO and Tom Phillips, vice president, Starwave Corp., September 1995.

Page 40: Interviews with Walter Isaacson, former editor of Time Warner New Media, current managing editor of *Time* magazine, September and December 1995.

Pages 40–41: Interviews with Andrew Anker, president of Hotwired, September 1995 and June 1996.

Pages 42–43: Fish Wrap demonstration at MIT Media Laboratory, May 1996.

Pages 43–44: Interview with John Zahner, vice president of business development, at Individual Inc., September 1995.

Pages 44–45: CyberAtlas Web Advertising Roadmap, published by Internet Profiles (I/PRO), San Francisco, September 1996, cites the median figure of forty bookmarks per Web surfer.

<CHAPTER TWO>

Pages 47–48: Interview with Bob Austin, Volvo Cars of North America, October 1995.

Page 49: Interviews with Emily Green and Josh Bernoff, Forrester Research, October 1995 and April 1996.

Pages 49–50: Interview with Rich Everett, Chrysler Corporation, October 1995.

Page 50: "Budget Bungle Puts McDonald's in a Pickle," by Richard Gibson and Sally Goll Beatty, the *Wall Street Journal*, July 8, 1996, page B6.

Page 53: Interview with AT&T's Mary Lou Floyd, October, 1995.

Pages 53–54, 55: Interview with Steve Coffey, PC Meter, June 1996. Ratings figures are from PC Meter's research sample of 10,000 U.S. Web-surfing households.

Page 55: Average click-thru rate figure has been determined both quantitatively and anecdotally. I/PRO and DoubleClick published a September 1996 study, "The Web In Perspective: A Comprehensive Analysis of Ad Response," which reports the typical click-thru rate at about 3 percent. Meanwhile, PC Meter's Coffey says: "The figures you've quoted I've heard repeated throughout the industry, both from people selling space and from advertisers. Click-thru rates above 5 percent are very likely anomalies, and I think in the real world, there are a lot running well below 2 percent."

Pages 55–56: Interview with Bob Ivins, I/PRO, June 1996.

Pages 57–58: *Being Digital,* by Nicholas Negroponte, (Knopf, 1995), page 84.

Page 60: "Program Involvement: Are Moderate Levels Best for Ad Memory and Attitude Toward the Ad?"; *Journal of Advertising Research,* September–October 1995 v35 n5 p61(12). Article states that "advertising effectiveness is affected by behaviors such as talking, leaving the room, muting of commercials, or 'channel surfing.' "

Page 61: "Network's Advance Sales of Ads Expected to Match Last Year's," by Sally Goll Beatty, the *Wall Street Journal*, June 1996.

Page 61: Average agency commission figures confirmed by Martha Brown, communications manager, American Association of Advertising Agencies.

Page 61: *The Affluent Society,* by John Kenneth Galbraith, (Houghton Mifflin, 1958), page 131, Fourth Edition.

Page 64: Les Ottolenghi, Holiday Inn Worldwide, presentation at Harvard Conference on the Internet & Society, May 29, 1996. Ottolenghi has since moved to the Carlson Companies.

Pages 65–66: Mary Ann Campanetto, IBM's director of digital publishing and advertising, presentation at MIT Media Laboratory's News in the Future symposium, May 24, 1996.

Page 65: Denise Caruso statement about credibility from the Harvard Conference, May 29, 1996.

Page 66: "P&G Steps Up Ad Cyber-Surfing; Tide Could Have Major Effect," by Raju Narisetti, the *Wall Street Journal,* April 18, 1996, page B14.

Page 68: Figures from Forrester Research.

Page 70: Michael Bungey quote from BackChannel, the AAAA newsletter, February 1996, page 7.

<CHAPTER THREE>

Page 72: Interview with Rich Everett, Chrysler Corporation, October 1995.

Page 73: Interview with Mary Lou Floyd, AT&T, October 1995.

Page 74: *Wired* magazine's production and distribution costs from company's prospectus, September 1996, page 24.

Pages 74–75: Interviews with Andrew Anker, president of Hotwired, September 1995 and June 1996.

Pages 75–79: Interview with Firefly Network's Pattie Maes, May 1996; Interviews with Doug Weaver, Firefly's advertising sales chief, and Max Metral, Firefly's technology chief, June 1996.

Pages 79–80: Interviews with Bob Manni, group account director at Margeotes Fertitta & Partners, October 1995 and June 1996.

Pages 80–82: Interviews with Peggy Vessels, Jack Daniel Distillery, May and July 1996.

Page 83: "First Green Stamps. Now, Coupons (P&G Wants to Eliminate These Sales Boosters—and Rivals May Follow)," by Zachary Schiller, *Business Week,* April 22, 1996.

Pages 88–89: The Coalition for Advertising Supported Information & Entertainment was formed in 1994 as a joint program of the Association of National Advertisers and the AAAA.

Page 89: Interview with Ariel Poler, I/PRO, November 1995.

Page 90: "I/PRO Refocuses, Reduces Staff by 12 Percent," by Kathleen Murphy, *WebWeek,* September 23, 1996, page 56.

Page 90: "New Move to Protect Kids: Privacy Advocates Include the Young in Effort to Ban Sale of Databases," by Rory J. O'Connor, *San Jose Mercury News,* May 22, 1996.

<CHAPTER FOUR>

Page 93: Figures from the Chicago-based National Research Bureau published in the *Wall Street Journal,* March 14, 1996, page B1; Also: "Natural Selection and the Retail Industry: Curtailed Consumer Spending and an Imbalance Between Supply and Demand Persists, Putting Pressure on Centers to Redevelop," by Elyse Umlauf, *Building Design & Construction,* January 1994, page 30.

Page 94: Interview with Thomas W. Patterson, chief strategist, IBM's Electronic Commerce Internet Division, October 1996.

Pages 96–98: "What Makes Virtual Vineyards Rule?" by Fred Hapgood, Inc. Technology, 1996, No. 2, page 76.

Pages 98–101: Interview with Jeffrey Bezos, Amazon.com, September 1996.

Page 100: "A Literary Hangout—Without the Latte," by Kathy Rebello, *Business Week,* September 23, 1996, page 106.

Page 101: "How a Wall Street Whiz Found a Niche Selling Books on the Internet," by G. Bruce Knecht, the *Wall Street Journal,* May 16, 1996, page 1.

Page 101: "Amazon.com Forges New Sales Channel," by Susan Moran, *WebWeek,* August 19, 1996, page 46.

Pages 102–4: Interview with Rick Fernandes, CUC International, September 1995.

Page 104: "Retail's On-Line Advances," report by William Bluestein and Susan Sweet, Forrester Research, April 1996.

Pages 106–8: Interviews with Marisha Konkowski, JCPenney, May and October 1996; Presentation by Edward Sample, at MIT Media Laboratory's News in the Future symposium, May 24, 1996.

Page 110: "Making Money on the Net," by Kathy Rebello et al, *Business Week,* September 23, 1996, page 104.

Pages 111–13: Interview with Hans Koch, CEO of the Abele Owners' Network, October 1996.

Page 112: "Web Sites Provide Democratic Access to Home Listings," by Bradley Inman, *San Jose Mercury News,* August 31, 1996.

Page 113: Quotes by Becky Swann of the International Real Estate Directory from inter-active interview on the Boston.com site, July 1996.

Page 114: *The One-to-One Future,* by Don Peppers and Martha Rogers, (Currency/Dou-bleday, 1993), page 136.

Pages 114–16: "How Big A Bite?: On-line Grocery Stores Hope to Lead the Way into the Electronic Future . . . ," by Bill Richards, the *Wall Street Journal,* Selling in Cyberspace, Re-port on Technology, June 17, 1996, page R10.

Pages 114–15: Interview with Geoffrey E. Moore, Prodigy's director of market programs, May 1991.

Pages 115–16: "Peapod Picks, Delivers Groceries Ordered by PC; Time-pressed Families Use Computer Delivery Service," by Ed Rubinstein, *Discount Store News,* September 18, 1995, page 99.

<CHAPTER FIVE>

Page 120: "Trends in the World Wide Web Marketplace," ActivMedia, Inc., January 1996; Full research reports can be purchased from ActivMedia, Peterborough, N.H.

Pages 121–24: "Poised for Takeoff: The Travel Industry Is a Natural When It Comes to Cy-berspace Sales . . . ," by Scott McCartney, the *Wall Street Journal,* Selling in Cyberspace, Re-port on Technology, June 17, 1996, page R4.

Page 122: "Airlines Settle with Agents," by Mary R. Sandok, Associated Press, Septem-ber 4, 1996.

Page 124: "Segmenting the U.S. Travel Market According to Benefits Realized," by Stowe Shoemaker, *Journal of Travel Research,* Winter 1994, page 8.

Page 125: Interview with Henri Poole, CEO, Vivid Studios and the Vivid Travel Network, June 1996.

Pages 127–28: Gallup Poll reported in the *Sacramento Bee,* May 31, 1996, "Banking Com-petitors Moving in After Wells Fargo-First Interstate Merger," by Gilbert Chan.

Pages 128–30: Interview with Gailyn Johnson, Wells Fargo Bank, September 1996.

Page 135: "IRS to Lay Off Up to 4,800 in Wake of Budget Cuts," the *Wall Street Journal,* August 8, 1996.

Pages 135–36: "Registry Gets on Infobahn," by Simson Garfinkle, the *Boston Globe,* Au-gust 22, 1996, page C4.

Page 136: Interview with Ross Burger, LifeQuote of America, September 1996.

<CHAPTER SIX>

Page 139: Interview with David Reed, formerly with Interval Research, July 1995.

Page 140: "Free Airline Miles Become a Potent Tool for Selling Everything; 'Second Na-tional Currency' Even Used by Charities, Is a New Profit Center," by Scott McCartney, the *Wall Street Journal,* April 15, 1996, page A1.

Page 141: "AOL Fights to Keep Its Customers On-Line," by Thomas E. Weber et al, the *Wall Street Journal,* August 8, 1996, page B1.

Page 147: "Payments on the Web," report by David Weisman et al, Forrester Research, March 1996. States that 84 percent of forty-two Web merchants surveyed accept credit card payments online. Some merchants report a slightly lower percentage of customers ordering with credit cards online, while others report a slightly higher percentage. The range of 75 to 95 percent covers most of these merchants.

Pages 149–50: Visa and MasterCard figures from interview with Visa USA CEO Carl Pas-carella, in story titled "Branding Digital Cash: Visa Plans the Leap from Value Exchange to Information Exchange," Michael Schrage, *MediaWeek,* May 29, 1995.

Page 150: "The Buck Starts Here: Will Nanobucks Be the Next Big Thing, or Are We Just Talking Pocket Change?" by Tom Steinert-Threlkeld, *Wired,* August 1996, page 133.

Page 151: "Authors Sell, Write Stuff in Cyberspace," by Dwight Silverman, *Houston Chronicle,* June 15, 1996.

Page 151: Interview with Brock Meeks, May 1996.

Page 153: Talk given by John Donegan, First Virtual Holdings, Harvard Conference on the Internet & Society, May 29, 1996.

<CHAPTER SEVEN>

Page 156: "The *Business Week* 1000: America's Most Valuable Companies," March 25, 1996, page 88.

Pages 156, 157, 161: Interview with Mark Kvamme (pron. Quah-me), CEO of the CKS Group, August 1996.

Page 159: Jupiter Communications data on the top twenty-five Web advertisers and top twenty-five Web publishers from "The Web Ads Up," *InformationWeek*, August 5, 1996, page 44.

Page 160: Scott McNealy quotes from speech at Harvard Conference on the Internet & Society, May 28, 1996.

Pages 163–64: "Now Serving Boomer Burger: McDonald's Debuts Fast Food Aimed at Making Adults Happy," by Bruce Horovitz and Dottie Enrico, *USA Today*, May 9, 1996, page 1.

Pages 165–66: Virgin Group information researched by author and published in "The 21st Century CEO: Imperatives for Growth," by the Index Vanguard Team, CSC Index, 1996.

Page 167: Interview with Walter Isaacson, managing editor, *Time* magazine, December 1995.

Pages 171–72: Interview with Heather Keenan, Annie's Homegrown Inc., May 1996.

Pages 172–73: J. Walter Thompson and Kraft advertising history from the agency's corporate Web site, at www.jwtworld.com/corporate/clients/kraft.html, and from *Advertising Age*'s History of TV Advertising, www.AdAge.com/Features/TV/index.html.

<CHAPTER EIGHT>

Page 174: "Managing in the Marketspace" and "Exploiting the Virtual Value Chain," by Jeffrey F. Rayport and John J. Sviokla, *Harvard Business Review*, November-December, 1994 and 1995, respectively.

Page 176: Nicholas Negroponte talk at CSC Vanguard conference, April 3, 1996.

Pages 176–77: "The Real Numbers Behind Net Profits," a July 1996 report by ActivMedia Inc., details the differences between profitable and unprofitable sites and examines Web performance by product sector, market sector, promotional techniques, sales processes, country, and many other factors.

Page 178: "The Web in Perspective: A Comprehensive Analysis of Ad-Supported Web Sites," Internet Profiles (I/PRO) Research, June 1996.

Pages 178–79: Web Media figures from interview with Tarnya Norse, December 1996.

Page 180: Dell Computer figures from company reports.

Pages 181–83: Killen & Associates' country-by-country data on Internet host systems around the world can be found at the company's Web site, www.killen.com.

Pages 183–84: Interview with Bill Washburn, Killen & Associates, August 1996.

Page 185: Domino's survey published in *Food & Wine* magazine, September 1996.

Pages 185–89: "I-Phone: Will Telephony on the Net Bring the Telecos to Their Knees? Or Will It Allow Them to Take over the Internet? (And, Oh Yes, It's Damn Hard to Tap)," by Fred Hapgood, *Wired*, October 1995, page 140; "A Call to Phones," by Roderick Simpson, *Wired*, March 1996, page 84; "Silencing Internet Voice," by Craig A. Johnson, *Wired*, June 1996, page 122.

<CHAPTER NINE>

Page 190: Quote by Mitch Ratcliffe, *Technology Review*, April, 1992.

Pages 190–91: David Ogilvy quote from *In Search of Excellence*, by Tom Peters, et al., (Warner Books, 1982).

Pages 191–93: Interview with Nancy Raileanu, Webmaster at Federal Express, October, 1996.

Pages 193–94: "Disruptive Technologies: Catching the Wave," by Joseph L. Bower and Clayton M. Christensen, *Harvard Business Review*, January–February 1995, page 43.

Page 194: "Microsoft Morphs into a Media Company," by Denise Caruso, *Wired*, June, 1996, page 126.

Page 195: Teleconference with Christopher Hassett, CEO of PointCast, October 1996.

Pages 197–98: "Tuning in to Marimba," by Jesse Freund, *Wired,* November 1996, page 122.

Pages 198–99: Interview with Tim Berners-Lee, October 1996.

<EPILOGUE>

Page 202: Talk by John Sviokla, associate professor at the Harvard Business School, at Harvard Conference, May 29, 1996.

Pages 202, 214: Interview with Jeffrey Bezos, Amazon, September 1996.

Page 203: *The End of Economic Man,* by George P. Brockway, (Norton, Third Edition, published 1995).

Pages 204–6: Profile and interview with Paul Romer: "Cheap, powerful technology and 'free' information transforms the science of economics. But just how? This young economist knows," by Peter Robinson, Forbes ASAP, Spring 1995; "The Economics of Ideas: Economist Paul Romer sees a world of nearly unbounded opportunity. Nobel, anyone?" by Kevin Kelly, *Wired,* June 1996, page 148.

Page 206: Interview with Arthur Andreassen, a senior economist with the U.S. Bureau of Labor Statistics, July 1996.

Pages 206–7: "High-Tech Is Forming a Role As an Indicator," by G. Pascal Zachary, the *Wall Street Journal,* September 30, 1996, page A1; "High-Tech Explains Widening Wage Gaps," by G. Pascal Zachary, the *Wall Street Journal,* April 22, 1996, page A1.

Page 207: "Top Regional Home Sellers Reflect on How They Became the Best in the Business," by Tina Cassidy, the *Boston Globe,* September 29, 1995, page F1.

Pages 208–9: "Annual Webmaster Survey: Rewards, and Duties, Trend Up for Keepers of Corporate Webs," by Elizabeth Gardner, *WebWeek,* September 23, 1996, page 1.

Page 210: "Court KO's Internet Decency Law," by Dave Ivey, Associated Press, June 12, 1996.

Page 210: "Internet Braves Singapore's Tight Censorship Rule," By Siti Rahil and Shuichi Nakamura, Kyodo News Service, August 24, 1996.

Pages 211–12: Keynote speeches by Microsoft CEO Bill Gates and Sun CEO Scott McNealy, Harvard Conference, May 28–29, 1996.

Pages 212–13: "This $300 Gizmo Could Turn the Web into a Medium for Mass Entertainment," by Stephen H. Wildstrom, *Business Week,* September 16, 1996, page 22.

Pages 213–14: "People Are Supposed to Pay for This Stuff?: Crisscrossing the country, our intrepid correspondent visits corporate labs, model living rooms, and actual sofas—to check out the megahyped interactive television prototypes and see just how real the 500-channel future really is," by Evan I. Schwartz, *Wired,* July 1995, page 148.

Pages 214–15: *The Medium Is the Massage: An Inventory of Effects,* by Marshall McLuhan, (Bantam Books, 1967); "Global village" definition on page 63.

Page 215: "The Wisdom of Saint Marshall, the Holy Fool: In the tumult of the digital revolution, McLuhan is relevant anew. But if you think you know Marshall McLuhan or what he stood for—think again," by Gary Wolf, *Wired,* January 1996, page 122.

Pages 215–16: Presentation by McCann-Erickson executives, MIT Media Laboratory's News in the Future Conference, May 24, 1996.

<APPENDIX>

A Directory of Important and Intriguing World Wide Web Sites

<A>

<ADVERTISING & MARKETING>

Advertising Age magazine	www.AdAge.com
Amer. Assoc. of Ad Agencies—member links	wwww.commercepark.com
Bates Worldwide agency	www.batesww.com
CKS—integrated marketing agency	www.cks.com
Cybergold—payments for consumer attention	www.cybergold.com
DoubleClick—Web ad placement syndicate	www.doubleclick.com
J. Walter Thompson	www.jwtworld.com
Museum of Advertising Icons— Green Giant, etc.	www.toymuseum.com
RazorFish—digital media design	www.razorfish.com
Web Media—digital media design	www.webmedia.co.uk
WebZeit—digital media design	www.webzeit.com

<ALCOHOLIC BEVERAGES>

Jack Daniel's whiskey	www.jackdaniels.com
Sam Adams/Boston Beer Company	www.samadams.com
Stolichnaya vodka	www.stoli.com
Zima malt beverage	www.zima.com
Virtual Vineyards—wine recommendations/sales	www.virtualvin.com

<AUTOMOBILES>

AutoByTel—online car shopping	www.autobytel.com
Chrysler	www.chryslercars.com
CUC Auto Vantage—car buyers club	www.cuc.com/auto
Ford Cars	www.ford.com
Honda	www.honda.com
Mercedes-Benz	www.mercedes-benz.com
Saturn Cars	www.saturncars.com
Toyota Motors	www.toyota.com
Volvo	www.volvocars.com

\<B>

\<BANKING>

Bank of America	www.bofa.com
BankBoston (merged BayBank and Bank of Boston)	www.bankboston.com
CheckFree—electronic bill payments	www.checkfree.com
Citibank	www.citibank.com
Quicken Financial Network	www.intuit.com
Wells Fargo	wellsfargo.com

\<BOOKS>

Amazon	www.amazon.com
Bantam Doubleday Dell	www.bdd.com
BookWire—industry news, author appearances	www.bookwire.com

\<C>

\<COMPUTERS>

Dell Computer	www.dell.com
Gateway 2000 Computer	www.gw2k.com
IBM	www.ibm.com
Sun Microsystems—creator of Java	www.sun.com

\<CONSUMER GOODS>

Gillette	www.gillette.com
Hot Coupons	www.hotcoupons.com
Kodak	www.kodak.com
Levi's	www.levi.com
Tide detergent	www.clothesline.com

\<D>

\<DIGITAL CASH/PAYMENT>

CyberCash—online debit and credit accounts	www.cybercash.com
ClickShare—micropayment settlement service	www.clickshare.com
DigiCash—online credit accounts	www.digicash.com
First Virtual—online credit accounts	www.fv.com

MasterCard   www.mastercard.com
Mondex—smart card payment system   www.mondex.com
NetCheque—online check payments   www.netcheque.com
Visa   www.visa.com

<E>

<ENTERTAINMENT>

CDnow—music shopping   www.CDnow.com
Walt Disney   www.disney.com
Discovery Channel   www.discovery.com
Firefly—music and movie recommendations   www.firefly.com
MovieLink—reviews and links to film
    promo sites   www.movielink.com
Playbill Online—theatre information   www.webcom.com/~broadway
Seinfeld—info and sound clips   www.seinfeld.mogul.no
The Spot—Web soap opera   www.thespot.com
The Mind's Eye—unpublished fiction
    for sale   www.tale.com
TicketMaster   www.ticketmaster.com

<F>

<FOOD & DRINK>

Annie's Homegrown—macaroni & cheese   www.annies.com
Eastern Meat Farms—sausage, breads,
    cheese   www.salami.com
Frito-Lay—chips and snacks   www.frito-lay.com
Coca-Cola   www.cocacola.com
Kraft   www.kraftfoods.com
Milk   www.whymilk.com
McDonald's   www.mcdonalds.com
Ragu—Italian cooking and culture   www.eat.com

<G>

<GAMES>

Happy Puppy—online games/contests   www.happypuppy.com
Sandbox—fun and games with
    "integrated" ads   www.sandbox.net
Sega of America   www.segaoa.com

Smart Games—games software   www.smartgames.com

Virgin Interactive Entertainment   www.vie.com

\<GOVERNMENT SERVICES\>

Department of Commerce   www.doc.gov

Federal Trade Commission   www.ftc.gov

Internal Revenue Service income tax
documents   www.irs.ustreas.gov

Massachusetts Dept. of Motor Vehicles   www.mdmv.gov

U.S. Patent & Trademark Office   www.uspto.gov

SEC Edgar investment database   www.sec.gov

The White House   www.whitehouse.gov

\<H\>

\<HOBBIES\>

Pez collecting   www.easysource.com/toys/pezlink

Outdoors Network   www.ono.com

\<I\>

\<INVESTING\>

Charles Schwab—discount brokerage   www.schwab.com

E*Trade—stock trading   www.etrade.com

Fidelity Investments   www.fid-inv.com

The IPO Insider   www.capmarkets.com/ipoinsid.html

NASDAQ   www.nasdaq.com

New York Stock Exchange   www.nyse.com

Prudential Securities   www.prusec.com

Stock quotes   www.quote.com

T. Rowe Price   www.troweprice.com

\<INSURANCE\>

InsureMarket—Intuit's insurance site   www.insuremarket.com

LifeQuote—life insurance policies   www.lifequote.com

QuickQuote—life insurance quotes   www.quickquote.com

\<M\>

\<MAGAZINES\>

The Atlantic Monthly   www.theAtlantic.com

Business Week   www.businessweek.com

The Electronic Newsstand—dozens of
   magazines   www.enews.com
Magazine industry study   www.mediacentral.com
Pathfinder, including Time Inc. magazines   pathfinder.com
Slate   www.slate.com

<N>

<NEWS & NEWSPAPERS>
The Boston Globe—local
   news/culture/events   www.boston.com
CNN   cnn.com
Individual Inc.'s NewsPage   www.newspage.com
MSNBC   www.msnbc.com
The New York Times   www.nytimes.com
PointCast—software retrieves
   personalized news   pioneer.pointcast.com
Reuters News Service   www.reuters.com
San Jose Mercury News   www.sjmercury.com
The Wall Street Journal   www.wsj.com
USA Today   www.usatoday.com

<NEW MEDIA>
HotWired—digital culture reports   www.hotwired.com
C/Net—The Computer Network   www.cnet.com

<P>

<POLITICS>
AllPolitics—political updates by CNN
   & Time   www.allpolitics.com
Christian Coalition   www.cc.org
PoliticsNow—comprehensive political news   www.politicsnow.com
Reform Party   www.reformparty.org
TANN CyberDemocracy Network   www.duc.auburn.edu/~tann

<R>

<REAL ESTATE LISTINGS & INFORMATION>
Abele Owners' Network—for sale by owner   www.owners.com
International Real Estate Directory   www.ired.com
National Association of Realtors   www.realtor.com
Coldwell Banker   www.coldwellbanker.com

<RESEARCH REPORTS, STUDIES, SURVEYS>

A. C. Nielsen—ratings services	www.nielsen.com
ActivMedia—Web research	www.activmedia.com
CSC Vanguard—business & technology	www.csc.com/vanguard
EPIC Privacy Archives	www.washofc.epic.org/privacy
Forrester Research—industry research	www.forrester.com
Georgia Inst. of Tech.—semiannual users surveys	www.gatech.edu/gvu/user_surveys
Global Information Infrastructure Commission	www.gii.com
Killen & Associates—international Web data	www.killen.com
KMPG—electronic commerces and taxes	usserve.us.kmpg.com
Pew Foundation—studies on media	www.people-press.org
Markle Foundation—public interest media	www.markle.org

<S>

<SEARCH ENGINES & DIRECTORIES>

Alta Vista	www.altavista.digital.com
AtHand—Pacific Bell's value-added yellow pages	www.athand.com
Excite	www.excite.com
Four-One-One—E-mail address directory	www.four11.com
HotBot	www.hotbot.com
InfoSeek	www.infoseek.com
Lycos	www.lycos.com
Switchboard—national white pages directory	www.switchboard.com
Yahoo!	www.yahoo.com
World Pages—people and business search	www.worldpages.com

<SEX & SMUT>

Bianca's Smut Shack	www.bianca.com/shack
Playboy magazine	www.playboy.com

<SHIPPING>

Federal Express	www.fedex.com
United Parcel Services	www.ups.com
U.S. Postal Service	www.usps.com

<SHOPPING>

CUC NetMarket—buyers' club	www.netmarket.com
Internet Shopping Network	www2.internet.net/directories.html
Home Runs—online grocery orders	www.homeruns.com
JCPenney	www.jcpenney.com
Land's End	www.landsend.com
L. L. Bean	www.llbean.com
OnSale—live online auctions	www.onsale.com
Peapod—online grocery orders	www.peapod.com
Streamline—online grocery orders	www.streamline.com
World Avenue—IBM's cybermall	www.worldavenue.com

<SPORTS>

ESPN SportsZone	espnet.sportszone.com
SportsLine	www.sportsline.com
Golf Web	www.golfweb.com

<T>

<TELECOMMUNICATIONS>

Ameritech	www.ameritech.com
AT&T	www.att.com
Internet Phone (I-Phone)—online audio chats	www.vocaltec.com
MCI	www.mci.com
Net2Phone—calls from Web to phones	www.net2phone.com
Sprint	www.sprint.com

<TRAVEL>

American Airlines	www.americanair.com
Conde Nast Traveler magazine	www.cntraveler.com
Delta Airlines	www.delta-air.com
Holiday Inn	www.holiday-inn.com
Internet Travel Network	www.itn.net
Preview Travel	www.reservations.com
Status of frequent traveler accounts	www.status.com
United Airlines	www.ual.com
TravelWeb	www.travelweb.com
Virgin Atlantic	www.virginatl.com
Vivid Travel Network	www.vivid.com
Travelocity (by Sabre Group)	www.travelocity.com

<W>

<WORLD WIDE WEB INFORMATION>

Tim Berners-Lee bio, Web history

                  www.w3.org/hypertext/WWW/People/Berners-Lee-Bio.html/

Better Business Bureau	www.BBBonline.com
Center for Democracy & Technology	
—privacy snoop	www.13x.com/cgi-bin/CDT/snoop.pl
Center for Media Education	www.cme.org
Interactive Age magazine	techweb.cmp.com/techweb/ia
Internet World magazine	www.iworld.com
Webonomics—get your Web site rated!	www.webonomics.com
Web Week magazine	www.webweek.com
WWW domain name registration service	www.rs.internic.net
ZD Net—Ziff Davis publications	www.zdnet.com

<INDEX>

Abele Information Systems Inc., 111–12
A. C. Nielsen Company, studies by, 16, 52, 53
Active Desktop, 196
ActivMedia research studies, 120–22, 176, 177, 182
Adolph Coors Company, 169
Advertising
  for cigarettes, 61–62
  consumer privacy and, 88–89
  consumer ranking of Web, 77
  deconstruction of, through consumer control, 56–58
  diminishing returns on mass-market, 59–61
  economics of, 68–70
  "impressions" as basis of, 50, 52–53, 56
  ineffectiveness of mass-market, on Web, 47–49
  of new brands, 159
  new psychology of, on Web, 61–63
  rewards for viewing, 86–87
  subscriptions vs., 40–42
  targeted Web, 77–78
  user control and deconstruction of, 56–58
  Web site "banners" as, 47, 50–51, 53, 55, 64–66, 77
  of Web sites, 63–68
  Web sites as, for print publications, 23–24
Advertising agencies, Web sites created by, 68–70
Africa, Internet infrastructure in, 182
Agility, maintaining competitive advantage through, 190–200
Airline industry
  flier miles as value-based currency offered by, 139–40
  online self-service applications of, 120–26
Alcoholic beverages
  brands and consumer identity, 169–70
  Web marketing of, 79–82, 96–98
Allen, Paul, 36
Alta Vista (search engine), 54, 158, 159, 179
  top ten search terms used on, 21

Amazon.com online bookstore, 98–101, 104, 158, 179–80, 202
American Airlines, 123, 139–40
American Express, 122, 149, 166
America Online, 54, 102, 121, 166
  exchanging time for customer data by, 85–86
  time on, as value-based currency, 141
  Web access from, 16, 17
America's Carriers Telecommunication Association, 188–89
Anderman, Rich, 109
Anderson, Laurie, 184
Andreassen, Arthur, 206
Andreessen, Marc, development of Mosaic browser by, 11–12
Anker, Andrew, 40, 66, 74–75
Annie's Homegrown Inc., as Web-based brand, 171–73
Anonymity and Web monetary systems, 148–49
Apollo online reservation system, 122
Apple Computers, 193–94
Asia, Internet infrastructure in, 181–82
AT&T
  Instant Answers technology, 187
  value-based currencies offered by, 141
  Web site, 53, 73, 133
Atkinson, Jill, 25
Atlantic Monthly, 6
Attention. *See* Users, sustaining attention of
Austin, Bob, 48
AutoByTel Web site, 110
Autodesk company, 8
Auto industry, 85, 109–10, 206
  car brands and consumer identity, 167–69
  Chrysler, 49–50, 72–73
  Saturn, 167–69
  Volvo, 47–49
Automated teller machines (ATM), 127
Automation, jobs and effects of, 131–36, 206–9
AutoVantage Web site, 110

Balance of trade in global Web marketspace, 176–78

Banking industry, online self-service in, 126–31

Banners
as advertising, 50–56, 64–66, 77
clicks on, 50, 55, 66–67
fees for, 47, 53, 66–67

Bantam Doubleday Dell, 77

Banyan Systems, 133

Barnes & Noble stores, 93, 101, 158

Battelle, John, 218

Berkeley Systems, Inc., 196

Berners-Lee, Tim, 188, 212
hypertext and World Wide Web developed by, 8–10
on information push/pull, 198–99

Bezos, Jeffrey, 98–101, 202, 214

Bianca's Smut Shack, community and interactivity at, 24–26

Big-ticket purchases, online shopping and, 109–13

Blockbuster Video stores, 110

Bookmarks, Web site, 44–45

Books
Web advertising of, 77
Web marketing of, 98–101, 158, 202

Bookstores, online, 98–101, 158

Borders stores, 101, 158

Boston.com Web site, 42

Boston Globe (newspaper), news on Web site from, 42

Bradlees stores, 104

Brand names and brand images, 155–73
advertising and, 59
extending, into new products, 158, 165–67
forging connection between consumers and online, 170–73
as identity badge, 167–70
importance of, to Web businesses, 155–56
translation of global, to Web, 160–64
Web-based, 157–60

Branson, Richard, 165–66

Bridal registry online, 106–8

Browser programs, 10–14, 147, 184
Internet Explorer, 13, 147, 194, 196
Netscape Navigator, 12–13, 74, 147, 184

Bungey, Michael, 70

Burger, Ross, 136

Burke, Raymond, 114

Bush, Vannevar, vision of world-wide information network from, 6–7, 9, 217

Business(es). *See also* Marketers; Marketing; Marketspace
agility required for competitive advantage of, 190–200
linking consumers to, 49–52
size of, and response to Web's global marketspace, 178–80

Business Week, 35

Caldor stores, 104

Campanetto, Mary Ann, 65, 68

Carillon Importers, 80

Carlyle, Thomas, 203

CASIE advertising industry coalition, 88–89

Castanet (software), 197–98

Catalogs, online, 106

Center for Media and Democracy, 87–88

Center for Media Education, 90

CERN (European Particle Physics Laboratory), 8

Charges. *See* Fees

Chaum, David, 145

CheckFree Corp., 130

Children, personal data and privacy concerns for, 90–91

Chrysler Corporation Web site, 49–50, 72–73, 177

Cichowski, Lorraine, 29, 31

Circuit City stores, 93, 109

Cisco Systems, 122

CKS Group, 34, 156, 161

Clark, Jim, 12

Clickshare Corp., 152

Click-thru's, 66

Clinton, Bill, 209

C/Net, 159–60

CNN, 28

Coca-Cola brand, 25, 156, 161–62

Coffey, Steve, 54, 133

Coleridge, Samuel T., 7

Communications Decency Act, 210

Communications services
effect of Webphone on international, 185–89
telephone, 131–34, 186
Web site domains, 134–35

Community on Web, 24–26

Competitive advantage, agility required for, 190–200
effect of disruptive technologies on, 193–94
Federal Express as example of, 191–93
information push/pull and, 195–97

trends for future in, 197–200
Comp-U-Card company, 102
CompUSA stores, 93
CompuServe online service, 16, 54, 102, 106, 121
Computerization, jobs and effects of, 131–36, 206–9
Consumers. *See also* Users
  control exercised by, and deconstruction of advertising, 56–58
  effect of disruptive technologies on, 194
  E-mail from, 48–49, 192
  examples of information-rich products marketed to, 96–103
  expectations of, 4, 20
  forging connection between online brand names and, 170–73
  fostering loyalty of, 81–82, 106–8, 141, 143, 164
  large purchases made online by, 109–13
  linking businesses to, 49–52
  motivations of, 3
  new psychology of advertising and needs of, 62–63
  product brands integrated with identity of, 167–70
  relationship between retail stores and, 93–96, 103–8
  research on Web usage patterns by, 53–56
  rewarding, in exchange for personal data, 72–91
Content creators
  challenge for, to create unique and valuable Web sites, 21–24
  disclosing personal user data to, 73–79
  motivations of, 3
Coopers & Lybrand, studies by, 16–17
COSMOS Federal Express tracking system, 118
Costco stores, 93
Cost per thousand (CPM) of advertising impressions, 52–53, 56, 66–67
Coupons, 83–84
Credit card companies, 144, 147, 149–50
CUC International, 102–3, 104, 110
Currencies. *See* Monetary systems online
Customized products, 4
  filtered news, 32–33, 44
  telephone calling plans, 133
CyberCash, Inc., 145, 153
Cybergold, Inc., 86

Cybermalls, 94–95
Cyberwire Dispatch column, 151–52

Deconstruction, user participation and, 33–35, 56–58
Dell Computer, 180
Dietsch, Jeanne, 120, 122, 177
DigiCash, 145, 149
Digital cash, 5, 138, 144–46
Digital certificate, 147
Digital Equipment Corporation, 159, 179, 193. *See also* Alta Vista (search engine)
Direct-mail advertising, 67
Discounts on products, 83–87
Disney Web site, 90, 133
Disruptive technologies, business response to, 193–94
Donegan, John, 153

Easy Sabre travel reservation system, 121
Ecash, 145, 149
Economics, 201–17
  government policies related to, 209–10
  jobs and, 206–9
  media and, 214–17
  New Growth Theory of, 201–6, 207
  technological change and, 210–14
  traditional, 1, 2
  on Web (*see* Webonomics)
Economy, global Web. *See* Marketspace
Electronic bill paying services, 129–31
Electronic currency. *See* Monetary systems online
Ellison, Larry, 212
E-mail services, 48–49, 86, 192
Employment
  auto industry, 206–7
  software industry, 206–7
English language in Web marketspace, 183–84
Entertainment
  Firefly Web site for recommendations related to, 75–77
  shopping malls as, 105
ESPN Sports Zone, 36–38, 158
Europe
  Internet infrastructure in, 181
  Web businesses in, 177
European Particle Physics Laboratory (CERN), 8
Everett, Rich, 49–50, 72
Excite (search engine), 21, 158

Experience, user's
    of community, 24–26
    creating unique user, 21–46
    of interactivity, 26–28
    quality of, emphasized in Web
        marketing, 52–56
    of television watching vs. Web
        browsing, 16–18
Expertise as factor in information-rich
    products, 96–98
Export sales, Web and U.S., 176–78

Federal Express
    agility and competitive advantage
        maintained by, 191–93
    online self-service applications of,
        117–18
Federal Communications Commission, 61
Federal Reserve Automated
    Clearinghouse, 130
Federal Trade Commission, 87
Fees
    for banners, 47, 53, 66–67
    currencies used to pay (*see* Monetary
        systems online)
    deciding on what to charge for, 36–39
    for membership at Web sites, 26, 37
    subscriptions for news services, 29–33,
        36, 44
    subscriptions vs. advertising as, 40–42
Fernandes, Rick, 102, 104
Filo, David, 157
Financial online sites, 51, 126–31
Firefly Network Inc., 75–79
Firefly Web site, 75–79
First Interstate online banking services,
    129
First Virtual Holdings, 145, 150–51, 153
Fish Wrap Web site, 42–43
Floyd, Mary Lou, 53, 73, 133
Forbes, Walter, 102
Forrester Research, 104
Four11.com Web site, 132
Frankel, Max, 29
Franks, Bob, 90
Freund, Jesse, 198

Galbraith, John Kenneth, 61
Gartner Group, studies by, 19
Gates, Bill, 13, 194. *See also* Microsoft
    Corporation
    on future computer technology, 211–12
Gateway 2000, 180, 213
Georgia Tech, studies by, 16

Global brand icons, translation of, to
    Web, 160–64
Global economy. *See* Marketspace
Globalink company, 184
"Global village" concept, 214–15
Goldhaber, Nat, 86
GoldMail Web site, 86–87
Goods and services. *See* Products
Government
    online services of agencies of, 135–36
    technology investment by, 209–10
Granoff, Peter, 96–97
Green, Emily, 49
Greenspan, Alan, 207
Groceries, online services for ordering
    and delivering, 114–16
Gross ratings points, advertising
    "impressions" measured in, 50

Hannaford's Home Runs, 116
Harvard Business Review, 174, 193
Hassett, Christopher R., 195–96
Hassett, Gregory, 196
Holiday Inn Web site, 64, 68
Home Shopping Network, 95, 160–61
HotBot (search engine), 21, 158
H.O.T.! Coupons, 84
Hotwired Web site, 47, 159
    rewards for user data provided by,
        73–75
Hyperlinks. *See* Links
Hypertext. *See also* Links
    T. Berners-Lee's concept of Web and,
        8–10
    T. Nelson's concept of, 7–8
HyperText Markup Language (HTML), 8,
    9
HyperText Transfer Protocol (HTTP), 8, 9

IBM Corporation, 147, 193, 205
    banner ads from, 65–66, 68
    World Avenue cybermall from, 94–95,
        166
I/Code, 89–90
Ideas as cause of economic growth,
    204–5
Individual Inc., 43–44
InfoHaus, 150
Information
    news (*see* News)
    products rich in (*see* Information-rich
        products)
    privacy in personal, 72, 87–91
    quality of, 2

rewarding users for disclosing
  personal, 72–91
value-added, 28–33, 41, 42–46
Information-poor products, 113–16
Information push/pull, 57–58, 195–97
  future trends in, 197–200
Information-rich products, 92–116,
  202–3. *See also* Value-added
  products
  big-ticket purchases as, 109–13
  enhancing bond between consumer and
    retailer with, 106–8, 171–73
  expertise as factor in, 96–98
  impact of, on retail stores, 103–5
  information gap in traditional retail as
    opportunity for, 93–96
  information-poor products vs., 92–93,
    113–16
  price as factor for, 101, 102–3
  product delivery as, 114–16
  selection as factor for, 98–101
InfoSeek (search engine), 21, 54, 158,
  159, 160, 166, 204
Infrastructure companies, Web, 208–9
  consumer brand Web sites created by,
    68–70
  motivations of, 4
Insurance industry, online services of, 136
Intellectual property, Web composed of,
  201–3
Interactive Edition of *Wall Street Journal*,
  35
Interactive television, 213
Interactivity on Web, 18, 26–28
  tourism and, 125–26
Internal Revenue Service (IRS), 135
International Discount
  Telecommunications (IDT), 188
International Real Estate Directory, 113
Internet. *See also* Web
  development of, 14
  hypertext programs placed on, in 1991,
    9
  imbalance in global infrastructure of,
    180–83
  technological change and, 210–14
  telephone services on, 185–89
Internet Explorer (browser software), 13,
  146, 194
Internet Network Information Center
  (InterNIC), 134–35
Internet Phone (software), 187
Internet Profiles Corp. (I/PRO), 55–56,
  89–90, 178

Internet Shopping Network (ISN), 95,
  160–61
Internet Travel Network (ITN), 122
InterNIC, 134–35
Interval Research Corp., 139
Intranet market, 159, 196
Intuit Corporation, 131, 166
Isaacson, Walter, 40, 42, 167
Ivins, Bob, 56

Jack Daniel Distillery Web site, 80–82
Japan, Internet infrastructure in, 181–82
Java (programming language), 160, 212
JCPenney stores, 148
  online services of, 106–8
Jobs, effects of automation and online
  self-service on, 131–36
Johnson, Gailyn, 128, 129, 131
Journal of Travel Research, 124
Jupiter Communications, 104

Kasparov, Gary, 68
Keenan, Heather, 171
Keller, Jamie, 61
Kent, Eileen, 23
Keynes, John Maynard, 209–10
Killen & Associates, 181, 182
Kinsley, Michael, 40
Koch, Hans, 112
Konkowski, Marisha, 106, 108, 148
Kraft Foods brand, market presence of,
  171–73
Krueger, Alan, 207
"Kubla Khan" (poem), 7
Kvamme, Mark, 34, 156, 157, 161

Language
  Java programming, 160, 212
  in Web's global marketspace, 183–85
Latin America, Internet infrastructure in,
  182
Library, concept of Web as global, 5–10
LifeQuote of America, Inc., 136
LifeQuote Web site, 136
Links, 47. *See also* Hypertext
  of consumers to businesses, 49–52
  trading or purchasing, to promote Web
    sites, 64
Local news, value-added, 30–33,
  42–45
Lycos (search engine), 21, 54, 158

McCann-Erickson Worldwide, vision of
  future by, 215–17

McDonald's Corporation, advertising by, 25, 50, 163–64
McLuhan, Marshall, 214–15
McNealy, Scott, 2, 160, 212
Maes, Pattie, 75, 76, 77
Magellan (search engine), 21, 158
Maldutis, Julius, 123
Malls, 105
    in cyberspace, 94–95
Malthus, Thomas, 1, 203
Manni, Bob, 79–80
Margeotes Fertitta & Partners, 79–80
Marimba, Inc., 197–98
Market, agility required for adaption to changes in, 190–200
Marketers
    disclosing personal user data to, 79–82
    motivations of, 3–4
Marketing, 19–20, 47–71
    diminishing returns on mass-market advertisements affecting, 59–61
    economics and challenge of Web, 68–70
    effects of consumer control on Web, 56–58
    fees and (*see* Fees)
    global (*see* Marketspace)
    ineffectiveness of mass marketing paradigm in Web, 47–49
    of information-rich products (*see* Information-rich products)
    monetary systems and (*see* Monetary systems online)
    new psychology of Web, based on consumer needs, 61–63
    promoting Web sites for, 63–68
    quality of experience emphasized over quantity of site visitors in Web, 52–56
    for results, not for exposure, 49–52
MarketplaceMCI, 94
Marketspace, 174–89
    balance of trade in, 176–78
    effect of Webphone on, 185–89
    imbalances in Internet infrastructure and, 180–83
    language patterns in, 183–85
    size of company and responses to, 178–80
    Web economy as move from marketplace to, 174–76
Martin, Steve, 18
Massachusetts Institute of Technology (MIT), 42–43, 176

Massachusetts Registry of Motor Vehicles, 135–36
Mass marketing paradigm
    diminishing returns on, 59–61
    ineffectiveness of, on Web, 47–49
    shift to needs gratification in, 61–63
Mass media. *See also* Newspapers and magazines; Television
    advertising in, 50, 51, 52–53
    deconstruction of, on Web, 33–35, 56–58
    future trends in, 214–17
    promoting Web sites in, 63–64
    Time-Warner on Web, 39–42
    Web as different from, 18–19, 26–27
MasterCard, 147, 149
MCI 1-800-Music Now, 78
Medium Is the Massage, The (McLuhan), 215
Meeks, Brock, 151–52
Melton, William, 153
Membership fees at Web sites, 26, 37
"Memex," 7, 9
Metromail, 90
Micropayments online, 150–52
Microsoft Corporation, 13, 54, 131, 166, 194, 196, 205. *See also* Gates, Bill
Microsoft Network (MSN), 194
Miller, Chris "Freeform," 25
Mind's Eye Web site, 151
Modem Media company, 169
Mokyr, Joel, 207
Monetary systems online, 4–5, 138–54
    anonymity as benefit of, 148–49
    digital cash, 5, 144–46
    fees and (*see* Fees)
    micropayments as benefit of, 150–52
    security concerns affecting, 146–48
    trust and credibility as issues affecting, 153
    value-based currencies as, 138–43
Money Mailers, 84
Monier, Louis, 22, 27
Monopolies, Paul Romer on, 205
Mosaic (browser software), 11–12
Movie and music recommendations, Firefly Web site for, 75–77
Murdoch, Rupert, 94
Mutual fund services, 131, 132

Nanobucks, 150
National Association of Realtors, 112
National Purchase Diary (NPD), 53–54
NC (network computer), 211, 212

Negroponte, Nicholas, 176
on information push/pull, 57–58
Nelson, Ted, hypertext concept developed
by, 7–8
Net2Phone service, 188
NetMarket (formerly Shopper's
Advantage), 102–3
Netscape Communications Corp., 12–13,
54, 122, 159, 218, 205–6
Netscape Navigator (browser software),
12–13, 74, 146, 184
"Network computer" devices, 211, 212
News, 27–28
information push in, 195–97
sports, 36–38
television, 34
value-added, 28–33, 35, 41, 42–45
News Corp., 94
News-filtering programs, 32
NewsHound, 32
NewsPage Web site, 44
Newspapers and magazines, 27–28
charging for subscriptions vs.
advertising for Web, 40–42
deconstruction of, on Web, 33–35
value-added news at Web sites of,
28–33, 41, 42–45
Web sites as advertisements of, 23–24
New York Times, 30, 197
Nike brand, 165
Nineteen Eighty-Four (Orwell), 217
Nixon, Richard, 209
Norse, Tarnya, 178

Odyssey, studies by, 16
Ogilvy, David, 190–91
Oil industry, 143
Olson, Robert, 96
OneCast (software), 196
One-to-One Future, The (Peppers,
Rogers), 114
Online information services, 16, 17. *See
also* America Online; CompuServe;
Prodigy
time on, as value-based currency, 141
time on, traded for consumer data,
85–86
Orwell, George, 217
Ottolenghi, Les, 64, 163
Owners' Network (Owners.com) Web site,
111–12

Parkinson, Andrew, 115
Parkinson, Thomas, 115

Parr, Barry, 33
Pathfinder Web site, 39–42, 47, 80, 85
Patterson, Thomas W., 94
"Pay to Play" vision of media future, 216
PC Meter, 53–55, 132–33
Peapod online grocery store, 115–16
Peppers, Don, 114
Philip Morris, 172
Phillips, Tom, 38
Playboy Web site, 15–16, 22–24, 25, 26,
47, 56
PointCast, Inc., 27–28, 195–97
Point of sale, security concerns at,
146–47
Poler, Ariel, 89
Polese, Kim, 197
Poole, Henri, 125
Price as factor in information-rich
products, 100, 102–3, 202
PriceCostco stores, 110
Pricing. *See* Fees
Privacy, 72, 87–91
Procter & Gamble
discount coupons offered by, 83
Web advertising by, 66
Prodigy online service, 16, 102, 106,
114–15, 121, 128
Products
brand name (*see* Brand names and
brand images)
customized (*see* Customized products)
deciding what to charge for, 36–42
delivery of, 114–16, 197
exchanging discounts on, for consumer
information, 83–87
information-rich, vs. information-poor,
92–116
marketing of (*see* Marketing;
Marketspace)
providing uniquely valuable, 21–24
value-added, 28–33, 42–45
Prudential Corporation, 51
Pure-Bred Puppynet Web site, 101

Ragu Italian food Web site, 84, 88
Raileanu, Nancy, 118, 191–93
Rayport, Jeffrey F., 174
Real estate industry, 42, 58, 207
online services of, 110–13
Rebates, 85
Reed, David, 139
Registration
centralized, 89–90
at Web sites, 73, 74

Retail stores
  effect of information-rich products on,
    103–5
  enhancing bond between consumers
    and, with information-rich products,
    106–8
  information gap in traditional, 93–96
"Revolution du Jour" vision of media
  future, 216
Rewards to users for disclosing personal
  data, 72–91
  from content creators, 73–79
  discounts as, 83–87
  from marketers, 79–82, 99–100
  privacy concerns and, 72, 87–91
Ricardo, David, 203, 205
Rogers, Martha, 114
Romer, Paul, New Growth Theory of,
  204–7
Roosevelt, Franklin D., 6, 209
Rudenstine, Neil, 5
Runyon, Marvin, 119

Saatchi, Maurice, 179
Saatchi & Saatchi research, 17
Sabre travel reservation system, 121
SAIC Network Solutions, 134–35
Sample, Edward W., 107
Samsung Corporation, 179
Samsung Human Resources Development
  Center, 179
Samuelson, Paul, 209
San Jose Mercury News (newspaper),
  value-added news at Web site of,
  31–33, 39
Saturn cars, 167–69
Scarcity of demand, 2
Scarcity of supply, 1, 2
Screen savers, news on, 196
Search engines. See also Alta Vista;
  Yahoo!
  top search terms used in, 21
  as top Web sites, 54
  as Web-based brands, 157–58
Secure electronic transaction (SET), 147
Secure Sockets Layer, 147
Security
  online banking and, 128
  online monetary systems and, 145,
    146–48
  Webphone, 189
Selection as factor in information-rich
  products, 98–101
Self-service online applications, 117–37

in banking industry, 126–31
effects of automated, on jobs, 131–36
in shipping industry, 117–19
in travel industry, 120–26
Services and goods. See Products
Sex, Web-user interest in, 21–27
"Shared whiteboard," 187–88
Shipping industry
  agility and competitive advantage in,
    193–94
  online self-service in, 117–19
Shopper's Advantage, 102–3
Shopper's clubs, 102–3
Shopping online, 102–3
  digital cash and, 144–46
Singapore, 210
Slade, Mike, 36–37
Slate (Web magazine), 40
Smart cards, 142, 143
Smith, Adam, 204
Spiders (software), 64
SportsLine, 38
SportsZone (ESPN), 36–38, 47, 158
Staples stores, 93
Starwave Corp., 36, 158
Stolichnaya vodka Web site, 79–80
Streamline Inc., 116
Subscription fees at Web sites. See also
  Fees
  advertising vs., 40–42
  for news services, 29–33, 44
  for sports news, 38
Sun Microsystems, 160
Sutton, Willie, 131
Sviokla, John J., 174, 202
Swann, Becky, 113
Switchboard.com Web site, 132–33

Technology
  accelerating changes in, 210–14
  as factor of production, 204
  future of media and, 214–17
  responding to disruptive, 193–94
"TechnoUtopia" vision of media future,
  215–16
Telephone directories, national, 132
Telephone services
  automation and, 131–34
  effect of Webphone on international,
    185–89
  value-based currencies and, 141
Television
  advertising on, 52–53, 60, 69
  cable, 44, 60, 95, 157, 211

interactive, 213
news programs on, 34
Web experience vs. experience of,
16–17, 213–14
"Web TVs," 212–13
Thau, David, 25
Thompson, J. Walter, 51, 172
Time (magazine), 39, 40
Time-Warner, Pathfinder Web site of,
39–42, 47, 80
Tobacco industry, 61–62, 161
Tourism, online services for, 124–26
Trade, Web and global balance of,
176–78
Translation software, automatic language,
184
Travel industry, online self-service in,
120–26
Tribe Z and marketing of Zima beverage,
169–70
True Rewards program (AT&T), 141
Trust and credibility issues affecting
online monetary systems, 153

Uniform Resource Locator (URL), 8, 9
United Parcel Service (UPS), 192
online self-service applications,
118–19
U.S. Bureau of Labor Statistics, 206
U.S. companies, Web export sales from,
176–78
U.S. Patent and Trademark Office, 135
U.S. Postal Service, 192
online self-service applications of,
119
U.S. Treasury, 138
USA Today (newspaper), Web site of,
29–30, 32
Users, 14–20. *See also* Consumers
business and corporate, 15–16
control of, effects on marketing, 56–58
demographic data on, 15–16
experience of (*see* Experience, user's)
rewarding (*see* Rewards to users for
disclosing personal data)
Web marketing to, 19–20 (*see*
Marketing)
Users, sustaining attention of, 2, 21–46
advertising vs. subscriptions and,
39–42
by creating community experience,
24–26
by creating sites with unique value,
21–24

deciding on fees, and 36–39
deconstruction and user participation
for, 33–35
interactivity and, 26–28
value-added products for, 28–33, 42–45

Value-added products. *See also*
Information-rich products
in financial sites, 51, 126–31
from news services, 28–33, 35, 41,
42–45
self-service and (*see* Self-service online
applications)
Value-based currencies, 4–5. *See also*
Monetary systems online
defining, 138–39
examples of, 139–43
security concerns affecting, 146–48
Vessels, Peggy, 80–82
"Video streaming," 212
Virgin Group, extension of brand names
from, 165–66
Virtual Vineyards, 96–98, 104, 179–80
Visa, 147, 149
Vivid Travel Network, 125
Vlahos, Len, 101
VocalTech Inc., 187
Voice recognition software, 132
Volvo Cars of North America, Web site of,
47–49

Walker, John, 8
Wall Street Journal, 30, 35, 36, 61
Wal-Mart stores, 93
Walt Disney Company, 142
Disney Web site, 90, 133
Warhol, Andy, 18
Washburn, Bill, 183, 184
Weaver, Doug, 78
Web
browser programs for, 10–14
economics of (*see* Webonomics;
Webonomics, principles of)
as example of disruptive technology,
194
experience of television vs. experience
of, 16–17, 213–14
four groups on, 3–4
historical development of, 8–10
jobs produced by, 208
potential size of, 18
products on (*see* Products)
sites (*see* Web sites)
users of (*see* Consumers; Users)

Web-based brands, 157–60
Web Crawler, 158
Web Media, 178–79
Webonomics, 1–5
    development of this book on, 218–20
    government policy and, 209–10
    job shifts and, 131–36, 206–9
    new economic theory and, 201–6
    new media landscape and, 214–17
    technological change and, 210–14
Webonomics, principles of, 20
    agility and adaptation to market,
        190–200
    brand name and brand image, 155–73
    global "marketspace," 174–89
    information-rich products, 92–116
    marketing for results, not exposure,
        47–71
    rewarding users for disclosing personal
        data, 72–91
    self-service applications, 117–37
    sustaining user attention with quality
        experiences, 21–46
    value-based currencies, 138–54
Webphone, effect of, on international
    communications, 185–89
Web sites
    bookmarks for, 44–45
    challenge of creating unique and
        valuable, 21–24
    community in, 24–26
    deciding fees on, 36–39
    design and creation of, 68–70, 82,
        178–79

domain names for, 134
membership and subscription charges
    at, 26, 29–33 (*see also* Fees)
noted in this book, 227–34
page design for, 14
personal, 18, 78
promoting, 63–68
registration at, 73, 74, 89
regulations and, 161, 210
Web Translator (software), 184
Web TVs, 212–13
Wells Fargo online banking services,
    128–29
Wholesale shopper's clubs, 102–3
Williams, Roy, 18
Wired (magazine), 73, 159, 218, 219
Wire services, 27, 28
Withey, Ann, 171
World Avenue cybermall, 94–95, 166
World Wide Web, development of, 8–10.
    See also Web
World Wide Web Consortium, 9

Xanadu (software), 7–8

Yahoo! (search engine), 21, 54, 66, 204
    as Web-based brand, 157–58, 166
Yang, Jerry, 157
Yoxsimer, Bruce, 122

Zima beverage, 169–70